# A NEW EARTH

*From Conflict to Unity: The Road to
Permanent Peace*

## By

## Seymour Lessans

# A New Earth

Seymour Lessans

Published by Safeworld Publishing Company, 2022.

# Table of Contents

# To my mother, IDA;

my wife, MADELINE;
our three children —
LINDA, JANIS, and MARC;
and in memory of my father,
DAVID.

## SEYMOUR LESSANS

A New Earth took five years to complete. It was the author's 3rd attempt to reveal a scientific discovery capable of preventing war, crime, discrimination, and many other evils plaguing mankind. This knowledge reveals that the long-awaited Messiah (the solution to all our problems) is nothing other than a psychological law of man's nature which has remained undiscovered, like atomic energy, until now. By discovering this well-concealed law and demonstrating its power, a catalyst is introduced into human relations that compels a fantastic change in the direction our nature has been traveling. Very few people, upon first reading the Preface that follows, will believe these changes possible. However, mathematical proof is undeniably established as the text is read and understood.

## PREFACE

No words can more adequately express the general tenor of this book than those written by Eric Johnston in the November 6, 1960 issue of This Week magazine of The Baltimore Sun. And they go as follows:

"If there is one word which characterizes our world in this exciting last half of the twentieth century, the word is change.

Change in political life... change in economic life... change in social life ... change in personal life... change in the hallmark of our times. It's not gradual, comfortable change. It is sudden, rapid, often violent. It touches and often disrupts whole cultures and hundreds of millions of people.

Behind it all lies an explosive growth in scientific knowledge and accomplishment. Some 90 percent of all the scientists who ever lived are living today, and the total accumulation of scientific knowledge is doubling every ten years.

But this is reality. If we remember that, then we will never flinch at change. We will adjust to it, welcome it, meet it as a friend and know it is God's will."

However this may be, the question arises: Is there a Supreme Intelligence guiding this universe? Julian Huxley, in his book Man Stands Alone, says, "No, there isn't." But A. Cressy Morrison, who titled his book Man Does Not Stand Alone as a challenge to Huxley's conclusions, says there is. Who is right? Now, before I reveal the purpose of my book, I should like to quote the chapter on Chance from Morrison's work. He writes:

"Chance seems erratic, unexpected, and subject to no method of calculation, but though we are startled by its surprises, chance is subject to rigid and unbreakable law. The proverbial penny may turn up heads ten times running, and the chance of an eleventh is not expected but is still one in two, but the chance of a run of ten heads is very small. Suppose you have a bag containing one hundred marbles, ninety-nine black and one white. Shake the bag and let out one. The chance that the first marble out being the white one is exactly one in one hundred. Now put the marbles back and start again. The chance of the white coming out is still one in a hundred, but the chance of the white coming out first twice in succession is one in ten thousand (one hundred times one hundred).

3

Now try a third time, and the chance of the white coming out three times in succession is one hundred times ten thousand or one in a million. Try another time or two and the figures become astronomical.

The results of chance are as clearly bound by law as the fact that two and two make four.

In a game in which the cards are shuffled and an ace of spades was dealt to one of the players, ace of hearts to the next, clubs to the third, and diamonds to the dealer, followed by the deuces, the threes and so on, until each player had a complete set in numerical order, no one would believe the cards had not been arranged.

The chances are so great against such a happening that probably it never did happen in all the games played anywhere since the game of whist was invented. 'But it could happen.' Yes, it could. Suppose a little child is asked by an expert chess player to beat him at chess in thirty-four moves and the child makes each move by pure chance exactly right to meet every twist and turn the expert attempts and does beat him in thirty-four moves. The expert would certainly think it was a dream or that he was out of his mind. 'But it could happen.' Yes, it could.

To repeat, my purpose in this discussion of chance is to bring forcibly to the attention of the reader the fact that the purpose of this book is to point out clearly and scientifically the narrow limits within which any life can exist on earth, and prove by real evidence that all the nearly exact requirements of life could not be brought about on one planet at one time by chance. The size of the earth, the distance from the sun, the thickness of the earth's crust, the quantity of water, the amount of carbon dioxide, the volume of nitrogen, the emergence of man and his survival — all point to order out of chaos, to design and purpose, and to the fact that, according to the inexorable laws of mathematics, all these could not occur by chance simultaneously on one planet once in a billion times. It could so occur, but it did not so occur. When the facts are so overwhelming, and when we recognize, as we must, the attributes of our minds which are not material, is it possible to flaunt the evidence and take the one chance in a billion that we and all else are the result of chance?

We have found that there are 999,999,999 chances to one against a belief that all things happen by chance. Science will not deny the facts as stated; the mathematicians will agree that the figures are correct. Now we encounter the stubborn resistance of the human mind, which is reluctant to give up fixed ideas. The early Greeks knew the earth was a sphere, but it took two thousand years to convince men that this fact is true.

New ideas encounter opposition, ridicule and abuse, but truth survives and is verified.

The argument is closed; the case is submitted to you, the jury, and your verdict will be awaited with confidence."

Well, do you still believe there is no Supreme Intelligence guiding this universe through mathematical laws, which include the relation of man with man, and that everything happens by chance? Do you believe that your faith in God has been in vain? You are in for the surprise of your life.

Thousands of years ago it was prophesied that sometime during the 20th century a New Earth would commence, an age that would see a permanent end to all war, crime, hate, prejudice, and the domination of man by man. When first hearing this, shortly after Hitler had slaughtered six million Jews, I laughed with contempt because nothing appeared more ridiculous than such a statement. Since then, however, something happened in my life which has made me realize that I, myself, am going to be partly responsible for making this prophecy into a reality. Are you skeptical? You should be, if you're not.

In the early part of 1959, after 15 years of extensive reading, my dissatisfaction with a certain theory that had gotten a dogmatic hold on the mind, compelled me to spend nine strenuous months in the deepest analysis; and in November of that year I made a finding that was so difficult for me to believe, it took me two years just to understand its significance for all mankind, and three additional years to put it into the kind of language others could comprehend. It is the purpose of this book to reveal this finding — a fantastic, scientific discovery about the nature of man, whose life, as a direct consequence of this mathematical revelation, will be completely revolutionized in every way for his benefit, bringing about a transition so utterly amazing that if I were to tell you of all the changes soon to unfold, without also demonstrating the cause as to why these must come about, your incredulity would be aroused sufficiently to consider this a work of science-fiction, for who would believe it possible that all evil (every bit of hurt that exists in human relations) must decline and fall the very moment this discovery is thoroughly understood? Who believed the first astronomer when he predicted an eclipse, and who believed Einstein when he revealed the potential of atomic energy?

However, as Morrison wrote, "we encounter the stubborn resistance of the human mind, which is reluctant to give up fixed ideas. The early Greeks knew the earth was a sphere, but it took two thousand years to convince men that this fact is true." To overcome this "stubborn resistance" and bring about this new world, it is imperative that the knowledge in this book be adequately comprehended, which requires that the reader does not apply himself and his ideas as a standard of what is true and false, but that he understand the difference between a mathematical relation and an opinion, belief, or theory. As an example of what I mean, and to clarify that in this book the words scientific and mathematical only mean undeniable, if it is <u>absolutely impossible</u> for something to be proven true, whatever it may be, is it possible to prove the opposite of this something false? Isn't it obvious that the answer must be "no, it is not possible," unless the person asked does not understand the question, simply because to prove the opposite false would also prove this something true, and we began with the statement that this is an impossibility. Such reasoning is not a form of logic, <u>nor is it my opinion of the answer</u>. It is mathematical, scientific, undeniable, and it is not necessary to deal in what has been termed the exact sciences in order to be exact and scientific. Yet to show how confused is the thinking of the average person who is not accustomed to perceiving mathematical relations of this nature, when I told someone that his answer was incorrect, he replied, with a tone of resentment, "That's your opinion, but I believe it is possible," as if the answer could be one or the other. The earth can't be round and flat; it has to be one or the other, and your opinion can never change what is.

Now before I proceed, because this is a very crucial point, do you understand there is only one correct answer to what was just given, and that is, "No, it is not possible," which has nothing whatever to do with my opinion? The reason it is necessary to belabor this point is to preclude the possibility of someone adducing the rank of his education, or the long tenure of an accepted belief, as a standard from which he thinks he qualifies to disagree with anything that contains within itself proof of its veracity. Remember, I am going to bring about an unprecedented change in human conduct, but I can only do this if you understand what I am about to reveal. If you can't follow my reasoning as to why the earth is round, you will be compelled to continue believing it is flat, for it gives you satisfaction not to be wrong. Therefore, it is imperative that you know, well in advance, that my reasoning will be completely mathematical, scientific, and undeniable, so if you find yourself in disagreement, you had better reread that with which you disagree; otherwise, your "stubborn resistance," your inability to perceive these relations, will only delay the very life you want for yourself.

The dialogue of the text will be like a game of chess in which every one of your moves will be forced, and checkmate inevitable, but only if you don't make up your own rules as to what is true and false. The laws of this universe, which include those of our nature, are the rules of the game, and the only thing required to win, to bring about this New Earth that will benefit everyone... is to stick to the rules. But if you decide to move the king like the queen because it does not satisfy you to see a pet belief slipping away, or because it irritates your pride to be proven wrong or checkmated, then it is obvious that you are not sincerely concerned with learning the truth, but only with retaining your doctrines at all costs. However, when it is scientifically revealed that the very things religion, government, education and all others want — which include the means as well as the end — are prevented from becoming a reality only because we have not penetrated deeply enough into a thorough understanding of our ultimate nature, are we given a choice as to the direction we are compelled to travel, even though this means the relinquishing of ideas that have been part of our thinking since time immemorial?

I know you are quite curious as to what I am about to reveal, but it shouldn't be necessary to jump to conclusions because you will know this soon enough. Therefore, to preclude this jumping as much as possible, I am urging you not to read in a desultory manner since it is vitally important (in fact, absolutely necessary) that this book be read chapter by chapter in the sequence it was written. The first two chapters are most fundamental, upon which the rest is based. If you cannot understand them, or if you should skip over these and read other chapters, this work could appear like a fairytale; otherwise, the statement that "truth is stranger than fiction" will be amply verified by the scientific world, or by yourself, if you are able to follow the reasoning of mathematical relations.

Well, would you like to see what happens when science, the perception and extension of undeniable observations, takes over the problems of human conflict as the result of a fantastic discovery? Would you like to see that the mankind system has been obeying an invariable law just as mathematically harmonious as that which inheres in the solar system, a law that allowed a prophecy to be made thousands of years ago and verified in the 20th century? Would you like to learn, though this book has nothing whatever to do with religion or philosophy, that your faith in God will finally be rewarded with a virtual miracle, one that will shortly deliver us from all evil? If you are sincerely interested in seeing this fantastic transition to a new way of life, which must come about the moment this discovery is thoroughly understood, then do not judge this book in terms of your present knowledge, but do everything in your power to understand what is written by following the mathematical relations implicitly expressed throughout. Once you see, for the very first time, what is truly better for yourself (this applies to all mankind, regardless of race, color, creed, or manner of earning a living), you will be given no choice as to the direction you must travel.

However, in spite of everything, in spite of the fact that my discovery is completely scientific, it is a very difficult task to break through the beliefs, opinions and theories that have gotten a dogmatic hold on the mind. Therefore, in concluding this preface, and to exclude the type of reader who might be more of a hindrance than a help (those people who offer "stubborn resistance" because of their fallacious ideas; those who also judge a book and its author by certain standards, even before it is read), I should like it to be known that I am Jewish, that I have little formal education (seventh grade, to be exact), and that I intend to be my own publisher. Now if this disturbs your prejudices, if you are more concerned with who I am, the extent of my formal learning, the manner in which I express myself (punctuation, vocabulary, grammar, style and the general format of my book) rather than with what I have to relate, then you will know immediately that this is not the type of book you want. But when, for the very first time, the proverbial cart is placed after, not before, the horse, what difference does it really make when the knowledge I am about to reveal is for the benefit of all mankind, not just certain groups, and when all the education in the world can never teach what you are about to learn through my discovery? Are you going to be bitter and resentful and nail me to a cross for revealing, out of necessity, how unconsciously ignorant of the truth you have always been, for which you are not being blamed, or are you going to overlook this and thank God, as I have done, for showing the way at last?

This is a very serious work that has been put into a form that allows it to be understood, and it will start an atomic chain reaction of thought more powerful than anything yet produced. But despite all efforts to make it easier to read, it is still deep and will require that you go at a snail's pace, reading many things over and over again. However, if you would like to learn that Man Does Not Stand Alone, as Morrison understood from his scientific observations, that God, this Supreme Intelligence, is a mathematical reality of infinite wisdom, then what do you say we set sail on a voyage that will literally change the entire world. Shall we begin?

# PART 1

# THE FOUNDATION AND DEVELOPMENT OF A

# MATHEMATICAL STANDARD

# CHAPTER 1 — WORDS, NOT REALITY

Many years ago, long before man understood anything about the solar system, the Earth was considered flat, although there were several thinkers even then who were wondering about this.

"Say, Jim," said one of them to start up a conversation, "what is your opinion about the shape of the earth? Do you believe it is really flat or do you go along with my conception that it is round?"

"What difference does it really make what I think, Larry? The shape of the earth is what it is, and regardless of what I think, this will not be altered."

"That part is true, Jim, but if the earth is definitely round, isn't it obvious that just as long as we think otherwise, we will be prevented from discovering those things that depend on this knowledge for their discovery? Consequently, it does make a difference, how much so we are not in the position to know, but thousands of years hence, perhaps in the 20th century, there may be all kinds of scientific achievements attributed directly to knowing the true shape of the earth. Right?"

"This is very possible."

The scene now shifts to the present time, and a similar dialogue is started on another subject.

"Say, Jim, do you believe that man's will is free, or do you go along with my thoughts on the subject — that man's will is not free and never was?"

"What difference does it really make what I think, Larry? The will of man is certainly not going to be affected by my opinion, isn't that true?"

"That part is true enough, but if the will of man is definitely not free, isn't it obvious that just as long as we think otherwise, we will be prevented from discovering those things that depend on this knowledge for their discovery? Consequently, it does make a difference... how much so, we are not in the position to know at this moment but it is very possible that years hence there may be a new world attributed directly to this knowledge that man's will is not free. Right?"

This is very possible. But Larry, the other day when I was in Temple, a rabbi, during the course of his sermon, made it very clear that man has free will. What is more, professors, doctors, lawyers, and just about everybody I know, with the exception of you, agree that man has free will. If this is a theory, you would never know it by talking to them. Well, is it a theory, or is this established knowledge?"

"Of course it is a theory, Jim, otherwise there would be no believers in determinism. Is it possible for a person to believe that the Earth is flat now that we have mathematical knowledge of its circular shape? The only reason we still have opinions on both sides of this subject is simply because we don't know for a mathematical fact whether the will of man is or is not free."

But these theologians don't agree with you, Larry; they say that man's will is definitely free. Look, here comes a rabbi; ask him if man's will is free, just for the heck of it, and see for yourself how dogmatic he is in his answer."

"Rabbi, we have been discussing a subject and would appreciate your opinion. Is it true, false, or just a theory that man's will is free?"

"It is absolutely true that man's will is free because nothing compels an individual to choose evil instead of good; he prefers this only because he wants to partake of this evil, not because something is forcing him."

"Do you mean, Rabbi, that every person has two or more alternatives when making a choice?"

"Absolutely. That bank robber last week didn't have to rob the bank; he wanted to do it."

"But assuming that what you say is true, how is it possible to prove that which cannot be proven? Let me illustrate what I mean. Is it possible for you not to do what has just been done?"

"Naturally, it is impossible for me not to do what has just been done, because I have already done it."

"This, Rabbi, is a mathematical or undeniable relation and is equivalent to asking, is it possible for anyone not to get four as an answer to two plus two. Now if what has just been done was the choosing of B instead of A, is it possible not to choose B, which has already been chosen?"

"Impossible, naturally."

"Since it is absolutely impossible (this is the reasoning of mathematics, not logic, which gives rise to opinions) not to choose B instead of A, once B is selected, how is it possible to choose A in this comparison of possibilities when in order to make this choice you must not choose B, which has already been chosen?"

"Again, I must admit it is something impossible to do."

"Yet free will, in order to prove itself true, must do just that, the impossible. It must go back, reverse the order of time, undo what has already been done, and then show that A, with the conditions being exactly the same, could have been chosen instead of B. Since it is utterly impossible to reverse the order of time, which is absolutely necessary for mathematical proof, free will must always remain a theory. In other words, Rabbi, the most you can say is that you believe the bank robber had a choice, but there is absolutely no way this can be proven."

"I may be unable to prove that he was not compelled to rob that bank and kill the teller, but it is my opinion that he didn't have to do what he did."

"I'm not in the mood to argue that point, Rabbi, but at least we have arrived at a bit of knowledge that is absolutely undeniable, for we have just learned that it is mathematically impossible for any person to prove, beyond a shadow of doubt, that the will of man is free, yet a moment ago you made the dogmatic statement that man's will is definitely free."

"My apologies, dear Sir. What I meant to say was that it is the consensus of opinion that the will of man is free."

"Thank you, Rabbi. And now one other question and I will let you go. If it is mathematically impossible to prove the will of man free, is it possible to prove determinism, as the opposite of free will, false?"

"Yes, it is possible."

"No, Rabbi, it is not possible."

"That, my friend, is your opinion, not mine."

"Let me show you it is not an opinion. If you could prove that determinism is false, wouldn't this prove that free will, which is the opposite of determinism, is true, and didn't we just prove that it is mathematically impossible to prove free will true, which means that it is absolutely impossible to prove determinism false?"

"I see what you mean, and again I apologize for thinking this was a matter of opinion."

"This means that we have arrived at another bit of mathematical knowledge, and that is, although we can never prove free will true or determinism false, there still exists a possibility of proving determinism true or free will false. Now tell me, Rabbi, supposing your belief in free will absolutely prevents the discovery of knowledge that, when released, can remove the very things you would like to rid the world of, things you preach against, such as war, crime, sin, hate, discrimination, etc., what would you say then?"

"My friend, if this is true, and you can prove it, then all I can say is that God's ways surpass my understanding. I enjoyed talking with you, Son, and perhaps I shall live to see the day when all evil will be driven from our lives."

"Even if you don't live to see it, Rabbi, please rest assured the day is not far away, and that it must come about the very moment certain facts pertaining to the nature of man are brought to light because it is God's will. If you would like to see how this is accomplished by extending mathematical relations, then buy a copy of my book when I get it completed."

"Hey, Larry, I didn't know you could reason and think like that; you almost sound like old Socrates himself. Boy, that was really something to see. Just imagine, you actually got the rabbi to admit that free will is nothing other than an opinion. But you weren't serious about getting rid of all the evil in the world, were you?"

"I was never more serious in all my life."

"But how is it possible for you, just with your reasoning, nothing else, to put an end to all war, crime, sin, hate, etc.? If I must say so, Larry, this does sound kind of ridiculous."

"Are you asking if it is possible, or telling me that you know it is impossible?"

"After what you just demonstrated to the rabbi, I certainly would never tell you it is impossible when I don't know if it is, but it seems so incredible to hear someone say he is going to remove all evil from the entire earth, that I cannot help but be skeptical. Well, what is your first step? How do you go about making a start?"

"The first step is to prove conclusively, beyond a shadow of doubt and regardless of any opinions to the contrary, that the will of man is not free."

"But Larry, if you plan to use the knowledge that man's will is not free as a point from which to start your chain of reasoning, couldn't you get the same results without demonstrating that man's will is not free, simply by showing what must follow as a consequence?"

"Yes I could, Jim, and that was a very sharp question; but my purpose in proving that man's will is not free is not so much to have a sound basis from which to reason, but to show exactly why the will of man is not free. Now, this dictionary I have with me states that free will is 'The power of self-determination regarded as a special faculty of choosing good or evil without compulsion or necessity. Made, done, or given of one's own free choice; voluntary.' But this is only part of the definition, since it is implied that man can be held responsible, blamed and punished by others for doing what is considered wrong or evil, since it is believed he could have chosen otherwise. He is held responsible not for doing what he considers right, better, or good for himself under his particular set of circumstances, but for doing what others judge to be wrong or evil from their point of view, and they feel absolutely certain he could have acted otherwise had he wanted to. Isn't this the theme of free will, Jim?"

"I think you hit the nail right on the head."

"But take note, supposing the alternative judged right for him by others is not desired by himself because of conditions known only to him, what then? Does this make his will free?"

"Of course not; it only means that he disagreed with those who judged what was right for him."

"Bravo, Jim! I don't think you will have any trouble at all in following my reasoning, but let's pursue this a little bit further. Supposing a father is desperately in need of work to feed his family, but can't find a job. Let us assume he doesn't come under the consideration of unemployment compensation or relief and can't get any more credit for food, clothing, shelter, etc.; what is he supposed to do?"

"If he has no friends, he's in a bad way. Under conditions like these, he might even lend an ear to the principle of communism or socialism, or he might even be tempted to steal."

"But if he steals a loaf of bread to feed his family, the law can easily punish him by saying he didn't have to steal if he didn't want to, which is perfectly true. Others might say stealing is evil, that he could have chosen good, which in this case was almost any other alternative, according to their judgment. But supposing this individual preferred the risk of stealing, which took into consideration the possibility of punishment if caught, because he judged this act good for himself in comparison to the evil of asking for charity or further credit, which has already been denied; does this make his will free because he preferred stealing?"

"Absolutely not, Larry. It still only means that he disagrees with those who tell him what to do. But why is religion so hostile towards those who disagree with the belief in free will?"

"To theologians, God is the creator of all goodness. Since man does many things considered evil, and God is all goodness, they were given no choice but to endow him with freedom of the will so that God could be absolved of all responsibility for what man does of his own free will. The same thing occurs in society. The government holds each person responsible for obeying the laws, and then punishes those who do not, while absolving itself of all responsibility; but how is it possible for someone to obey that which appears to him worse? It is quite obvious that a person does not have to steal if he doesn't want to, but under certain conditions he wants to, and it is also obvious that the laws do not have to punish unless they want to, but both sides want to do what they consider better for themselves under the circumstances. The Russians didn't have to start a communist revolution against the tyranny that prevailed; they were not compelled to do this; they wanted to do it. The Japanese didn't have to attack us at Pearl Harbor; they wanted to. We didn't have to drop an atomic bomb among their people; we wanted to. In other words, it is an undeniable observation that man does not have to commit a crime or hurt another in any way if he doesn't want to. The most severe tortures, even the threat of death, cannot compel or cause him to do what he makes up his mind not to do. Since this observation is mathematically undeniable, the words 'free will,' which have come to signify this aspect that nothing can compel man to do what he doesn't want to do, are absolutely true in this context because they symbolize what the perception of this relation cannot deny, and here lies in part the unconscious source of all the dogmatism and confusion because man is not caused or compelled to do to another what he makes up his mind not to do. The words 'free will' contain an assumption or fallacy for they imply that if man is not caused or compelled to do anything against his will, it must be preferred of his own free will. This is one of those logical, not mathematical, conclusions. Consequently, determinism was faced with an almost impossible task because it assumed that heredity and environment caused man to choose evil, but in reality, so thought the other side, he was not caused or compelled to commit a crime; he did it of his own free will; he wanted to do it, he didn't have to."

"Say Larry, this is getting kind of confusing. Are you telling me that though you know man's will is not free, he is not caused or compelled to do what he does?"

"You see, Jim, the words cause and compel are the perception of an improper or fallacious relation because in order for them to be developed and have meaning it was absolutely necessary that the words free will be born as their opposite, as tall gives meaning to short, beautiful to ugly, intelligent to stupid, etc. The expression 'I did it of my own free will' is perfectly correct when it is understood to mean 'I did it because I wanted to do it; nothing compelled or caused me to do it since I could have acted otherwise had I desired.' But the truth of the matter is that at any particular moment of time, the motion of man is not free, for all life obeys an invariable law which I shall prove in an undeniable manner. It is extremely important, however, that you understand the expression — 'I did it of my own free will' is correct when qualified, but in no way indicates that man's will is free. In fact, I shall use it frequently myself!'

"You must be kidding, Larry. Here you are in the process of demonstrating why the will of man is not free, and in the same breath you tell me you're doing this of your own free will."

"Let me clarify. The phrase 'I was compelled, of my own free will' only means that I was not being coerced to do anything against my will. It is also important to understand that a great many motions of man are under the normal compulsion of living and therefore do not play any part in what pertains to the belief in free will because no choice is involved; consequently, these are not my consideration. For example, free will does not hold any person responsible for what he does in an unconscious state like hypnosis, nor does it believe that man can be blamed for being born, growing, sleeping, eating, defecating, urinating, etc. Obviously, a great part of our lives offers no choice and therefore it is unnecessary to prove that these actions, which come under the compulsion of normal living, are beyond control. In reality, we are carried along on the wings of time or life during every moment of our existence, and we have no say in this matter. We cannot stop ourselves from being born, getting older, and are compelled to either live out our lives or commit suicide if not satisfied. Is it possible for anyone to disagree with this?"

"Not unless he doesn't understand the question."

"However, to prove that what we do of our own free will, of our own desire because we want to do it, is also beyond control, it is necessary to employ mathematical reasoning. Therefore, since it is absolutely impossible for man to be both dead and alive at the same time, and since it is absolutely impossible for a person to desire committing suicide unless dissatisfied with life, we are given the ability to demonstrate a revealing and undeniable relation.

Life is all motion and never satisfied to remain in one spot. Every motion of life, from the beating heart to the slightest reflex action, from all inner to outer movements of the body, indicates that life is never satisfied or content to remain in one position for always, which, in this context, shall be termed death.

I shall now call the present moment of life or time — here, for the purpose of mathematical clarification, and the next moment coming up — there. You, Jim, are now standing on this present moment of time called here and are given two alternatives: either live or kill yourself; either move to the next spot called there or remain where you are without moving a hair's breadth, which is death or here. Which do you prefer, Jim, here or there, suicide or life?"

"I prefer... "

"Excuse the interruption, but the very fact you didn't commit suicide at that moment makes it obvious and mathematically undeniable that you are not satisfied to stay in one position forever and always, which is death, and prefer moving off that spot here to there, which motion is life. Consequently, the motion of life, which is any motion from here to there, is a movement, however slight or imperceptible, away from that which dissatisfies; otherwise, had you been satisfied to remain here in this one position, which is death or suicide, you would never have moved to there. Since the motion of life constantly moves away from here to there, which motion is an expression of dissatisfaction with death, or a motion away from that which dissatisfies, it must obviously move constantly in the direction of satisfaction. This reasoning is completely mathematical in every way, not logical, and does not require man's approval or agreement for its validity, although his understanding is necessary for recognition of the facts."

"I can't understand all this clearly, Larry, but I'm going to take your word for it that life is compelled to move constantly in the direction of satisfaction."

"This simple demonstration, Jim, proves conclusively that from moment to moment, all through life, man can never move in the direction of dissatisfaction, and that his every motion, conscious or unconscious, is a natural effort to get rid of some dissatisfaction or move to greater satisfaction, otherwise, as has been shown, not being dissatisfied, he could never move from here to there. Every motion of life expresses dissatisfaction with the present position. Scratching is the effort of life to remove the dissatisfaction of the itch, as urinating, defecating, sleeping, working, playing, mating, walking, talking, moving about in general, are unsatisfied needs of life pushing man always in the direction of satisfaction. It is easy, in many cases, to recognize things that satisfy, such as money when funds are low, but it is extremely difficult at other times to comprehend the innumerable subconscious factors often responsible for the malaise of dissatisfaction. Your desire to take a bath arises from a feeling of uncleanliness or a wish to be refreshed, which means that you are dissatisfied with the way you feel at that moment, and your desire to get out of the tub arises from a feeling of dissatisfaction with a position that has suddenly grown uncomfortable. Well, Jim, believe it or not, this simple demonstration proves conclusively that man's will is not free because satisfaction is the only direction life can take, which offers one possibility only at each moment of time."

"You mean there is nothing else, and this is supposed to satisfy me? Let's assume for the sake of argument, Larry, that other people are just as thick as me. Frankly, you could never prove to me that man's will is not free because I can't follow your reasoning. Isn't there something else you can add to prove your equation, just as we can prove that two from six leaves four because four plus two equals six?"

"To satisfy you, Jim, I shall put this to a mathematical test for further proof and clarification. Let us suppose that you wanted very much of two alternatives, the one labeled A, which we shall designate something considered evil by society, instead of B, the humdrum of your regular routine. Could you possibly pick B at that particular moment of time, if A is preferred as a better alternative, when nothing could dissuade you from your decision, not even the threat of the laws?"

"Not if I made up my mind that this is what I really want."

"Let's change it around now for a better understanding. Supposing the clergy wanted of two alternatives, the one labeled A, which shall now represent something considered good by society, instead of B, that which is judged evil. Is it possible for them to prefer the latter when the former, at that very moment of time, is considered the better choice? If it is utterly impossible to choose B when one of the two must be chosen at that particular moment of time, are they not compelled, by their very nature, to prefer A; and how can they be free when the favorable difference between A and B, regardless of the reason it is preferred, is the compulsion of their choice and the motion of life in the direction of that which gave them greater satisfaction? To be free, according to free will, man would be able to prefer of two alternatives, either the one he wants or the one he doesn't want, which is an absolute impossibility because selecting what he doesn't want when what he does want is available as an alternative, is a motion in the direction of dissatisfaction. Let us examine this further, Jim.

"Supposing you were taken prisoner in wartime for espionage and condemned to death, but mercifully given a choice between two exists: A, is the painless hemlock of Socrates, while B is death by having your head held under water. Which do you prefer, and have I given you a choice? Is it humanly possible to prefer exit B if A is offered as an alternative?"

"You know you haven't given me any choice, Larry."

"Once it is understood that life is compelled to move in the direction of satisfaction, and two such alternatives are presented, what choice can anybody possibly have but to accept the lesser of two evils? Since it is absolutely impossible to prefer something considered still worse in your opinion, regardless of what it is, are you not compelled, completely beyond your control in this set of circumstances, to prefer A; and since the definition of free will states that man can choose good or evil without compulsion or necessity, how is it possible for the will of man to be free when choice is under a tremendous amount of compulsion since B was evil, as the worse alternative, and could not be selected in this comparison of possibilities?"

"But this is ridiculous, Larry, because you know you are not giving me any choice."

"That's where you are wrong, Jim. I most certainly am giving you a choice, and if your will is free, you should be able to choose B just as well as A. The reason you are confused is because the word 'choice' is very misleading, for it assumes that man has two or more possibilities; but in reality this is a delusion because the direction of life, always moving towards satisfaction, compels man to prefer of differences what he considers better for himself; and when two or more alternatives are presented for his consideration he is compelled, by his very nature, to prefer not that one which is considered by him worse, but what gives every indication of being better or more satisfying for the particular set of circumstances involved. The purpose of thinking things through very carefully is to avoid, as much as possible, making a mistake, which is hindsight recognition of what should have been done where the unfavorable reactions of others are concerned. The purpose of choice is to compare meaningful differences to decide which alternative is preferable. A and B, representing small or large differences which include the blame, criticism, and punishment that follow in the wake of certain preferences, are compared. The comparison is absolutely necessary to know which is preferable. The difference, which is considered favorable, regardless of the reason, is the compulsion of greater satisfaction desire is forced to take, which makes one of them an impossible choice in this comparison, simply because it gives less satisfaction under the circumstances. Consequently, since B is an impossible choice, you are not free to choose A, for your preference is a natural compulsion of the direction life is compelled to take, over which you have absolutely no control. The word choice itself indicates there are preferable differences, otherwise there would be no choice in the matter at all, as with A and A. Choosing, or the comparison of differences, is an integral part of man's nature, but he s compelled to prefer of alternatives the one he considers better or more satisfying under the circumstances, which is why suicide, in many cases, has been preferable to remaining alive. Consequently, even though he chooses various things all through the course of his life, man is never given any <u>free</u> choice at all."

"Boy oh boy, Larry, that's terrific. I'm beginning to understand now that will is really not free. But yet it seems to me that it is still possible to give an example of how man can be made to move in the direction of dissatisfaction. If I could do this, then all your reasoning is shot to hell."

"That's true, Jim, but I defy you or anyone else to give me an example of this. Go ahead and try."

"Well let's suppose that of two apples, a red and a yellow, I actually can't stand to eat the red because I'm allergic to it; consequently, my taste lies in the direction of the latter which gives me greater satisfaction. In fact, the thought of eating the red apple makes me very dissatisfied. Yet in spite of this, I am going to eat it to demonstrate that even though I am dissatisfied and prefer the yellow apple, I can definitely move in the direction of dissatisfaction."

"And do you honestly think this demonstrates a motion in that direction? Isn't it obvious that regardless of the reason you decided to eat the red apple, even though it would be distasteful in comparison, this choice, at that moment of time, gave you greater satisfaction; otherwise, you would have definitely selected and eaten the yellow? The normal conditions under which you frequently ate the yellow apple in preference were changed by your desire to prove a point, and it gave you greater satisfaction to eat what you did not like in an effort to prove that life can be made to move in the direction of dissatisfaction. No matter how many examples you may experiment with, the results will always be the same because this is an invariable law."

"But Larry, there are many times when I have been terribly dissatisfied with things that I have done, and at that exact moment, isn't it obvious that I am not moving in the direction of satisfaction because I am very dissatisfied?"

"No, because the very moment before you thought of your dissatisfaction, you were dissatisfied not to think of this; consequently, it gave you greater satisfaction to think about your dissatisfaction with what you did. Remember, each moment of time you are standing on this spot called here, and if you move, think, or do anything, it is obvious that you are not satisfied to remain on that spot; consequently, your motion to there, even though you contemplate something that gave you dissatisfaction, is more satisfying than not thinking about it at that particular time. The very next moment you may discover that thinking about it is so terribly dissatisfying that you will think about something else, which again is a motion in the direction of satisfaction; and if you find that you can't go on to the next spot called there, because the thought of continuing to live is worse than killing yourself, then you would be forced to commit suicide because you are terribly dissatisfied with life, but yet your motion to there, which in this case is killing yourself, is still in the direction of greater satisfaction."

"In spite of all that you say, Larry, I know that I am not satisfied with my job. There are many things I don't want to do because they do not satisfy me at all, but I have to do them."

"Your words are not accurate, Jim. You also want to do the very things you do not like, simply because the alternative is still worse. How many times in your life have you remarked, 'You give me no choice,' or 'It makes no difference?' Just because some differences are so obviously superior in value where you are concerned that no hesitation is required to decide which of the alternatives is preferable, while other differences need a more careful consideration, doesn't change the direction of life which moves always and ever towards satisfaction. The truth of the matter is that all through life, man is compelled to choose what he considers good for himself, but what you may judge bad or good for yourself doesn't make it so for others, especially when it is remembered that a juxtaposition of differences in each case presents alternatives that affect choice. Now Jim, just take careful note of this simple mathematical reasoning that proves conclusively, beyond a shadow of doubt, that man's will is not free.

Man either doesn't have a choice because none is involved, as with aging, and then it is obvious that he is under the normal compulsion of living, regardless of what his particular motion at any moment might be; or he has a choice, and then is given two or more alternatives of which he is compelled, by his very nature, to prefer the one that gives him greater satisfaction, whether it is the lesser of two evils, the greater of two goods, or a good over an evil. Therefore, it is absolutely impossible for the will of man to be free because he never has a <u>free</u> choice."

"Larry, I am absolutely convinced that man's will is not free, but this doesn't mean anything to me. It's just like I said before, what difference does it really make? If I sock you in the jaw because this gives me greater satisfaction, and you, in turn, sock me, what difference does it make whether my will is free or not? Besides, this demonstration of yours would have no meaning whatsoever for philosophers like Will Durant, nor would it have for religion. Spinoza and Spencer knew that man's will is not free, and each of them had their own form of proof, so what did it get them? Spencer is criticized by Durant who concludes his analysis of free will with a statement that is obviously inaccurate since you have just demonstrated that it is mathematically impossible to prove free will true or determinism false, because he writes on page 103 in the Mansions Of Philosophy which I happen to have with me: 'For even while we talked determinism we knew that it was false; we never treated ourselves, or our children, as machines. If there is an almost eternal recurrence of philosophies of freedom, it is because direct perception can never be beaten down with formulas, or sensation with reasoning.' I've been carrying this book around with me for some time. Did you ever read it?"

"Yes I have, several times in fact; but Durant is anything but a scientist and an accurate thinker. In the two sentences just quoted, he assumes that free will is true because, in his mind, determinism is false, and the reason he thinks determinism is false is because man is not a machine.

Then, not realizing how mathematically impossible is his next statement, he claims that philosophies of free will eternally recur because reasoning and formulas can't beat down the obvious truth of direct perception. Take a look at that last statement very carefully, Jim, and see if you can't tell me why it is mathematically impossible, forgetting all the things you just learned from me."

"I give up, Larry. In fact, to be honest with you, I always agreed with Durant in everything he had to say. To me, he has always been a great thinker and a great writer."

"I certainly don't want to take anything away from this man, Jim, but when he makes statements that are obviously inaccurate, once certain facts are clarified, we can't continue to live a lie. Now observe very carefully. If free will was proven, once and for all, to be that which is nonexistent (and let's take for granted that you know this for a fact), and accepted as such by our scientific world at large, simply because the proof cannot be denied by anyone anywhere, would it be possible, according to Durant's statement, for 'philosophies of freedom' to recur anymore? Isn't it obvious that the recurrence of the belief in free will is a mathematical impossibility once freedom of the will is proven to be a figment of the imagination, or to phrase it differently, a realistic mirage? Is it humanly possible for the belief that the world is flat to eternally recur when we have mathematical knowledge that it is round? Consequently, the continued return of this belief in free will can only be due to the fact that it is still a logical theory, or plausible conception, that has never been analyzed properly, allowing the belief and its philosophies to persist. But Durant states that 'philosophies of freedom eternally recur' not because of the explanation I just gave, an explanation that cannot be denied by anyone anywhere, even by this philosopher himself, providing it is understood, but 'because direct perception can never be beaten down with formulas, or sensation with reasoning.' Isn't it apparent to you now, Jim, that such words have no relation to reality whatsoever?"

"I have to agree with you, Larry, and I think your reasoning is terrific."

"You know, Jim, if this is a sample of what Durant calls direct perception, and he considers it superior to reasoning, is it any wonder he is so confused and his reasoning so fallacious, since the word 'because', which denotes the perception of a relation, whether true or false, indicates that he is criticizing reasoning while reasoning. This simple paraphrase will clarify a point: 'If there is an almost eternal recurrence of' four equaling two plus two, 'it is because' two equals one plus one, and one plus one plus one plus one totals four. He unconsciously uses syllogistic reasoning (he criticizes this somewhere in his books), which is logical though completely fallacious, by setting up an understandable assumption for a major premise. But when a person perceives, with direct perception, certain undeniable relations, is it necessary to make an equation out of four equaling two plus two, or out of the fact that once free will is proven untrue it can no longer exist and its philosophies of freedom return? He begins with the assumption that direct perception (two words that have confused him) is superior to reasoning in determining the truth, which made a syllogistic equation necessary to attempt to prove the validity of an inaccurate observation. Then he reasons thusly in his minor premise: free will is not a matter of reasoning, like determinism, but is the result of direct perception; therefore (and here is his fallacious conclusion), since philosophies of freedom employ direct perception, which can never be beaten down by the reasoning of determinism, the belief in free will must eternally recur."

"I must say it again, Larry; you are simply terrific. If this is a sample of your power to perceive mathematical relations, there is no telling what you may accomplish."

"I wasn't kidding, Jim. I'm prepared to perform a virtual miracle, something so fantastic that you will be compelled to catch your breath in absolute amazement, and we have already finished the first step."

"Do you mean that proving man's will is not free is essential to this miracle you are about to perform? Couldn't you have just started with the assumption that man's will is not free and still accomplished the same thing?"

"Yes, as I told you before, but now you know why man's will is not free; otherwise, you might have been influenced by Durant and interjected a remark about man not being a machine. Is there anything about my demonstration, Jim, that would make you think he is now a machine?"

"Nothing at all."

"What time do you have, Jim?"

"What! Is it that late already? I told my wife I'd be home at five-thirty. I really have to run, Jim, but I just want to point out one thing. The fact that will is not free demonstrates that man has been unconsciously developing at a mathematical rate, and during every moment of his progress was doing what he had to do because he had no free choice. Building cities, developing scientific achievements, writing books and laws, composing music, going to war, arguing and fighting, committing terrible crimes, praying to God — all these things are mankind at a particular stage of his development, just as children were sacrificed at an earlier stage. These activities or motions are the natural entelechy of man who is always developing, correcting his mistakes, and moving in the direction of greater satisfaction. He is constantly compelled by his nature to make unfree choices, decisions, and prefer of whatever is available during each lifetime that which he considers better for himself. But this knowledge, the facts just presented that prove conclusively man's will is not free... and the knowledge that I will reveal to you tomorrow, if you're interested . . ."

"I am."

. . ."were not available before this, and what is revealed as each individual becomes conscious of his true nature is something fantastic to behold, for it not only gives ample proof that evil is no accident, but it will also put an end to every conceivable kind of hurt that exists in human relations."

"Do you mean that God caused the evil so that we could develop ourselves?"

"I mean that evil was part of a harmonious operation called the mankind system, and that it was compelled to come into existence by the very nature of life itself; but once certain facts are understood, it will also be no accident that this evil will be compelled to take leave of this earth."

"I believe it is mathematically impossible, to use your pet expression, Larry, to remove all evil from our lives."

"Don't bet your life on it, Buddy Boy, or you'd be a dead duck. We have been gravitating, in an unconscious manner, toward this New Earth, which many prophets foresaw, but now no more prophecies, conjectures, or philosophies are necessary, for this long-awaited, wonderful moment we have been looking forward to with prayers, hope, and great anticipation has arrived at last. There will take place a virtual miracle of transformation as each person consciously realizes <u>what it means</u> that his will is not free, which has not yet been revealed.

This discovery I will soon make known to you, Jim, is not only that long sought standard and touchstone of truth and reality, but also that elixir of alchemy, for with it the baser metals of human nature are going to be magically transmuted into the pure gold of genuine happiness for every individual on this planet, and for all generations to come.

"Now be perfectly honest with me, Jim, who can object to relinquishing the belief in free will when this is the key to the decline and fall of all misery and unhappiness?"

"Only an absolute fool, Larry, no one else."

"See you tomorrow at the same time and place, OK?"

"Right you are."

# CHAPTER 2 — THE GREAT IMPASSE OF BLAME

# AND PUNISHMENT

That evening, Jim could not sleep for the longest time. He kept reflecting on the conversation with Larry, and the more he dwelt on this, the more amazed he became with the realization that although 98% of the world believed in freedom of the will, man's will was actually not free at all. He then began to understand how this belief, or any fallacious conception that had gotten a dogmatic hold on the mind, could very easily prevent the discovery of knowledge hidden behind it, because no one takes thorough pains to look. "But that in itself could not be accurate because Spinoza and many other philosophers also knew that man's will is not free," he thought to himself, "and yet they didn't make any discoveries. I also know the same thing, now, yet I wouldn't know what to do with this knowledge if my life depended on it. I suppose that these men, with all their potential as deep thinkers, just didn't think deeply enough, that is, if Larry really and truly has made a sensational discovery. Somehow or other, despite his apparent seriousness, I believe he's pulling my leg. Well, tomorrow I'll know the truth once and for all," and Jim finally dozed off with this on his mind.

The next day, they met at their usual place, and Larry could see that Jim was all excited to learn what it meant that man's will is not free.

"Well, Buddy Boy, did you have a good night's rest?"

"Are you kidding? Say, Larry, will you please not beat around the bush any further, and kindly tell me what your discovery is?"

"Don't get impatient, Jim. There are certain things that must be understood first in order to comprehend this discovery, and one of them is the realization that all my reasoning of yesterday could never, in itself, dethrone the belief in free will, simply because there is a force that compels the belief to remain in existence. Durant, all theologians and other philosophers, and all forms of government would never be shaken by my demonstration thus far."

"I can understand why religion would want free will to remain in existence, because otherwise God would have to be blamed for the evil in the world."

"Let us be more accurate with our words, Jim, and say that religion thinks God would have to be blamed if man's will is not free. But what about the philosophers and governments who are compelled to reason that man's will is free despite everything?"

"I give up, Larry. What is responsible for the 'almost eternal recurrence of philosophies of free will?' And that was from memory, too."

"The responsibility lies with the fact that the corollary thrown up by the knowledge that man's will is not free presents an impasse which no thinker, including the deepest of all time, has been able to understand and overcome. The belief in free will came into existence out of necessity because it was mathematically impossible for man to solve his problems without blame and punishment, which required the justification of this belief in order for him to absolve his conscience. But once it is established, beyond a shadow of doubt, that will is not free because life is constantly moving in the direction of satisfaction, completely beyond control (this is an invariable law which cannot be denied or disproved by anyone anywhere), compelling man to always prefer of available alternatives that which he, not someone else, considers more satisfying for himself, it becomes absolutely impossible to hold him responsible for anything he does, regardless of what."

"You must be joking, Larry. You know it's impossible not to blame and punish people for committing murder, rape, stealing, the wholesale slaughter of 6 million Jews, etc. Does this mean that we are supposed to condone these evils, and wouldn't man become even less responsible if there were no laws and threats of punishment to control his nature? Doesn't our history show that if man wants something badly enough, he will go to any lengths to satisfy his desire, even commit murder and pounce down on other nations with talons or tons of steel? What is it that prevents the poor from walking into stores and taking what they need and want, if not the fear of punishment? Do you fully realize that what you just said strikes at the very heart of all civilization, the teaching of what is right and wrong, good and evil, for how is it humanly possible not to blame a person for hurting others? No, Larry, there is no way out of this, and unless you perform some kind of miracle, I'm afraid that I, too, will have to continue believing in freedom of the will, that is, unless this corollary is untrue."

"Well, Jim, is it any wonder free will has never been dethroned when the solution has been beyond the capacity of every thinker thus far? Can't you see when a thinker is faced with this problem, he is given two alternatives: either admit his ignorance or pretend to knowledge he doesn't possess? Do you know the answer, Jim?"

"I certainly do not."

"Then why do you pretend to knowledge you do not possess?"

"I didn't say I knew the answer."

"But your whole attitude clearly indicates that you believe it is mathematically impossible to solve this problem, which means that you are pretending to possess the knowledge that I don't have the solution. What difference does it make whether you say something can be done or it can't be done; don't you clearly indicate that you possess the knowledge to know this?"

"You're right, Larry. I did imply that I know this cannot be accomplished, but I take back what I said on the grounds that I do not have the knowledge of your knowledge."

"Which is nothing but the truth, right, Jim?"

"Don't rub it in, Larry. I admitted I was wrong."

"Well, then, let's continue. You see, Jim, I fully realize that my explanation thus far is inadequate, but you jumped to a conclusion right away without even letting me clarify the corollary. I know that your knowledge that man's will is not free will not prevent you from continuing to blame and punish despite this fact, if it gives you greater satisfaction under the conditions that demand such a reaction. I repeat, I know that this is certainly not a sufficient explanation as to why there should be no blame and punishment, especially when these corrective measures were definitely the lesser of two evils as a solution to the many problems that always confronted mankind."

"I apologize again, Larry. I realize how wrong I was to jump to the conclusion that you were not aware of the inadequate explanation."

"Thank you, Jim. If it had not been for the development of laws and a penal code, for the constant teaching of right and wrong, civilization could never have reached the outposts of this New Earth. Yet despite the fact that we have been brought up to believe that man can be blamed and punished for doing what he was taught is wrong and evil (this is the cornerstone of all law and order up to now), the force that makes us move in the direction of satisfaction (or this invariable law of God) states explicitly, as we perceive these mathematical relations, that since man's will is not free — Thou Shall Not Blame anything he does."

"There you go again, Larry, and I can't help myself because that statement rubs me the wrong way since I can think of many situations where blame and punishment are absolutely necessary as the lesser of two evils. However, it's true that I don't know what you have up your sleeve, but if the average person is anything like me, you would have one heck of a time getting him to listen to what appears to be plain nonsense."

"How well I know this. I tried to engage a rabbi once in a discussion about free will, and when he said: 'If man's will is not free, then you can't blame or punish anything he does, is that correct?' And when I answered, 'Right,' he actually got up and walked out of the room. Now you tell me, Jim, how is it possible to explain the solution when nobody wishes to listen because they think they know there isn't any?"

"I will listen, Larry, and the whole world will listen if you really can put an end to all war, crime, and evil in general."

"That's just it, Jim; it requires the entire world to listen and understand so that this evil in our lives can be done away with. Do you still have that book, Mansions of Philosophy, in your car?"

"Yes I do."

"Will you get it, please? I'd like to read you just part of a sentence to show that Durant is no different than the rabbi, and that his mind is also closed to what to him is already a foregone conclusion. Here it is: 'Let the determinist honestly envisage the implications of his philosophy,' which demonstrates that all reasoning in favor of free will is the result of inferences derived from the inability of logic to accept the implications. Right at this point, Jim, lies the crux of a problem so difficult of solution that it has kept free will in power as far back as we can remember, for how was it humanly possible for government, religion, education, even philosophy and psychology to strike at the very heart of all civilization, or even look in that direction for an answer."

"That's exactly what I have been saying, Larry. It is impossible for anyone to think otherwise."

"Yes, Jim, but that doesn't imply there isn't any solution because we are faced with what appears to be an impossible impasse. There is even another implication that will only complicate matters still more; do you know what it is?"

"I think I do, but I didn't want to mention it for fear I would only make a fool of myself."

"Actually, you wouldn't be making a fool of yourself, Jim, that is, assuming that you are thinking what I'm thinking, because even Durant thought the same thing. Well, what are you thinking?"

"It occurred to me that if man knew his will is not free, he would use this knowledge to excuse himself by saying, 'I could not help myself because my will is not free.'"

"That's right, Jim. That is the other implication. Durant expresses it on page 87 by saying — here it is — 'if he committed crimes, society was to blame; if he was a fool, it was the fault of the machine, which had slipped a cog in generating him.' In other words, he assumes that this kind of knowledge allows a person to shift his responsibility for what he does. One individual blames society for his crimes, as he rots in prison, while another blames the mechanical structure of the machine which slipped a cog and made him into a fool. However, you will soon see that not only Durant but all mankind are very much confused by the misleading logic of words that do not describe reality for what it is.

It is important to remember, Jim, that just as long as it is believed man's will is free, that's just how long it is possible to blame and punish as a solution to our problems. Nobody would think of blaming a baby for being born, but shortly thereafter, the parents and society will blame and punish this child for not acting as he should. Society judges what is right and wrong and then holds man responsible to these standards. In other words, just as long as man has this safety valve of blame and punishment, he is permitted to strike the first blow of injustice with impunity."

"What do you mean, Larry?"

"Every standard of right blames someone in advance for doing what is judged wrong; but supposing this yardstick itself is wrong? Then the person who judges the conduct of another according to this measurement is permitted to strike the first blow of injustice with impunity, while being permitted to blame any retaliation. A perfect example is when parents tell a child that it is wrong to do certain things. The child, desiring to do what they said not to do, is blamed and punished, while they justify their own conduct by saying his actions were wrong since he didn't have to do what he did because man has free will to act otherwise. Are you beginning to see what takes place in our present world, Jim?"

"But Larry, isn't it obvious that parents have to teach a child something, and regardless of what this is, it must be a standard of some sort? Supposing your son, while visiting some friends, was to jump on their brand new sofa with his shoes and use it as a trampoline, wouldn't you blame and punish him for embarrassing you and hurting their furniture in this manner? And supposing he was in the habit of doing this, wouldn't you warn him in advance that if he does it, he will be severely punished? Isn't it obvious that we must have standards of some kind so that a child can be taught the difference between right and wrong, good and evil? Supposing all individuals in a society are told that it is wrong to steal (I hope you're not going to tell me this is right), yet certain ones deliberately ignore this and take what belongs to someone else, isn't it obvious that we must blame them because they were warned in advance that should they steal, they will be punished? Are you trying to tell me there is no such thing as a standard of right and wrong?"

"Bravo, Jim! You're not so bad yourself. However, my fine feathered friend, if you know the difference between right and wrong, and you also know that a person cannot be blamed or punished for what he does because his will is not free, isn't it obvious that we are given only one alternative, and that is to prevent the desire to do what is wrong from arising, which then makes it unnecessary to blame and punish? In other words, just as long as man has this safety valve of blame and punishment, he doesn't have to find the solution to this doing of what is wrong. Parents can be very careless and excuse themselves by blaming their children, as governments can be careless and excuse themselves by blaming their citizens, while plunging the entire world into war."

"But supposing they are not careless, and they are doing everything in their power to prevent children and citizens from doing what is wrong so that blame and punishment are not necessary, what then, are we not supposed to blame and punish them for our own protection when they do something wrong?"

"That's just the point, Jim. Once it is discovered, through mathematical reasoning, that man's will is definitely not free, then it becomes impossible to blame an individual for what he is compelled to do; consequently, it is imperative that we discover a way to prevent his desire to do the very things for which blame and punishment were previously necessary as the lesser of two evils."

"In other words, Larry, your discovery, whatever it is, will prevent man from desiring to commit murder, rape, start a war, annihilate 6 million people, etc., is that right?"

"That's correct, Jim. The corollary Thou Shall Not Blame doesn't mean, when it is extended, that we will be forced to condone what hurts us, but only that we will be shown how to prevent these evils by mathematically extending the corollary."

"Do you mean there is absolutely no way all evil can be removed from our lives without a knowledge of your discovery?"

"That's absolutely true, Jim."

"Then your discovery must be the most fantastic thing ever discovered by man before."

"It is. To show you how fantastic, just take note of the infinite wisdom that directs every aspect of this universe, which includes the solar and mankind systems, through invariable laws that we are at last getting to understand. Follow this, Jim, it is very interesting. Now here is versatile man — writer, composer, artist, inventor, scientist, philosopher, theologian, architect, builder, mathematician, chess player, murderer, prostitute, thief, etc. — whose will is absolutely and positively not free despite all the learned opinions to the contrary, yet compelled by his very nature to believe that it is since it was impossible not to blame and punish the terrible evils that came into existence out of necessity, and then permitted, after reaching a sufficient degree of development, to perceive the necessary relations as to why will is not free and what this means for the entire world, soon to be revealed, which perception was utterly impossible without the development, and absolutely necessary for the inception of our New Earth. Where in all history have you heard anything more incredible?"

"Nowhere, Larry. This is really and truly the most fantastic thing I have ever heard, providing your discovery proves it, but this is still an unknown factor, right?"

"Not for long, Jim, because I'm getting ready to show you what my discovery is; but to solve this problem of evil with the aid of our enigmatic corollary — Thou Shall Not Blame (for this seems mathematically impossible since it appears that man will always desire something for which blame and punishment will be necessary), it is extremely important to go through a de-confusion process regarding words by employing the other scientific fact revealed to you yesterday. Consequently, as was earlier pointed out, and to reveal this relation, it is an absolutely undeniable observation that man does not have to commit a crime or do anything to hurt another person unless he wants to. Even the most severe tortures and the threat of death cannot make him do to others what he makes up his mind not to do. He is not caused or compelled against his will to hurt another by his environment and heredity but prefers this action because at that moment of time, he derives greater satisfaction in his motion to <u>there</u>, which is a normal compulsion of his nature over which he has absolutely no control. But though it is a mathematical law that nothing can compel man to do to another what he makes up his mind not to do (this is an extremely crucial point), he is nevertheless under a compulsion, during every moment of his existence, to do everything he does. We can't blame him for doing what he does because his will is not free, but he can't be made to do what he does — unless he wants to, or, to phrase it differently, unless he desires to do it of his own free will."

"Can you clarify that a little bit more, Larry?"

"Certainly. In other words, no one is compelling a person to work at a job he doesn't like or remain in a country against his will; he actually <u>wants</u> to do the very things he dislikes simply because the alternative is considered worse in his opinion, and he must choose something to do among the various things in his environment, or else commit suicide. Was it humanly possible to make Gandhi and his followers do what they did not want to do when unafraid of death, which was judged the lesser of two evils? They were compelled, by their desire for freedom, to prefer nonviolence, turning the other cheek as a solution to their problem. Consequently, when any person says he was compelled to do what he did <u>against his will</u>, because the alternative was considered worse in his opinion; that he really didn't want to do it but had to (and innumerable of our words and expressions say this), he is obviously confused and unconsciously dishonest with himself and others because everything man does to another is done only because he wants to do it, or, to be ironical once again, done of his own free will, which only means, in this context, that his preference gave him greater satisfaction at that moment of time for one reason or another. But remember, this desire is a compulsion beyond control for which he cannot be blamed. So bear in mind now, for this is that very crucial point I find necessary to repeat: man is never compelled to do to others what he doesn't want to do, but is compelled to want to do everything he does. This reveals that he has mathematical control over the former, since whatever he decides to do must be considered the preferable alternative under his particular set of circumstances. All I am doing is clarifying these terms so that you are not confused, but make sure you understand this mathematical difference before proceeding further."

"It is perfectly clear to me now, Larry, and I find it impossible to disagree."

"Therefore, to continue my reasoning, Jim, if someone were to say, 'I didn't really want to hurt that person but couldn't help myself under the circumstances,' which demonstrates that though he believes in freedom of the will he admits he was not free to act otherwise; that he was forced by his environment to do what he really didn't want to do — or should he make any effort to shift his responsibility for this hurt to heredity, God, his parents, the fact that his will is not free, or something else as the cause — he is obviously lying to others and being dishonest with himself because absolutely nothing is forcing him, against his will, to do what he doesn't want to do, for over this, as was just shown, he has mathematical control."

"Wait a minute, Larry, this is getting too much for my little brain. Do you mean to tell me that even though man's will is not free, there is absolutely nothing that causes him to do what he does, not environment, heredity, or anything else?"

"I didn't say that, Jim, not in those exact words. I said that nothing, absolutely nothing, can cause man to do what he doesn't want to do. The environment does not cause him to commit a crime; it just presents conditions under which his desire is aroused; consequently, he can't blame what is not responsible, but remember, his particular environment is different because he himself is different; otherwise, everybody would desire to commit a crime. But the reason he doesn't come right out and say, 'I hurt that person not because I was compelled to do it against my will, but only because I wanted to do it,' is that the standards of right and wrong prevent him from deriving any satisfaction out of such honesty when this will only evoke blame, criticism, and punishment of some sort for his desires. Therefore, he is compelled to justify those actions considered wrong with excuses, extenuating circumstances, and the shifting of guilt to someone or something else as the cause, to absorb, if not all, the responsibility, which allowed him to absolve his conscience in a world of judgment, and hurt others, in many cases, with impunity, since he could demonstrate why he was compelled to do what he really didn't want to do. You see it happen all the time, Jim, even when a child says, 'Look what you made me do,' when you know you didn't make him do anything. The boy, spilling a glass of milk because he was careless, and not wishing to be blamed, searches quickly for an excuse to shift the responsibility for what happened to something other than himself."

"But the boy didn't want to spill the glass of milk, Larry, it was just an accident."

"That's true, Jim, but why did he want to blame his own carelessness on somebody or something else if not to avoid the criticism of his parents?"

"But isn't it true, Larry, that the boy's awareness that he would be blamed and punished for carelessness, such as this spilling of the milk on the rug, makes him think very carefully about all that he does to prevent the blame and punishment he doesn't like? If he knew that he wasn't going to be blamed and punished, wouldn't he become even more careless? Isn't it also true that the dethronement of free will would allow him to shift his responsibility all the more, and take advantage of the knowledge that he will not be blamed, to excuse or justify any desires heretofore kept under reasonable control by the fear of criticism, blame, punishment, and public opinion which judged his actions with standards of right and wrong?"

"Your last question, Jim (don't get offended now), is a superficial perception of inaccurate reasoning, simply because it is mathematically impossible to shift our responsibility, to excuse or justify getting away with something, when we know in advance that we will not be blamed for what we do. Now observe this very carefully because it is another crucial point: Is it possible for you to say, 'I couldn't help myself because man's will is not free,' when you know in advance that no one is going to say you could help yourself or question your action, regardless of what you do? I repeat, think about this very carefully. If you try to justify or excuse your action, it is an indication that the person or people to whom you are presenting this justification must consider the action wrong in some way; otherwise, there would be no need for it. If you do what others judge to be right, is it necessary to lie or offer excuses?"

"No, it isn't necessary."

"It is only possible to attempt a shift of your responsibility for hurting others, or for doing what is judged improper, when you are held responsible by a code of standards that criticize you in advance for doing something considered wrong by them. They are interested to know why you could do such a thing, which compels you, for satisfaction, to think up a reasonable excuse to extenuate the circumstances and mitigate their unfavorable opinion of your action. But once it is realized, as a matter of positive knowledge, that man will not be held responsible for what he does since his will is not free, regardless of what is done (don't jump to conclusions, Jim, just follow the reasoning — my problem is difficult enough as it is), it becomes mathematically impossible for you to blame someone or something else as the cause for what you know you have done, simply because you know that no one is blaming you. Being constantly blamed and judged by the standards that prevailed, man was compelled, as a motion in the direction of satisfaction, to be dishonest with himself and others while refusing to accept his responsibility like a man. He blamed various factors or causes for the many things he desired to do that were considered wrong, because he didn't like being in the wrong. But the very moment the dethronement of free will makes it known that no one henceforth will be blamed, man is also prevented from making someone else the scapegoat for what he does, prevented from excusing or justifying his own actions since he is not being given an opportunity to do so, which compels him, completely beyond control but of his own free will or desire, not only to assume full responsibility for everything he does, but to be absolutely honest with himself and others. How is it humanly possible for you to desire lying to me or to yourself when your actions are not being judged or blamed, in other words, when you are not being given an opportunity to lie; and how is it possible for you to make any effort to shift your responsibility, when no one holds you responsible?"

"You win, Larry, there is absolutely no way, I agree, that the dethronement of free will would allow a person to shift his responsibility, which means that he is compelled to assume full responsibility for everything he does."

"We have been forcing our children to prefer lying as a solution to their problems, then we blame and punish them for what is not their responsibility, as a solution to our problems. We strike the first blow by judging what is right for others, and then when they strike back by disagreeing with our judgment, we blame and punish them for doing what they preferred under their set of circumstances, which included the advance knowledge that they would be blamed."

"But Larry, even though this reasoning demonstrates that man cannot desire to shift his responsibility when he knows in advance that no one is holding him responsible, why should this prevent him from taking more easily what he wants when the risk of blame and punishment is no more a condition to be considered? The boy who spilled the milk cannot desire to shift his responsibility when he knows his parents are not going to question what he did or blame him in any way, but why should this prevent him from spilling the milk every day if it gives him a certain satisfaction to watch it seep into the rug? Besides, if what someone does hurts another very much, how is it possible for the person hurt not to desire some form of retaliation, which blames and punishes? If the father just spent $1000 for carpeting, how is it humanly possible for him to say absolutely nothing when the milk is not carelessly but deliberately spilled?"

"These questions, Jim, are like asking: 'If it is mathematically impossible for man to do something, what would you do if it is done?' In other words, how is it possible for B to retaliate when it is impossible for B to be hurt? You have assumed that various forms of deliberate and careless hurt will continue, and I asked you not to jump to conclusions. Now take note of the most fantastic wisdom, which is not mine, any more than the knowledge that two plus two equals four, is yours.

At this present moment of time or life, you are standing on this spot called here and are constantly in the process of moving to there. You know as a matter of positive knowledge that nothing has the power, that no one can cause or compel you to do anything against your will, and this other, who is standing on this spot called there to where you plan to move from here, also knows positively that you cannot be blamed anymore for our motion from here to there regardless of what is done, because the will of man is not free. This is a very unique two-sided equation, Jim, which reveals that while you know you are completely responsible for everything you do — since it is mathematically impossible to shift your responsibility to an extraneous cause when no one holds you responsible — everybody else knows that you are not to blame because you are compelled to move in the direction of greater satisfaction during every moment of your existence.

Now if you know as a matter of positive knowledge that not only I but everyone on earth will never blame or punish you for hurting me in some way because you know we are compelled to completely excuse what we know is definitely beyond your control, is it mathematically possible (think very carefully about this because it is the most crucial point so far — the scientific discovery referred to) for you to derive any satisfaction whatever from the contemplation of this hurt when you know, beyond a shadow of doubt, that no one, including myself who is the one to be hurt, will ever hold you responsible, criticize or question your action, ever desire to hurt you in return for doing what must be considered a compulsion, completely beyond your control, since the will of man is definitely not free? But remember, you haven't hurt me yet, and you know (this is the other side of the equation), as a matter of undeniable knowledge, that nothing, no one, can compel you to hurt me unless you want to, for over this you have mathematical control, consequently, your motion, your decision as to what is better for yourself, is still a choice between two alternatives — to hurt me or not to hurt me. But the moment it fully dawns on you that this hurt to me, should you go ahead with it, will not be blamed, criticized, judged or punished in any way because no one wants to hurt you for doing what must now be considered a compulsion beyond your control (once it is established that man's will is not free), although you know it is not beyond your control, at this point, since nothing can force you to hurt me against your will unless you want to, you are compelled, completely of your own free will (to repeat: which only means that you are not being coerced to do anything against your will), to relinquish this desire to hurt me because it can never satisfy you to do so under these conditions, which proves conclusively that it is mathematically impossible for any person to hurt another as an alternative, when he knows in advance, as a matter of absolute knowledge, that no one will ever blame, criticize, or punish him for this act. Don't stop me now, Jim, I'm all wound up.

In order to hurt another, either deliberately or carelessly, man must be able to derive some satisfaction from this hurt, which means that he must be able to justify it in some way, but this justification either requires a previous hurt to him or the knowledge that he could be blamed and punished for this action. Blame itself, which is a condition of free will, is a part of the environment that permits and justifies any form of hurt to another, for this is the price man is willing to pay for the satisfaction of certain desires; but when it is removed so the knowledge that it no longer exists becomes a new condition of the environment, then the price he must pay to hurt someone is completely out of his reach because to do so he must move in the direction of <u>conscious dissatisfaction</u>, which is mathematically impossible. The solution to this impasse is now very obvious because the advance knowledge that man will not be blamed for the hurt he does to others, since his will is not free, which enters a condition or catalyst never before a factor in human conduct (this requires the complete removal of all forms of blame and judgment), mathematically prevents those very acts of evil for which blame and punishment were previously necessary as a normal reaction. Instead of being able to absolve his conscience by justifying an act of crime, or some other form of hurt, through the knowledge that he will be blamed and punished, which permitted efforts to shift his responsibility while encouraging what had to be criticized and condemned, he is prevented from deriving any satisfaction from the contemplation of this hurt by the realization that he will never be blamed, criticized, punished, or judged for doing what he knows everyone must condone, while denied a satisfactory reason with which to excuse his contemplated conduct. But remember, it takes two to tango, each person and the rest of mankind, and this discovery that man can be prevented from desiring to hurt others is only effective when he knows in advance, as a matter of positive knowledge, that he will never be blamed or punished no matter what he does. By following the corollary, Thou Shall Not Blame, which will act as an infallible slide rule and standard to what is right and wrong while solving the many problems that lie ahead, we will be obeying the mathematical wisdom of this universe, which gives us no choice when we see what is truly better for ourselves. Consequently, by removing all forms of blame, which include this judging in advance of what is right and wrong for others, we actually prevent the first blow of injustice from being struck. By judging that it is wrong to do something, whatever it may be, we are blaming the possibility of it being done, which only incites a desire to challenge the authority of this advance accusation that has already given justification. The corollary, Thou Shall Not Blame, is not only effective by your realization that we (all mankind) will never blame you for any hurt done to us, but also by our realization that any <u>advance blame</u>, this judging of what is right for someone else, strikes the first blow since it is impossible to prevent your desire to hurt us by telling you we will never blame this hurt, when we blame the possibility by telling you in advance that it is wrong. Consequently, to prevent the very things we do not want, which hurt us, it is absolutely imperative that we never judge what is right for you. But this will be understood much better as I proceed."

"Can I say something now, Larry?"

"Yes, Jim. I just didn't want to interrupt my train of thought before."

"Will you admit that if I strike you first, you are perfectly justified in striking back?"

"Of course you are not justified in striking a person who is compelled to do what he does by the laws of his nature."

"But Larry, you know that an individual doesn't have to strike another if he doesn't want to."

"But if he wants to, isn't it obvious that this desire is completely beyond his control because it is now known that man's will is not free?"

"Are you trying to tell me that if someone strikes me, I must turn the other cheek because he couldn't help himself?"

"That's exactly right, Jim. How is it humanly possible to justify some form of retaliation when you know that the person who hurt you is a mechanical man moved by laws over which he has absolutely no control?"

"But I'm not a mechanical man, Larry, and I do have mathematical control over not hurting you, if I don't want to."

"I don't know that, Jim, because it is impossible for me to judge what you can and cannot do since you are compelled to move in the direction of greater satisfaction, and I don't know what gives you satisfaction. Consequently, you are compelled to realize that should you desire to hurt me in any way whatsoever, you must also take into consideration the knowledge that under no conditions will I strike you back, because it can never satisfy me to hurt you for doing what I know you are compelled to do, since your will is not free."

"Now I get it, Larry. Then when I fully realize that under no conditions will you ever strike back because you must excuse what you know I am compelled to do, when I know that I am not compelled to hurt you unless I want to, for over this I have mathematical control, I am given no alternative but to forgo the desire to hurt you simply because, under the new conditions, it is impossible for me to derive even the smallest amount of satisfaction."

"Wonderful, Jim! If each reader would understand this basic principle, then he would be able to follow me as I extend the corollary into every part of our lives."

"I think he will, Larry. I'm just an ordinary guy, and I understood. But there is still one thing that puzzles me. Supposing this knowledge is released at a time when some government is actually abusing its people, and then, wishing to take advantage of this new knowledge, announces that henceforth there will be no blame and punishment for anything that is done. If the people are already being hurt, wouldn't this allow the government to control its citizens from blaming these abuses? Supposing a man and his family are starving, is this knowledge to prevent his desire from stealing because he knows he will never be blamed and punished for this theft?"

"No, Jim. The people who are doing the abusing, for which they cannot be blamed, will be prevented from continuing with their abuse because they will not be able to find satisfaction when knowing those who are being hurt will never blame them. However, any questions you ask at this point are premature, so please just bear with me. But before I begin extending the corollary, let me cite an example of how effective knowledge of this law is in changing our conduct.

Two children, old enough to understand what it means that man's will is not free, are given one bike between them. They decide to take turns using it for two hours each. They draw from a hat to see who goes first, and Joshua is allowed to use the bike from 1 to 3, while his brother, Jordan, will use it from 3 to 5. Now in the world of free will, Joshua knows that if he keeps the bike out longer than 3 he will be blamed, criticized, condemned, even punished by his parents, so he is given unconscious justification to stay out longer if this should be his desire, simply because he is prepared to pay the price of hurting his brother this way. Furthermore, knowing that he will be questioned as to why, he is given an opportunity to prepare a reasonable excuse or lie, which might mitigate the severity of the punishment. But when he knows, as a matter of positive knowledge, that his brother, though hurt should the bike be kept out longer, would never blame him, never criticize; and that his father and mother would never think to question or punish him in any way for doing what he knows they must excuse since man's will is not free, he is given no alternative, under these conditions, but to refrain from hurting his brother since it is mathematically impossible to derive any satisfaction whatsoever from being excused for doing what he knows he doesn't have to do, if he doesn't want to. Under these conditions, Joshua would make every effort possible to be on time, and if on the way home he met with an accident, which delayed him, Jordan would know immediately, without being told, that it was unavoidable."

"I must say, Larry, although I understand, I'm somewhat like a layman trying to grasp the reasoning of scientists who are trying to show him how a satellite could be launched after certain things are done. If what you told me so far is supposed to be a blueprint explanation of a coming New Earth, then I'm afraid I can't yet see how this will be accomplished."

"You are not supposed to see this yet, Jim, because all I have done thus far is lay the groundwork, but our mathematical slide rule and standard, our magic elixir Thou Shall Not Blame (when understood to mean that no one on our planet will ever blame another for what is done because man's will is not free, which includes the complete removal of all forms of advance blame), will adequately solve every problem we have, not only without hurting a living soul, but while benefiting everyone to an amazing degree. We can prepare to say goodbye to all the evil (anything that hurts another in human relations) that came into existence out of necessity, for which no one is to blame. However, the problems that confront us at this moment are very deep and involved, which makes it necessary to treat every aspect of our lives in a separate, yet related manner."

"You're really serious about this, aren't you, Larry? You actually believe you now have the power to literally change the entire world."

"You are wrong in your observation, Jim. I don't think or believe I have been given this power; I know beyond a shadow of doubt that I have it because it is absolutely impossible to deny these mathematical relations, which everybody can see and understand when they are extended properly. Mankind will be given no choice, Jim; this has been taken out of our hands, as was also the motion of the earth around the sun."

"Well, I'm ready to listen, Larry, if you're ready to start."

"I shall begin with the most difficult problem of all — the economic world — then go on to those problems of love and marriage; thence our slide rule shall attack the world of parenthood and education. Last but not least, though our magic elixir shall not apply here, I shall reveal something about death, in a mathematical, undeniable manner, which will make you very happy, Jim."

"Do you believe in all that business about an afterlife, Larry, a spiritual world of souls?"

"You probably didn't understand me, Jim. I said I shall reveal something about death in a mathematical, undeniable manner. Now, has anybody ever spoken on this subject in such a manner?"

"I suppose not. I do have that habit, Larry, of jumping to conclusions."

"So does everybody else, Jim. Anyway, you will catch your breath in utter amazement at the infinite wisdom that governs this universe, which includes man and all he can do, through mathematical laws, and you will be given no choice but to change your ways the very moment you discover that this is the only alternative open for needed satisfaction in your motion from <u>here</u> to <u>there</u>, once man sees what it means when the knowledge that his will is not free is mathematically extended. 'Know thyself,' said Socrates; but this was never possible — until now. Are you with me, Jim? Do you really want to see a miracle performed?"

"You bet I do, especially since I'm not at all satisfied with the way things are at present. When I get married, and my sons grow up, I certainly wouldn't want to see them killed in war, and I certainly wouldn't want to have any atomic bombs dropped where I'm living."

"You needn't worry anymore, Jim. God, not me, is finally going to reveal the solution. The amazing thing, and absolute proof that man's will is not free, is the undeniable fact that we are given no choice once it is understood that man can control man only by obeying the corollary —Thou Shall Not Blame — for then everything that came into existence which caused us to blame and punish, must, out of absolute necessity, take leave of this earth. What do you say we have lunch, and then I'll continue."

"Fine, Larry. I am a little hungry."

# PART 2

# THE EXTENSION OF THIS DISCOVERY INTO

# THE ECONOMIC WORLD

# CHAPTER 3 — THE DISPLACED

"Well, Larry, do you feel more inclined to talk now that you finished eating?"

"I'm rarin' to go, Jim."

"One question before you begin. Are you going to try and solve every problem that exists in economic relations, even those between countries?"

"No, Jim, I am not going to <u>try</u> to accomplish anything. From here on, each move I make is equivalent to the forced moves in a chess game; consequently, no attempt is necessary because checkmate cannot be avoided, nor can this New Earth be stopped."

"Do you mean that if a group of millionaires found this new way of life opposed to their best interest, or if Russia and China found it disagreeable, they wouldn't be able to stop it?"

"I don't mean that at all, Jim. I simply said it is mathematically impossible to stop the development of something everybody wants. If the rich and poor, the capitalistic and communist countries, plus everybody else not mentioned, desire what I am about to show, is it possible for this New Earth not to become a reality? How is it humanly possible to be dissatisfied with the solution, when it is impossible not to be satisfied?"

"I see what you mean. You are going to reduce the differences between people to a common denominator that satisfies the whole human race."

"You hit the nail right on the head, Jim; I couldn't have said it better myself."

"It seems impossible, Larry, but since talking with you, I realize it is very presumptuous to judge your capacity according to what I can and cannot do. Besides, you are in possession of a discovery that no one before ever knew about; therefore, the experts in every field are also inadequately prepared to judge what you are able to do with it."

"But if these experts didn't know that I possessed a fantastic slide rule, what do you think they would say if you told them that you have a buddy who is prepared to put an end to all war, crime, and other evils of human relations?"

"I think they would call you a nut, and me a bigger screwball for believing it."

"And you can't blame them, Jim, because there are all kinds of statements being made every day to attract attention. To show you how skeptical publishers are of anything that appears ridiculous or opposes what government and religion teach, after telling one about a book I planned to write which would not only reveal that man's will is not free, but also demonstrate how to put an end to all evil throughout the entire earth — you know, Jim, the very things we're discussing now — he looked at me as if I was completely nuts, and quietly said, 'I'm not interested in that kind of material.' And can you blame him? Wouldn't you, ordinarily, react that way?"

"Ordinarily, yes, but not after listening to you talk, and to your proof that man's will is not free and what this means when understood properly. So you go right on and talk to me, Larry; if you sell me on the value of what you have, I'll help you carry the ball, fair enough?"

"I'll just turn it over to you and let you spread the gospel."

"Do I get a commission?"

"I'll work out something satisfactory."

"You've got a deal, let's shake on it. If you can do what you say you can do, you'll sell as many books containing this knowledge as there are Bibles. But you have to prove it to my satisfaction first, so let's get going, Larry; this has suddenly become that much more interesting."

"Well, Jim, the first step is to understand that the solution requires that we work our problem backwards, which means that every step of the way will be a forced move that in itself will be a loose end, and only when all these ends are drawn together will the blueprint be complete. However, it is only by extending our slide rule — Thou Shall Not Blame — which is the key, are we given the means to unlock the solution. Remember, everybody on this entire earth must be satisfied.

As an example of what I mean about following a key fact to solve any mathematical problem that is solvable (the problems that exist in human relations are purely mathematical, once it is understood that man's will is not free), and as an example of working a problem backwards, if you were told that a woman with a pocketbook full of money went on a spending spree to 10 stores, paid a dollar to get in every one, a dollar to get out, spent half of what she had in each and came out of the last place absolutely broke, it would be very simple to determine the amount of money she had to start because the dollar she paid to get out of the last store, which broke her (this is the key fact, as is Thou Shall Not Blame because man's will is not free and because this prevents what is not desired), must represent one-half of the money spent there. Consequently, she had two dollars left after paying a dollar to get in, giving her three just before entering. Since she paid a dollar to get out of the penultimate store, this, added to the three, gives her four, which represents one-half of the money spent there. Continuing this process eight more times, it is absolutely undeniable that she must have begun her spending spree with $3,069. In other words, Jim, when a key fact is available from which to reason, it is then possible to solve a problem, but when it is not, we must form conjectures and express opinions with the aid of logic. At first glance, it appears impossible not to blame an individual for murder, etc., but when we extend this key fact, it can be seen that these acts of evil are not condoned but prevented. Regardless of a person's opinions on the rightness or wrongness of the answer to the problem I just gave, an opinion that would have to be based upon a logical conclusion, as is that of our experts when considering the impossibility of removing all evil from our lives, we know that our answer is correct because we have positive proof."

"I'm with you, Larry; just keep going."

"By a similar process of working our problem backwards, which necessitates the removal of all forms of blame so that each person knows he is completely free to do what he wants to do, the answer becomes apparent of how it is possible to satisfy all people regardless of their financial, economic, social, or religious position. What I am about to reveal is nothing other than a blueprint of the solution, and when everybody recognizes that they are satisfied, then it will be a simple matter to officially launch our New Earth; but to balance an equation of such magnitude, it is absolutely necessary to please every person alive, not just certain groups. However, this is not difficult when we have an infallible slide rule that God gave us as a guide. Shall I begin?"

"Please do, Larry. I'm getting tired of this beating around the bush. But why did you have to say that God gave us this slide rule when I know you are not a religious person?"

"Religion doesn't have a monopoly on that word, Jim. I only use it as a symbol for the source of everything that exists, whereas theology draws a line between good and evil, using the word God only as a symbol for the former. Actually no one gave me this slide rule, that is no one handed it to me, but the same force that gave birth to my body and brain compelled me to move in a direction of satisfaction, and for me to be satisfied after reading Will Durant's analysis of free will, it was necessary to disagree with what obviously was the reasoning of logic, not mathematics. Every time I heard a rabbi or priest dogmatically say that man's will is free, the hair used to stand up on my arms, and though I didn't know exactly why, I was very dissatisfied, which forced me to get rid of this dissatisfaction by proving that these people didn't know what they were talking about. To say that God made me do this is like saying I was forced by my nature to move in this direction. Have I made myself clear?"

"Yes you have, perfectly. Does this also mean that God is responsible for the evil in the world?"

"We are the result of forces completely beyond our control, but by understanding that our will is not free and what this means, we are able to veer in a different direction without blaming anybody, but still towards greater satisfaction. Actually, there is no such thing as evil when everything is understood, nor is there such a thing as beauty (you will understand this much better shortly), for these words do not symbolize anything externally real. For now, what do you say we get on with the problem at hand?"

"I agree, Larry, so shoot away."

"If you don't understand anything, Jim, don't hesitate to ask."

"I won't."

"Now at the present time, the capitalist and communist countries, diametrically opposed in their ideologies, and in serious competition for foreign markets, cannot afford the risk of disarmament because they are filled with distrust, and fear a treacherous attack. But once the people in each country are taught the truth, that man's will is not free, which means that a person can be mathematically prevented from hurting others by knowing in advance that his action will never be blamed, criticized or punished, those who have been considering an offensive attack, or contemplating a crime, will be prevented from so doing by the full realization that they will not be blamed or retaliated upon for this action, because it is now known that they cannot help themselves, that they must take people's lives, and steal their property, as a solution to their problems; but they also know that they don't have to do these terrible things unless they want to, for over this they have mathematical control, and when it fully dawns on them that no one will ever desire to hurt them in return for doing what must be considered a compulsion beyond control, when they know it is not beyond their control since they don't have to do it unless they want to, they are given no choice but to forgo the contemplation of an attack or crime because it can give them no satisfaction under these conditions. However (don't interrupt me, Jim, I've anticipated your question), it must be understood that in the world of free will, innumerable wars, revolutions, and crimes were a reaction to various forms of hurt, which did not allow any alternative but to retaliate. Therefore, when those about to fight back discover that they will no more be retaliated upon, it is also necessary for them to realize that the factors responsible for this consideration of war and crime as an alternative will be removed; and are we given any choice but to remove these when we know that those whom we have been hurting will never blame us for this?"

"But you say, 'remove these,' as if I and others know what to remove. When consumption slows up, and production is forced to lay off thousands of employees, what are we supposed to do? Are we given a choice? And if this layoff creates a condition that arouses man's desire to move in the direction of crime because his family has been hurt by the loss of his income, how can I and others remove these factors when we don't know how? If these people, about to commit a crime, must also know that these factors are going to be removed."

"Excuse the interruption, Jim, but this job was delegated to me; does that answer your question?"

"We would certainly be in a bad way if we had to depend on our experts and politicians to remove this condition, that's for sure."

"In other words, Jim, preventing war and crime by removing the justification necessary for their existence, does not also remove the factors that made, in the world of free will, those evils the preferable alternative. However, since this control of the desire to declare war and steal is only effective when those considering an attack or crime know positively that they will never be blamed or retaliated upon — since every defensive weapon or means is an accusation that obviously blames in advance the possibility of an attack or crime — mankind is given no alternative, if the desire is to seriously prevent what has never been successfully accomplished, but to remove the various things that try to prevent man from hurting man through threats of punishment and retaliation. Regardless of what is now being done towards this end, it must be destroyed, removed, or converted, so that this form of blame, which gives an additional motivation with justification, is no more an influencing factor. Can you think of anything more humorous or ironic, Jim? To prevent war, crime, and the desire to hurt others, it is <u>first necessary</u> (this is only the beginning of the solution) to remove everything that is trying in some way to prevent these through blame, punishment, and retaliation."

"You can't be serious, Larry. You don't expect the government of the United States to discharge all its troops and leave the field to communism."

"The sole purpose of disarming our defenses, as other countries can disarm theirs, is simply because, under the conditions just described, neither Russia nor the United States can find satisfaction in <u>physically</u> hurting those who refuse to hurt them in return for doing what must be considered a compulsion beyond control. But the people who are on the offensive know that this desire to hurt those who refuse to fight back is not beyond their control, and when they fully realize that their desire to strike a blow must be excused without the possibility of any justification, they are given no choice but to relinquish this desire to physically hurt others with the use of weapons. Remember, Jim, I didn't say that the removal of all defenses is a solution to the problem; I said it was only the beginning of the solution. However, this means that millions upon millions of people will be permanently displaced from their present jobs, businesses, and professions, because their services are no longer required. Of what value is having an army or police force when there is no possibility of war or crime?"

"Do you honestly believe that crime will cease when the police are removed? I think the crooks would have a ball."

"You must bear in mind, Jim, that you also thought removing blame and punishment would allow people to take advantage, but this is not true, so you must not jump to conclusions. We are working this problem backwards, and until other facts are revealed, certain things might appear ridiculous. Therefore, let me continue by asking the same question again. Of what value is having an army and police force when there is no possibility of war or crime?"

"Absolutely no value, and just a waste of the taxpayer's money."

"But remember (this is extremely important), to render these evils impossibilities, it is <u>first necessary</u> to remove the forces that try to prevent war and crime through threats of retaliation, because this kind of effort unconsciously motivates and justifies the very things these forces are trying to prevent. Now, how was it possible for the government to ever find the solution when the very first step required the dismissal of all forms of government?"

"Say Larry, is this supposed to satisfy our politicians? Do you expect them to calmly sit back while you take away their jobs?"

"Well, let me show you that every person who gets displaced, regardless of who he is or what his income is, will be completely satisfied. I shall ask all our politicians a very serious question. 'Gentlemen, would you have any objection to my removing every possibility of war and crime, which would render your services absolutely useless, provided the income you are now receiving would never decrease or stop as long as you live, although it could be increased?' Well, Jim, I kind of surprised you with that question, didn't I?"

"You sure did, Larry. You mean that every person who gets displaced will never have their income stopped or decreased, no matter how much he is earning?"

"That isn't all. I mean that every person who is employed at the time the transition gets underway (this includes all those who will be displaced) will be guaranteed their accustomed income for the rest of their lives, less taxes, of course. This not only includes the largest but also the smallest incomes, such as those from unemployment compensation, welfare, and relief."

"Be honest with me, Larry? Does this scheme have anything to do with socialism or communism?"

"Of course not, first because competition will still exist, and second because it is impossible to dictate to another what to do without blaming him for not doing it, which would be required under communism or socialism."

"But Larry, how is it possible to guarantee a businessman that his income will never decrease, when competition can very easily do the job?"

"At the moment, Jim, let's not be concerned with how I'm going to accomplish this, but with everyone's reaction to my doing it. Wouldn't it be a wonderful feeling to know that your income is secure, that it will never be stopped or decreased, only increased?"

"I'm satisfied, but I can think of plenty of people who would not be, like the insurance companies who make their living on the insecurity that exists, and the taxpayers whose jobs are secure without this security, but who might feel they will be overburdened with increased taxation."

"But supposing the insurance companies, instead of making less money, make more than they ever dreamed possible; and supposing the taxpayers, instead of paying more, end up paying less, what would you say then, my fine feathered friend?"

"Either you are truly a crackpot or you've been sent from heaven."

"That wasn't very nice, Jim. You know I didn't come from heaven."

"You know what I mean, Larry. By the way, does this hold true for all other countries? Will they also be guaranteed their income never to stop or decrease just as long each individual shall live?"

"Naturally. Aren't we all God's children?"

"For the moment I thought you were primarily concerned with solving the problems of the United States . . ."

"And the Whites over the Blacks, the Christians over the Jews, and the good guys over the bad guys... is that what you think, Jim?"

"Not exactly, Larry, and stop making fun of me. Everybody has some prejudices."

"Maybe so, Jim, but God shows no partiality, and since I have been sent here on a mission by God himself, everybody to me is equal regardless of his color, race, or anything else you care to throw in. Consequently, the United States, though I live here, is no more a problem to me than Russia, China, or Africa. Besides, nobody asked to be born, and once it is understood that man's will is not free, and what this means, how is it possible to blame an individual for anything when both sides of this human equation understand the principles?"

"You really can't, I know, but yet some people irritate the hell out of me, and I can't help blaming them for what they do, not so much for what they are."

"You will soon see how all the factors that gave rise to disrespect will be permanently removed, which will then prevent you from becoming irritated."

"You're too much, Larry. Well, how about continuing before the digression consumes too much time? Dinnertime is approaching, according to my stomach."

"Now the next step, Jim, once those to be displaced are assured that they will not be hurt financially, is to remove every form of advance blame, which will show us who are most, not all, of the people to lose their manner of earning a living. The first group to be displaced in our blueprint (our diagram of how it is possible to remove all evil from our lives) is the armed forces of defense, which renders useless the further need for weapons of offense. Is it possible for a potential criminal to use a gun for a holdup when nothing is going to stand in his way of taking anything he wants without force?"

"You're absolutely right, Larry, there is no need for weapons under these conditions."

"Therefore, not only are the armies, navies, and police of the entire world displaced, but so are all the laws, lawmakers, lawyers, judges, diplomats, foreign ambassadors, and every politician, putting an end to all politics everywhere. The manufacturers of war equipment will be out of work, as well as those who make burglar alarms, safes, vaults, armored cars, locks and keys, even cash registers that are designed to check on the honesty of cashiers. All windows and doors will be unlocked, prisons destroyed or converted, and prisoners, regardless of their crime, will be released because there will be no possibility they will ever commit another crime. Floor walkers, detectives, private eyes, guards, even all cashiers are displaced since they are employed to check on the honesty of buyers. We are going to make it very easy for every potential thief to steal and cheat all he wants, if he wants to when we are through with him. Remember, Jim, at the same time that the cops get displaced with a guarantee that their income will never stop or decrease, so do the robbers. If, for example, someone engaged in unlawful practices was earning an income of $25,000 or $250,000 per year, and because of this transition loses his profession, he will be treated with the same consideration as anyone else who gets displaced, simply because no one is to blame. This includes bank robbers, hired killers, etc.

The unions are displaced not only because they blame employers for not paying enough wages, but also because they try to prevent abuses by force to employees. Collection agencies are displaced because a creditor blames his debtors, who will be permitted to hurt him if they want to, while credit investigating agencies are displaced because they are employed to check on the honesty of others. Personnel departments and employment agencies are displaced because they are employed to check on the qualifications of an applicant for a job, which shows a distrust of the applicant's honesty."

"Now just a minute, Larry. Isn't it obvious that an employer must do everything in his power to get the most qualified person he can get for a position?"

"Certainly, Jim, and that's exactly what is being done when he ceases from all distrust of someone's honesty — under the new conditions, of course. This must be constantly borne in mind. For example, when employees know in advance that their employer will never discharge them for incompetence, no matter how much they hurt him with their mistakes, they will never get any satisfaction in taking a position for which they are not qualified. Consequently, the new conditions compel every applicant for a job to be perfectly honest with himself, making it unnecessary for employers to test his qualifications."

"Is this how all the other things work, Larry?"

"Yes. By the same psychology, you will soon see how all the other displacements bring about fantastic changes for the benefit of everyone. Even the Bureau of Internal Revenue is displaced as a collection agency since everyone will be given a golden opportunity to cheat all they want, but it is not displaced as an organization to keep records of taxes paid in and money paid out."

"Do you mean I will be able to send in the amount of taxes I want to pay, not what it is thought I should pay?"

"You will be told the amount of your taxes, but you will not be blamed or punished should you desire to pay less or none at all. You don't seem to understand, Jim. Once all the abuses that presently exist in government are completely removed, everyone will desire to pay what he knows and sees is truly for his own benefit."

"You have quite a lot of cleaning up to do, Larry."

"I know I do, Jim, but these people are not to blame for doing what gave them greater satisfaction, and that is why they are not going to be punished."

"If all government is removed, who will take care of the taxes paid in?"

"Various functions of government do not require that anybody govern; therefore, though they come under the heading of government, they are not a governing body. In fact, since anyone who tells others how to live, or what is wrong in their conduct, blames them in advance for doing otherwise — which is a judgment of what is right for someone else — all sermonizing and the giving of unasked-for advice are displaced."

"But what's the difference between telling people how much taxes they are supposed to pay, which blames them in advance for not paying, and telling people how they should act in society, which blames them for not acting as they were told. If they are not going to be blamed or punished for not paying the amount of taxes they were told is necessary, and they are not going to be blamed or punished for not heeding the advice of our experts, where is the difference?"

"The one is a mathematical standard that clearly shows that, should you not pay your share of the taxes, you would definitely be hurting the economy, for which no one would ever blame you for doing what you are compelled to do. But when your income is guaranteed, there is no way you can justify not paying, and under these conditions, it cannot satisfy you to hurt the economy when you know there will be no blame and punishment. However, there is no mathematical standard as to what is right and wrong in human conduct, except this hurting of others; and once this is removed, once it becomes impossible to desire hurting another, then whatever value existed in asking for, and giving advice, has been permanently done away with."

"Do you mean that all standards of human conduct are going to be removed, such as customs, conventions, etiquette, etc." And what about morals?"

"The problem of the sexes will be discussed separately, but as for habits of behavior that you have found preferable, Jim, no one is ever going to tell you what to do. If it gives you satisfaction to stand on your head as a yogi, bump your head on a wall, hold your knife and fork a certain way, or do any number of things, this is definitely your business, but the moment you tell others that they should do as you do, then you are blaming in advance their desire to do as they want to do, which means that you are minding their business, not your own."

"That's all well and good, Larry, but isn't it true that many people criticize, blame, and ridicule when a person doesn't conform to their way of thinking, which would be a serious hurt to him if he doesn't know what will be criticized, blamed, and ridiculed? Consequently, it is necessary to give advice. In fact, doesn't your wife often tell you not to wear a particular tie with a certain suit because the color combination will be laughed at?"

"Yes, Jim, but supposing my wife knew, as a matter of positive knowledge, that no one would ever again laugh at the way I dress, or ridicule me, because this would be a hurt for which there would be no blame or retaliation, then is it possible for her to make an effort to preclude what will never arise?"

"I see what you mean, Larry."

"Is it possible for a minister to preach against sin when there is no further possibility of committing a sin? In other words, how is it possible to desire telling others what is right, when it is mathematically impossible for them to do what is wrong? You see, Jim, this discovery draws a mathematical line of demarcation between hurt that is real and hurt that exists only in the imagination, which you will understand much better later on. The hurt of ridicule and criticism is real, but in the world of free will, there existed many forms of hurt that justified the ridicule and criticism. When the hurt that motivated them is removed, then there can be no justification, which means that any ridicule and criticism that exists thereafter strikes a first blow of hurt, but this is controlled by the realization that it will never be blamed or punished. Consequently, there is no further need to tell others what to do."

"But what about children, don't we have to guide them, and doesn't this require telling them what to do?"

"There are many loose ends, Jim, but I don't want to get ahead of myself. Just be patient, and rest assured that every problem will be solved to your complete satisfaction. You must constantly bear in mind that it is impossible for me to tell you everything at the same time."

"I understand, and I will try to be patient."

"Also displaced, and something you will find difficult to understand and accept immediately, is asking favors, simply because this blames in advance the possibility of being disappointed, which is a judgment of what others are expected to do. Mathematical proof that asking favors is a form of advance blame is easily demonstrated when it is realized that no one could possibly do this if he knew in advance that his request would be refused. Consequently, he blames this possibility the moment he asks."

"You're right, Larry, I don't understand. I'm not hurting you by asking a favor, and you certainly have the right to refuse. Besides, there are many things I cannot do for myself, and if I didn't ask, how would I get the help I need?"

"There are two facts that bring an end to asking favors. First, a great change takes place on the part of those who know that nothing will be asked of them; and second, asking favors is placed in the same category of stating that the world is flat when we know it is round, which reveals a certain amount of ignorance, and it can satisfy no one to reveal his ignorance. In the new world, if I asked you to do something for me, you would look at me as if I were not all there, just as you would look at me if I walked around mumbling that the world is flat or that two plus two equals five. It was necessary, in the world of free will, to ask favors because it was, in many instances, the lesser of two evils, but when this evil is removed, man is given no alternative. However, this will be explained in greater detail later on. For now, I only brought it up to show that every person who makes a living by asking for charity is completely displaced. This includes any form of passing around a hat. But remember, the total amount of collections taken in at the time the transition gets underway will be guaranteed. In other words, the income that every person is guaranteed takes this into consideration."

"You keep saying, 'when the transition gets underway,' as if this New Earth will be launched like a satellite."

"That's exactly right, Jim, and we will even have a countdown."

"Can you tell me how long it will take before we are ready for this launching?"

"Just as long as it takes to teach all mankind what it means that man's will is not free, which presents a tremendous problem in view of what I call the 'sound barrier of learned ignorance.'"

"That's a neat expression, but it sounds as if you are criticizing the educated for being ignorant, and isn't that a contradiction in terms?"

"I'm not really criticizing them because it is obvious that if they are ignorant of this knowledge I am revealing, they certainly can't help themselves in view of the fact that their will is not free, isn't that correct?"

"That's true, but an educated person is certainly not ignorant, right?"

"Completely wrong, Jim, because this is an assumption that what is taught is true. The rabbi was taught that man has free will, and just look at how many thousands upon thousands of years it took to break through this sound barrier of learned ignorance. You see, an educated person starts out with this assumption, and when something doesn't agree with what he was taught, then he compares the educational background of the person who disagrees with his own background, and if he considers himself the more learned of the two, then he is given justification to reject the disagreement as being unsound. This happens all the time, even when a doctor says to a layman, 'You do not know what you are talking about because you are not a doctor.' He sets up a fallacious standard for the unconscious purpose of protecting himself against others knowing that he is learnedly ignorant, which means that this group of educated people, who actually, at present, control the thinking of mankind, will react with hostility towards anything that shows them to be ignorant in spite of their education, unless it is presented in such a mathematical manner that it is impossible to disagree without revealing a still greater ignorance. But the great humor here is the fact that these educated people are actually trying to solve problems that are very much over their heads, and what will be revealed to them is only a method to accomplish the very things they have been unsuccessfully attempting. Shouldn't a psychiatrist welcome any knowledge that would help him in the treatment of his patients, even if it meant the removal of psychiatry?"

"I don't know about that, Larry. It seems kind of insulting to imply that psychiatrists don't know what they are doing."

"But if his 50 patients called him one morning with the most wonderful news, that they were completely healed overnight as if by miracle, shouldn't that make him very happy because this is what he was trying to do?"

"I don't think he would be happy since his income depends on their being mentally disturbed."

"Forget the income. Isn't he trying to make people well?"

"Definitely."

"Then why shouldn't he be happy if someone helps him to accomplish the very things he has been unsuccessful in? If you are having a difficult time changing a tire, and I walk over to lend you a hand, wouldn't you appreciate this?"

"I certainly would."

"Then why shouldn't a psychiatrist, or any kind of doctor, welcome my services if I can get rid of illness on a large scale?"

"You're not serious, Larry? You're not going to tell me that sickness also will be completely removed from our lives?"

"About 90%. But shouldn't this make our doctors very happy since this is what they are trying to do? Shouldn't it make our politicians very happy over the realization that all war and crime are soon coming to an end, when this is what they have been unsuccessfully trying to accomplish?"

"I'm a little confused. It seems that they should be elated, but I doubt if they would be because other factors are involved."

"That's right, Jim. A doctor, like any other person, is interested in earning a living, and his income depends on sickness, not health. The more patients a psychiatrist has, the larger is his income and the happier he is. If he lost his patients, how is it possible for him to be happy when this decreases his income?"

"But you just said that all incomes will be guaranteed."

"That's right, they will be, but if they weren't guaranteed, a doctor would be just as unhappy over losing his income as anybody else. However, there is this other side of a doctor's unhappiness. If I reveal that the medical profession itself is partly responsible for a great percentage of all the sickness that exists, the doctors will certainly not be satisfied to learn of their unconscious ignorance, even though they will be guaranteed their income. Does it make a priest happy to know that he himself, in an unconscious sort of way, is contributing to the sins he shrives in the confessional? Can't you see, Jim, that any revelation of a person's ignorance is bound to annoy him, unless he is not hurt, only benefitted by the revelation, and unless there is no chance for disagreement? No one can argue with what is undeniable. Socrates demonstrated to the intelligentsia of his time that they didn't know the truth at all, only thought they knew. Do you recall this? He said, 'I know that I don't know, whereas you don't know either but think you know.' However, this doesn't apply to me, for I know beyond a shadow of doubt that I do know, and I am prepared to demonstrate, with language that cannot be disputed, that this is a fact."

"You certainly are positive, Larry, but many people before you were also positive, only to learn that they were wrong."

"Do you see the standard hidden in your reasoning, Jim? Because others were wrong and also positive, there is a possibility that I could be wrong because I am positive. Edison was positive, and so were many other scientists, but they proved that they were right with an undeniable demonstration, which is what I am doing. If my demonstration doesn't prove me right, then and only then will I be wrong. Remember, there is quite a difference between being positive or dogmatic over knowledge that is questionable and being positive over something that is undeniable, such as two plus two equals four. Aristotle was also positive over various things he assumed were true, and his logic and renown delayed any immediate investigation of his theories because no one dared oppose the genius of this individual without appearing ridiculous for such audacity, which brought about almost unanimous agreement; and even today we are still in agreement regarding a fallacious observation about the brain and sense organs, but now this problem, which will be discussed later, is more difficult to overcome because this fallacious observation has graduated dogmatically into what is considered genuine knowledge for it is actually taught in school, and our professors, doctors, etc. would be ready to take up arms, so to speak, against anyone who would dare oppose what they have come to believe is the truth without even hearing, or wanting to hear, the other side. Before these people will even consent to listen, you must qualify not by what you are prepared to prove in a mathematical manner, but by your educational rank. To further illustrate this sound barrier of learned ignorance — for which these people are not being blamed because they cannot help themselves — I recently pretended I made up a problem and presented it, as if I was the originator, to a student of mathematics. I asked this person if it was possible to arrange 105 alphabetical squares divided equally between A and O into groups of 3, so that each of the 15 different letters on a line, and in all 35 groups, would never be twice with any other letter. Since he assumed that I did not know the answer, he worked on the problem to find out if he thought it could be solved. After two weeks, feeling inadequate to the task, he said, 'My own personal opinion is that it cannot be done; however, I'm not an expert, but my professor is. I'll give it to him. 'By the way,' he inquired, 'did you ever study higher mathematics in one of the universities, and if you didn't, how far did you go in school?' 'Only to the 7th grade, 'I replied. He then took the problem to his professor with this knowledge of the 7th grade, and after another two weeks told me very positively that his professor said it could not be done. In other words, just as long as these experts are permitted to use fallacious standards with which to judge what is true and false, that's how long it will take to break through this sound barrier of learned ignorance and launch our New Earth. Have I made myself clear, Jim?"

"But if your knowledge is completely scientific, why don't you just present it to a university for analysis?"

"I did, and the moment the professor who started to read my manuscript learned that I was trying to prove that man's will is not free, he handed it back to me and said, 'We're not interested in that.' I even called Durant long distance only to be told that I was on the wrong tack. You see, this learned ignorance presents quite a problem, and only by getting you and others to understand what it means that man's will is not free can I hope to break through this barrier. How long this will take, I don't know. I may be dead and gone by then."

"Not if I have anything to do with it, Larry. Posthumous recognition is better than none at all, but there is nothing like becoming famous for a worthwhile achievement. Well, come on, stop wasting time. Let's get moving with the rest of the facts."

"Take it easy, Jim, haste makes waste, remember? And if I move at too fast a pace, then I will only have to repeat myself, which would take perhaps twice as long.

Now, next on the list to be displaced, and quite surprising, are all salespeople, because when A, the salesperson, approaches B, the potential buyer, he must judge in advance that this individual needs or wants what he has to sell. The only possible way a sale can be consummated without advance blame is when B approaches A. Ironically enough, sales will soon increase all over the world but without salespeople. This means that all direct selling and canvassing become obsolete, all retail stores will have assistants to offer their services when needed, all wholesalers will employ buyers to contact the manufacturers for the purpose of buying, not selling, while retailers will employ buyers to contact the wholesalers and manufacturers. A buyer knows that a seller has something to sell, but a seller doesn't know that the various buyers around the earth want what he has. To knock at a door for the purpose of trying to sell something blames people in advance for not buying it, which is the case when a salesman walks in to see a merchant. But when merchandise is displayed or advertised, and this arouses the desire of an individual who then approaches the seller, this is a horse of another color. Therefore, advertising will become bigger than ever, and more competitive, but knowing that they can easily hurt a person by false statements for which there will be no blame or punishment, the advertisers are prevented from taking advantage of their freedom because there is no advantage when someone can get hurt for which there is no blame."

"Say Larry, even though I may be jumping to a conclusion, this sounds like a fairytale. At the rate you're going, half the population in the world will be unemployed with a guaranteed income. Besides, how is it possible for a merchant to sell what he has when he can't afford the expense of advertising, and when he isn't allowed to employ salespeople?"

"That's his problem, Jim. We're going to guarantee his income from ever decreasing whether he stays in this business or is forced out, but if he wants to make more money, then he will have to use his ingenuity to figure out ways and means to solve his own problem. Communism and socialism tell others what to do because it was assumed that Marx had all the answers, but in this new world, nobody will tell anybody what to do, although each person will be mathematically prevented from desiring to hurt others. However, if I can't knock at someone's door without blame, then the only alternative is to display what I have in a manner that attracts attention. If it then appeals to people in the neighborhood, they will approach me. But who am I to tell a businessman and advertiser what is best for them?"

"In other words, Larry, this new world will not deprive anyone of incentive or initiative, and will place no limits on the capacity of an individual, although everyone will be prevented from moving in the direction of hurting others."

"That's right, Jim. A businessman might think up all sorts of ways to advertise or display his wares for the purpose of attracting buyers, and the only limit to his thinking is this desire to hurt others, which has now been prevented. A woman in the millinery business might think it good advertising to wear her hat in a theater for everybody to see, but when she realizes that the person sitting behind her cannot get a clear view of the screen because of her hat, which hurts him, and when she further realizes that he would never tap her on the shoulder and say, 'Lady, would you mind removing that bonnet, it's in my way,' because she knows he would never blame her for inconveniencing him this way, she is given no alternative but to take it off because she can get no satisfaction in keeping it on when she knows he must excuse what she cannot justify."

"Beautiful, Larry, just beautiful! I just love the way you expressed that."

"Anyway, Jim, to continue... although banks, as a place to safeguard money, are displaced, they are not as a place to invest or borrow money, nor is there any other financial institution. Insurance companies are not displaced, but they will be affected tremendously for the better, causing premiums to be decreased quite considerably, while the risks will be decreased even more. However, all liability insurance is displaced, as you know it, because this requires that one person blame another, and no one is responsible to others anymore for what he does, remember?"

"Now wait a minute. Do you mean that if I had an automobile accident, and it was definitely my fault, the other party couldn't sue me for damages?"

"That's right, there would be no lawsuits."

"But what about the expenses of patching up a person's body or car, or replacing an auto if necessary; who is to pay that?"

"Perhaps you can better understand how this functions when you see how our slide rule virtually eliminates everything for which liability insurance came into existence. Let me demonstrate this.

Imagine an automobile accident in which two children were killed, but the parents were unhurt. You, the driver of the other car, had been drinking (not that this was the cause of the accident), and were thrown clear. The mother and father are weeping their heart out, bystanders are sick over the sight, yet no one questions or blames either you or the parents in any way for what happened, because everyone knows that you and they were compelled to have this accident. But you know you are not compelled to drink and drive, not compelled to pass on a curve or hill, not compelled to recklessly show off and race... unless you want to, for over this you have mathematical control, and when it fully dawns on you that should you hurt others with your carelessness you will still not be blamed or punished, because everyone knows you were compelled to do what you did when you know you were not compelled, you are given no alternative but to do everything in your power to prevent a situation from arising that gives you absolutely no satisfaction. How do you feel standing around while the parents of these children cry their eyes out with grief, while no one questions or blames you in any way? 'But Larry,' you might reply, 'it was really not my fault but the father's; he went through a red light.' Well, Jim, is anyone blaming you? So how is it possible for you to blame the father? You know he couldn't help himself, that he was compelled to go through that red light. The only way it is possible for the father to blame someone else, or excuse himself, is if someone blames him. Consequently, each person is compelled to be responsible for everything he does simply because he cannot shift his responsibility when no one blames him. The only reason we have had accidents as a result of carelessness is because every individual was able to extenuate the circumstances, thereby shifting their responsibility, and liability insurance didn't help because those with ample coverage felt they were prepared to pay for their negligence. But when it becomes mathematically impossible to blame someone or something else, there is no way carelessness can be justified. Therefore, under these conditions each person involved in any kind of accident will assume the cost of all damage, which means that when you hold yourself responsible for hurting others, you must also hold yourself responsible for hurting them all the more since the money they will spend on a new or repaired car could be used either by themselves or the insurance company, for other things. If a person doesn't have this insurance, or a sufficient cash reserve to cover his share of the damage, then we, all the people, will pay the cost because we know this person couldn't help himself, that he was compelled to neglect taking out this insurance, or else he couldn't afford it. But when each person is guaranteed his income, and when all accidents due to carelessness are virtually wiped from the face of the earth, reducing the risk of the insurance companies and the premiums, then everyone will desire to carry this protection for fear they will hurt others by making them pay for damages they should be sharing. But you will understand this much better in a little while."

This reasoning also explains why the ability to confess one's sins allows the confessional to be a place where the sinner can find the justification necessary to absolve his conscience.

Here is another example of how this knowledge that you will never be blamed or punished compels a change in your character — where driving is concerned. Just imagine that you are stopped at a traffic light and are in the habit of doing things when the light changes, compelling, in the world of free will, those behind you to blow their horns in protest. This gives you a certain satisfaction, and when a cab driver passes and yells, 'You idiot, why don't you do your reading at home,' you counter with 'go blow it out your rear end, you goof.' You've seen this happen many times, haven't you, Jim?"

"Not exactly that way, Larry, and certainly not with myself. If I held up cars and people started to blow their horns, I couldn't possibly be satisfied."

"Well, let that be as it may, when the light changes and no one blows his horn in blame to let you know, even though it hurts him to be late for something or other, you are very displeased with yourself when you suddenly look up from what you are doing to see a long line of cars held up by you, for which no one is holding you responsible — even though you know it is your responsibility — which compels you to desire preventing such a situation from ever arising again. By blowing horns in blame and by calling names, you not only find justification to repeat that for which you are prepared to pay the price, but you get a certain satisfaction in irritating those whom you know will criticize this annoying habit. But when it becomes impossible to pay a price for hurting or annoying others, in other words, when all justification for tying up traffic has been removed, then you are given no choice but to change your ways."

"According to what you just said, Larry, driving a car becomes a very hazardous profession in the new world because the very thought that someone might get hurt, for which there would be no blame or punishment, no questions asked, compels everyone to become an extremely skillful driver before undertaking what could very easily lead to the kind of accident you just described, and there is no more unbearable form of punishment than to know that you are responsible for someone's death, or serious injury, while also knowing that no one blames you in any way for doing what they are compelled to excuse and you are unable to justify. How am I doing? Don't I almost sound like you?"

"Say, Buddy Boy, that was pretty good. How about you taking over now?"

"I wish I could. But there is so much I still don't understand about the extension of the corollary."

"You're doing fine, Jim. I only hope others will grasp this basic principle when my book is finally published."

"Well, let's avoid another digression. So tell me, are there many more that get displaced?"

"Not too many more, but the most surprising item to be displaced because it is used as a means of checking on the honesty of others, not only as a medium of exchange, is the material aspect of money itself, not the purchasing power implicit in it."

"Are you really serious, Larry? Do you actually mean that the green stuff you and I passed to each other so many times over a pool table is definitely going to be displaced?"

"That's exactly what I mean, Jim, but try to understand why it must come to an end. When no one will ever blame you for what you do, permitting you to steal all you want, if you want to; when no one will ever check on your honesty in any way, the present manner of paying for merchandise and services comes to an end. Even if this material aspect of money were not displaced, here's what would happen. Instead of having a cashier check your purchases, receive your money, and give you change if needed, you would do this yourself. Several adding machines and cash drawers can easily replace the cashiers and cash registers, so when you have done your shopping at one of the supermarkets, for example, all you have to do is total up your items, put them in a bag or cart, go over to one of the cash drawers, and pay for what you bought by putting in the proper amount, taking your own change if necessary. Certainly, you can put a one-dollar bill in and take a twenty out. You could even clean out the drawer if you want to, but if it is food you want, why even bother with the cash when you can clean out the store — if you want to. Nobody is going to stop you, check on whether you paid for this merchandise, or question your honesty in any way. Consequently, what difference does it make whether you use this material aspect of money or slips of paper on which you record the amount you are spending? What difference does it make whether you receive cash, a check, or a slip of paper on payday, representing the purchasing power for your labor? What difference does it make to a businessman whether he deposits $2000 cash and checks in the bank, or records the total receipts in a book, throwing away the slips of paper? He is interested, like the rest of us, in what this money represents, its purchasing power; therefore, when the slips of paper are thrown away, it makes no difference to him, just so his purchasing power is not impaired. What difference does it make to you, Jim, whether you go up to a cash drawer and pay for merchandise with a $20 bill, taking your own change, or whether you write $18.50 on a slip of paper, put this in the drawer, and deduct this amount from your total cash reserve? What difference does it make whether you mail a check to pay a bill, or a slip of paper, just so your creditor acknowledges receipt of this, so you can deduct while he adds? What difference does it make whether you put a 5-cent postage stamp on an envelope, after buying it for a nickel, or just write 5 cents on the envelope, deducting this from your total, while the Post Office adds?"

"It would make a lot of difference, Larry, if the people would desire to take advantage of this opportunity to steal."

"But that's just the point, Jim. To prevent this desire to steal from ever arising, it is first absolutely necessary to remove all forms of advance blame, which requires the removal of this material aspect of money only because it becomes, under these conditions, a useless appendage, very cumbersome in comparison, that employs millions of people at jobs that have lost all significance, releasing this labor, as with the other displaced, in many different directions. Consequently, once all the cash in circulation is transferred to individual records, corporate, government books, etc., the manufacture of money is completely displaced along with money orders, traveler's checks, bonds, stamps, and checking accounts. Besides, when this New Earth gets officially launched (this, remember, will depend only on how long it takes to teach all mankind what it means that man's will is not free), each person will keep a record of his own purchasing power, and when he goes shopping or pays for services, he will simply subtract, and when he gets paid or totals up his profit, he will add. This, you will understand much better as we proceed. The only one you will have to account to for your actions is yourself, and under the changed conditions, it will be mathematically impossible to desire cheating or being dishonest with yourself."

"Am I to understand, Larry, that you are finally going to show me this amazing solution to the economic problem?"

"That's right, Jim, and it's completely undeniable. But I won't start until I've had a snowball, so what do you say we walk over to the drugstore, OK?"

"The way I'm perspiring it will be a pleasure. But I think I'll have a sandwich first. My stomach has been growling for something to eat."

# CHAPTER 4 — THE NEW ECONOMIC WORLD

"When we were kids, my mother used to always say, 'Don't eat snowballs, that ice and flavor are bad for your health.' I would rejoin with this annoying question, 'Why are they bad, Mom?' 'Never you mind. Mother isn't going to hurt you, and mother knows best.' 'But how can you be so positive, Mom?' I would persist. Then she would proceed to tell me that some gentleman, a virtual genius who knows everything there is to know about the effect of anything taken into the body, told her that it was bad. When I asked her if it was possible for this genius to be wrong, she wouldn't hear of it. Was your mother that way, too, Jim?"

"Yes, she was, in fact, still is when we pay her a visit. I suppose all parents are that way to a degree, and if they can't trust the advice of the experts, who then can they believe?"

"This is another problem that will be shortly cleared up, but, again, let's not get ahead of ourselves."

"Now, to get started on this new economic world in proper fashion, I would like for you to imagine that everybody was in the process of learning what it means that man's will is not free. The schools, churches, synagogues, just about everybody in a position to spread this gospel, exerted an effort to disseminate it from one end of the earth to the other, and the reason they were all so anxious was because the world of science had confirmed the discovery. It was known at last that our New Earth would commence the very moment all mankind understood that no one would ever be blamed, henceforth, regardless of how much he stole, or how much he hurt another in any way, for this knowledge disallowed these things. Is it possible to imagine this, Jim?"

"This is very simple, Larry."

"Also, imagine that the heads of all governments, after testing the people as to their understanding of this discovery, have agreed upon a specific day and hour as to when this New Earth will be officially launched, and today is the day. We are only ten minutes away from the start of the countdown, which will only take one minute."

"Gee, Larry, I'm starting to get excited already!"

"Now remember, Jim, as part of this preparation, everybody was required to have a record book of some kind so that they could record the exact amount of their gross income and the exact amount of cash on hand. Assuming that this has been done, and that an international holiday has been declared for the purpose of this launching, you and everybody else are hovering impatiently over your television sets and radios just waiting for the countdown to begin. Finally, an announcement comes over the air and the count is started....60, 59, 58, 57....... 10, 9, 8, 7, 6, 5, 4, 3, 2, 1, 0.... and the New Earth has begun.

At that moment, the material aspect of money has lost all value, and everyone who is displaced will return home to his family and try to get another job, or go into some business."

"Does this include all prisoners?"

"Yes. They will also have estimated their gross income while in prison, and they will record this amount in their book as that salary that will never be decreased or stopped, but naturally they can get a job and increase it. Now remember, Jim, it is impossible for me to put everything down at one time. However, continuing to follow the infallible veracity of our guide — our magic elixir and slide rule that instructs us to remove all forms of blame because this knowledge that we will not be blame mathematically prevents the desire to do those very things for which punishment came into existence — it is necessary to understand that if one penny in purchasing power is taken away from any individual in the entire world, regardless of his wealth, he would be blamed for having too much money. This not only means that everyone throughout this planet will be guaranteed that his income, whatever it is at the start of the transition, less taxes, will never be decreased, but also that all prices, including labor, material, and finished products, will never be increased. In other words, those who increase say to everyone who must pay this difference: 'We, the increasers, have a problem, and it is a shortage of money. Since we cannot solve this any other way, we must blame you for having what we need as a solution.' But once everyone is prevented from increasing prices and decreasing incomes — because this is a form of blame — no one can find justification to do so, for how is it humanly possible for you to blame me by increasing my expenses to live, when no one blames you by increasing yours?"

"You know, Larry, that's terrific, but are you absolutely sure a person's expenses to live couldn't increase?"

"What are expenses, Jim, but somebody's labor. If all prices are guaranteed never to increase, which includes the cost of labor that is employed at the start of the transition, how is it possible to increase expenses?"

"Do you mean that if I am earning $125 per week, my salary will never increase, and if someone is earning only $50 a week, his salary will also never be increased?"

No, Jim, that is not what I mean. It is true, however, that your salary will never be increased or decreased, unless you, yourself, want to decrease it, but your purchasing power, due to lowered prices and the desire of the business world to give a share of the profits........ "

"Wait a minute, Larry. How do you know a businessman would desire to give a share of his profits?"

"He will, you'll see, and of his own free will (or desire). Anyway, due to these things, your purchasing power will be increased. Consequently, once the price of all presently employed labor is never increased, the cost of living can never go up."

"Does this mean that if a bookkeeper is earning $100, everybody who thereafter takes a job as a bookkeeper will start at that figure?"

"Certainly not, because this will depend on what an employer wants to pay for a particular job. He may desire to offer $100 or $125, depending on the size of his business and how many bookkeepers are available, but this is his business, as it is your business if you want to take the job. He may advertise only $80 for this job, and he may get nobody to take it. However, Jim, it must always be remembered that when the prices of material things go down, $80 could be equivalent to $200 or better."

"I know that, Larry, but are prices going to come down?"

"Tremendously, Jim, but this takes some time, of course; everything doesn't happen overnight. Didn't I say you are going to see a fantastic solution, one that will satisfy all mankind, the communists, the capitalists, the rich, the poor, employees and employers — everybody?"

"Yes you did, but I still... never mind, I know. I haven't the right to judge your capacity by my own."

"Not so much that, Jim, as the realization that my slide rule allows us to see, for the very first time, what is truly better for ourselves. Without it, we could not proceed, and with it, any person capable of projecting mathematical relations is in a position to solve the problem."

"Don't be so modest, Larry."

"Modesty has nothing to do with it. Besides, how is it humanly possible for me to be proud of this discovery when it came about not of my own free will? I didn't ask to be born, nor did I ask to move in the direction conditioned by my heredity and environment. If anyone deserves credit, it is God, that ineffable force that gave us our bodies, our brains, the solar and the mankind systems."

"Do you really believe in God?"

"Do I believe man's will is not free, do I believe the earth is round, do I believe two plus two equals four? Of course, I don't believe in God, simply because I know, now that it has been discovered man's will is not free, and what this means, that God is a mathematical reality."

"Could you give me a definition of God?"

"Definitions mean absolutely nothing, Jim, where reality is concerned. Regardless of what words I use to describe the sun, regardless of how much there is I don't know about this ball of fire, does not negate the fact that it is a part of the real world; and regardless of what words I employ to describe God does not change the fact that He is a reality."

"But isn't there quite a difference between seeing the sun and seeing God? I know that the description of the sun could be inaccurate, but I know it is a part of the real world. However, we can't point to any particular thing and say this is God; therefore, we must assume, because of certain things, that God is a reality, correct?"

"We assumed the energy contained within the atom until a discovery was made that proved this, and we assumed or believed that there was a design to this universe by the fact that the solar system moves in such mathematical harmony. Did the sun, moon, earth, planets, and stars just fall into their order, or is there some internal urgency pushing everything in a particular direction? The evil that existed in the world compelled religion to separate God from the bad and assign Satan to the evil, while endowing man with free will so that this separation could be reasonable. But now that it has been discovered will is not free, and at the very moment this discovery is made a mathematical demonstration compels man to veer sharply in a new direction — although still towards greater satisfaction — then it can be seen, just as clearly as we see the sun, that the mankind system has always been just as harmonious as the solar system, only we never knew it because part of the harmony was this disharmony between man and man, which is now being removed on a permanent basis. In other words, this discovery of what it means that man's will is not free also reveals that God is a mathematical, undeniable reality. This means, to put it another way, that Man Does Not Stand Alone."

"Does this also mean that religion will flourish as never before?"

"On the contrary. Religion gets displaced along with evil, simply because one was the complement of the other. Of what value is having an organization to combat the evil and sin in the world, when there is no more evil, and what is the value of preaching faith, to have faith that God will one day reveal himself to be a reality, when we have discovered at last that he is? Of what value is continuing to pray for deliverance from evil, when we will soon be delivered from it?"

"But religion won't like the thought of giving up the tremendous satisfaction experienced for so many many years."

"How is it possible for these theologians to object to the very things they have been unsuccessfully trying to accomplish, without revealing that they don't want mankind to be delivered of all evil? This is the great humor and the very reason why religion and government could never approve of this book, in spite of its purpose, because they would be forced to relinquish what has always been a source of tremendous satisfaction. Consequently, science will have to confirm the accuracy of this book before these others will accept it."

"Say, Larry, are you sure you are the boy I grew up with, the boy I used to play football, basketball, chess, checkers, and many other games with? If you're not careful, somebody might call you the Messiah."

"I am just the messenger, Jim. As was expressed on the very first page, 'this knowledge reveals that the long-awaited Messiah is nothing other than a psychological law of man's nature which has remained undiscovered, like atomic energy, until now.' Even if I had never made this discovery, it would sooner or later come to light because what it reveals is a definite part of the real world and not a figment of the imagination. This is something else that annoys religion. It expects the Messiah to look like Christ or Moses, that he will come to earth not through ordinary channels, and especially not someone who never cared one iota about religious ritual. But that's enough about God, Jim. He wants me to get on with the work at hand; this is much more important.

Now the transition will be as smooth and uninterrupted as a well-oiled piece of machinery, for when payday rolls around, the displaced need only enter their weekly income in their book and then send a withdrawal slip to the local Bureau of Internal Revenue so that this guaranteed compensation can be acknowledged and deducted. No one will tell these people where or when they should work, and if they wish to retire on this income for the rest of their lives, this is their business. However, when they fully realize that the money with which they are being supported could be used for other things the moment they take an available job, and that when they don't, they would be hurting us — the people who are supporting them — they are given no alternative under these conditions."

"But Larry, supposing a person like the President of the United States, who is earning in the neighborhood of $100,000 per year, can't get a job paying that amount of money, what then?"

"If he can only get a job paying $5000, he will still receive his guaranteed income just as long as he lives by drawing the other $95,000, less taxes of course, from the Bureau of Internal Revenue."

"But wouldn't this make him desire to take the easiest job available, regardless of the salary, since he knows that the chances are very slim that he will ever earn more than this $100,000? Besides, wouldn't an employer take advantage of this knowledge to pay the President only $5000 to do a very important job, one worth much more money, since he knows the difference would be given in unemployment compensation, so to speak?"

"Your questions show signs of alertness, Jim, but you have not looked into this deeply enough; otherwise, you would not have asked them. In order for an employer to pay less than what a job is worth, to pay less to the same individual who would receive more under other circumstances, it would necessitate that he hurt the taxpayers, who would be compelled to pay this difference, because he cannot help hurting them this way. But he knows he is not compelled to hurt them this way unless he wants to, and it cannot satisfy him to do this when he knows they are compelled to excuse what he is mathematically unable to justify. This rule applies in every human relationship, although there will be a slight variation of this theme where children are concerned. As for a displaced person taking a job that is easier, or one that he likes better than another, this is his business."

"Do you mean to imply that it isn't the employer's business if he wants to hurt the taxpayers?"

"You're a shrewd one, Jim. You know it's his business, if he wants to hurt them."

"I know that, Larry, but you seemed to draw a line between what is a person's business and what isn't."

"There is a line, Jim. Whatever pertains to your desire is your business."

"But what if my desire conflicts with yours; what then?"

"This is like asking... I'll repeat the question... 'If it is mathematically impossible for man to do something, what would you do if it is done?'"

"Do you mean to say that there is no way the desire of two people could conflict?"

"That's exactly what I mean. Under the new conditions, it becomes mathematically impossible. But once again, Jim, you will understand this much better as we proceed."

"Is it true that each person will simply draw the amount of his displaced income from the Bureau of Internal Revenue, without any questions asked?"

"That's exactly right."

"Supposing someone made a slip with his pencil or pen, and instead of recording $100 per week, he adds an extra zero, giving himself $1000 per week, what then, Larry?"

"Remember, Jim, everyone is going to be given a golden opportunity to cheat and steal all he wants, if he wants to. This person doesn't have to make a slip of his pen; he can just as easily add in $10,000 or $100,000, but why is this even necessary when all he is going to do when buying something is hand somebody a piece of paper on which is recorded the amount of the purchase? If he wants to take a trip abroad, and he doesn't have the purchasing power, it isn't first necessary to enter in his book the amount he thinks he will need for the trip, because nobody is ever going to question his ability to pay, or ask to see his record book. Consequently, all that is necessary is to have a pad of paper and a pen or pencil for writing. He could board the plane or ship, get the best stateroom or accommodations, eat the best meals, tip the waiters very heavily, and live like a millionaire. In fact, he never has to work at all and could issue slips of paper from morning to night, but there is one other thing required for him to do this with a clear conscience and that is he must be absolutely certain he is not hurting others by what he does, because if he is, and he knows that he will never be blamed or punished for this — which the people who are hurt must excuse and he cannot justify — then he will be mathematically prevented from moving in this direction because the very thought of it will give him no satisfaction whatsoever."

"But Larry, how does he hurt the people when he is paying them for everything he buys, though the slips of paper are counterfeit? If I give you a slip of paper for a television set, and you record this in your book at the end of the day, you certainly are not being hurt, correct? In fact, you are pleased with the business for the day, right?"

"That part is very true, Jim, but the storekeeper is not the one being hurt at that moment. The people who are hurt are those who desire to buy the very things you have just stolen, but can't, because these things are now not available, which makes a mockery of their purchasing power. Of what good is money on a deserted island?"

"None whatsoever."

"Then what good is this purchasing power when the very things you want are suddenly not available anymore?"

"None whatsoever."

"Consequently, when a person steals, he upsets the balance between available merchandise, services, and the money with which to purchase these."

"I see what you mean. There would be less merchandise and services, and more money."

"Yes, and when that happens, everybody will be forced to take a decrease in their income, even the storekeeper who, at first, was so happy with what appeared to be a sale. Now once each person understands that he would be hurting everybody by stealing, and further knows that he will never be blamed or punished for doing what everyone knows he is compelled to do, when he knows he is not compelled to steal unless he wants to, then he is given no alternative but to relinquish the contemplation of his theft, because it cannot satisfy him to be excused for this hurt when he knows it would be his responsibility."

"Beautiful, Larry, just beautiful! But what about the many people in the world who are receiving a little bit more than a starvation income; they are being seriously hurt, and doesn't this justify some form of retaliation on the society that hurts them in this manner?"

"Jim! I thought you were following me. How is it possible for these poor people to blame others for their own misfortunes when nobody is to blame?"

"It may be true that nobody is to blame, but that doesn't put food in their mouths, clothes on their backs, and give them decent shelter in which to live. The employer can't pay out more unless he cuts his own guaranteed income. Now what are they supposed to do, go on suffering?"

"Say, Jim, since when are you a defender of the poor?"

"Aww, cut it out, Larry. Just because my father made several millions on the slave labor of his black employees has no bearing on this. Besides, you just got through saying that nobody is to blame."

"That's right, Jim, nobody is to blame, but is that going to stop us from increasing the income of the poor so that they can at least have a livable wage?"

"But what is a livable wage, and who is going to determine the amount of the increase and, more importantly, who is going to pay it? What are you trying to do, start a union all your own?"

"Take it easy, Jim, don't get so excited. No one is going to force your father to do anything. Besides, his income is guaranteed never to decrease, so your weekly allowance is pretty secure. As for determining this subsistence wage, it will simply be that amount necessary to feed, clothe, and shelter one adult, two adults, one child, two children, and so on."

"But I distinctly heard you say that no one will judge what is right for another, once the transition gets underway, at least I thought I heard you say this. And if someone judges how much this subsistence wage should be, wouldn't he be blaming in advance the possibility that those to receive it might need still more? One adult might eat twice as much as another, isn't that right?"

"You're so right, Jim."

"The only person I can think of who would be an accurate judge of what he needs as a minimum for his family is the father, the mother, or both, but then that couldn't be right because someone might take advantage of a good thing."

"You were going along just fine, Jim, until the thinking under free will crept into your reasoning. Each person who feels he is receiving an inadequate income for the minimum needs of his family will simply enter in his book the amount he thinks he should have as his guaranteed income, and when payday comes around, and he receives this inadequate amount, he will simply add the difference by sending a withdrawal slip to the Bureau of Internal Revenue so it can be deducted. Now your father can't complain about this increase to his employees . . ."

"That's right, but the taxpayers can, and he is one of them, Larry, let's be sensible."

"Do you mean to imply that I am not being sensible, and does this mean that you are jumping to conclusions again, and that you think you know what I know? Do you know what I know, Jim, my boy?"

"I suppose I really don't, Larry, but what I meant to say is how is it possible for the taxpayers to be satisfied when this entails a gigantic increase in taxation?"

"Sometimes I wonder about you, Jim. Aren't you jumping to a conclusion when you assume that taxes will be increased?"

"Well, won't they?"

"Are you asking or telling me?"

"I'm asking."

"Well, if you're asking, then why do you say my solution isn't sensible when you haven't even heard the answer, and why do you say this will entail a gigantic increase in taxation when you don't know until you've heard my solution? You're getting to sound just like the many rabbis I spoke to who refuse to let me explain what I know to be a fact because they have already jumped to the conclusion that what I have to say is of no value since it is based upon the knowledge that man's will is not free. Every expert does the same thing when using a fallacious standard; he jumps to the conclusion that he knows when in reality he doesn't know, only thinks he does. Please, Jim, don't make it more difficult than it already is to break through this sound barrier of learned ignorance."

"If I'm ignorant, Larry, it isn't because I'm learned since I only went to high school... but just because I really don't know."

"Then if you don't know, admit it; don't pretend to knowledge you do not possess, especially now when every minute counts."

"What do you mean, 'every minute counts?'"

"Just what I said. How would you feel if you were behind a barrier that prevented you from getting out, and you saw a baby getting ready to crawl in front of an oncoming car? Can it satisfy you to watch the baby get killed?"

"What a horrible thing to see, especially when you know you could stop it if only you could get out from behind that barrier."

"That's exactly how I feel, Jim, when knowing that I can prevent any more wars and crimes, any more hurt between people, providing I can get out from behind this sound barrier of learned ignorance. It actually hurts me to see what I see. Consequently, I am under a great deal of pressure to get this knowledge into the proper hands before an atomic explosion takes millions of lives or, in other words, just as soon as humanly possible."

"Do you mean somebody like the President of the United States?"

"Of course not. The proper hands are those who understand this knowledge, anybody's hands. Then I will be able to start an atomic chain reaction of thought that will move from one end of the earth to the other with unprecedented speed, and unless you stop jumping to conclusions, you will delay the lighting of this fuse, because you, Jim, are the fuse. Now remember, there is a big difference between asking me if taxes will be increased or decreased, and telling me that they will definitely be increased if I do certain things. The first shows that you are sincerely interested in understanding my thoughts, while the second demonstrates that you think you already know what my thoughts are. Have I made myself clear, Jimmy boy?"

"Once again, I apologize, and henceforth I shall phrase my questions so as not to assume that I know when I only think I know. OK Larry?"

"Good enough, Jim. However, before I demonstrate that taxes will be decreased, it is important to understand certain facts about what displaces an individual, either altogether or in part, from earning his accustomed income.

Let us suppose that you were earning $100 per week at a job that was completely displaced, but you have $500 that is not being used in any capacity as an investment. In other words, it is money that is not even drawing interest from a savings account. Under this condition, you are actually not completely displaced because you have money that could be put to use to help pay for your own guarantee. However, if you don't wish to use this money as an investment, that is your business, and then you will simply draw from it, each and every week, your $100 until the $500 is exhausted."

"But supposing I don't want to use this money that way. Supposing I want to spend it all at one time."

"You can, providing you get a job immediately after you become displaced, paying the same amount as your previous job or more."

"I don't understand. You just got through saying that each person will do what he wants to do, and now you are dictating what must be done."

"This is a shortcut, Jim. What difference does it make if I show that any other method would result in a hurt, compelling those involved to refrain from it, or if I just dictate what must be done; isn't it all the same?"

"I see what you mean."

"If a displaced person doesn't use money that is not invested to help pay for his own guaranteed income, then he is taking advantage and hurting those whose taxes will be increased. In other words, he would actually be stealing. Now, if he wants to steal, this is his business, and no one will ever blame or punish him, no matter how much it hurts everybody's purchasing power; but if he doesn't want to steal, then he will only be considered displaced when he has no money with which to finance, or help finance, his own guarantee. To put it another way, each person who gets displaced will be given two alternatives — either spend any non-invested money towards their own guarantee, or else invest it towards the same end. The advantage of investing it lies in the fact that you then have two things going for you that might exceed this income of $100 per week — your own labor and your investment — but if you cannot invest it, then you have no choice but to draw your unemployment compensation from it at the rate of your guarantee. Furthermore, if you should get a job that pays only $85 per week, then, providing this $500 is still not invested, you will continue to draw $15 each week from the $500 to make up the difference. Once the $500 is consumed, then you can start to draw the $15 from the Bureau. If you wish to spend the entire $500 on something you have been saving for while only making $85 per week, $15 short of your guarantee, then you would not be permitted to draw the $15 from the Bureau until 33 and one-third weeks have passed, unless you desire to steal. If you get a job for the same amount or more than your displaced income, then what you do with this $500, for example, doesn't conflict with the desires of those who are compelled to pay when you fall below this amount because no unemployment compensation will be necessary, therefore it is 'your business,' and yours only. Certainly you can cheat and steal all you want, but how is it possible to desire hurting the very people who are now doing everything in their power not to hurt you, especially when you know they will never blame or punish you, no matter how much you hurt them?"

"Not me, Larry, I couldn't steal under these conditions in a million years. But tell me, supposing, as an example, a person has $13,000 in a savings account from which he has been deriving 4% interest or 10 dollars a week, and is displaced from a job that was paying him $100. Does this mean that his displaced income would only be 490 per week?"

"Of course not, because his guaranteed income is the amount he was earning at the start of the transition. In this case, he was earning $110 per week, but $10 of this amount is not displaced; consequently, this individual would draw $100 in unemployment compensation. If he wishes to spend the source of this $10 income, that is his business, but then this is a voluntary move, and there would be no guarantee to replace this $10. By the same reasoning, if someone voluntarily quits his job, he is not displaced and cannot expect to receive unemployment compensation."

"Well, supposing the place where he had this money went bankrupt and he lost his $13,000, what then?"

"He would draw $110 each and every week until he gets another job, and if the job pays less, he will draw the difference. But remember, Jim, any cash that is not invested must be used towards his own guarantee, either by investing or spending it. The same holds true with employees and people in business for themselves who are not displaced. For example, supposing you and several others own a steel mill that employs 10 thousand workers, and your salary is $25,000 per year, which will be guaranteed should you get completely or partially displaced. If you are forced to lay off employees because a decrease in consumption has slowed production, you needn't fear for these employees because they will receive unemployment compensation just as soon as they have exhausted their surplus cash."

"But if these employees know that they will have to consume their own cash before they can draw this compensation, of what advantage is it for them to hang on to this money?"

"None whatsoever, unless for the purpose of investing it."

"Then if they didn't have a place to invest it, wouldn't they just have a grand time spending it?"

"They certainly would, but this is their business. I know that if there was a possibility of my getting laid off or displaced, and I knew that I would have to use my reserve cash towards my own guarantee, I would spend every nickel I had, that is, providing I couldn't increase my income by investing it."

"But what about the employer, Larry, who is receiving $25,000 per year; what happens when business slackens off?"

"He, like the others, has two alternatives: either consume all his reserve capital to meet his accustomed income, or invest whatever reserve he has for the purpose of trying to meet it. If he doesn't want to sell his business for what he can get out of it, in order to meet his guaranteed income, this is his business, and under those conditions he would have to try and build up his business where he can again receive this amount or more; but if he is forced to close his doors then he would settle up with his creditors, and if anything is left over it would be used either as an investment towards the $25,000, or it will be spent at the weekly rate towards this guarantee. Once it is consumed or put to use, the difference — or if it was not invested, the entire $480 per week — could be drawn in unemployment compensation. Should he still owe some creditors after settling up, instead of having anything left over, we, the balance of the population, will assume this obligation, so no one gets hurt. However, Jim, you will soon see how everybody will be compelled to desire taking out every conceivable kind of insurance, not to protect themselves against getting hurt, but to protect others from having to pay.

A man going into business will want to get an insurance company to assume the risk of his failing. The insurance company will want to look into the facts, and if everything is agreeable, will charge this man a monthly premium to cover the risk. However, if he goes out of business and is unable to pay his creditors after selling his equipment and merchandise for what he can get, then he wouldn't be hurting the people by forcing them to pay his debts because the insurance company will assume his obligations."

"But supposing the insurance company doesn't want to assume the risk, or only part of it, what then?"

"Then this individual will have to think like he never thought before, because if his business doesn't succeed, and others will be forced to pay his creditors while guaranteeing his income, the realization that he is solely responsible for hurting those who will never blame or punish him in any way, is never a source of satisfaction under the conditions. In other words, unless a person can think mathematically, can see that he isn't risking a hurt to others, then he had better forgo what he has been contemplating, because it is the worst form of punishment imaginable to be excused for doing what he knows is his responsibility while also knowing that the ones who are hurt will never desire to hurt him for doing what he was compelled to do. Well, was this man compelled to go into this business for himself and risk hurting others?"

"If he decided to go, yes, he would be compelled."

"Wonderful, Jim, but he may think twice now before he does, right?"

"As you explain this, I can see where an individual in the world of free will would not mind taking all kinds of risks because there was always some form of justification that could be used to excuse himself. If someone borrowed a thousand dollars and was then unable to pay all of it back, he just says, 'Sue me for the rest.' If he tries to hold up a bank, however, and fails, the laws didn't allow him to excuse himself, and he went to prison, but without the knowledge that he would be blamed and punished should he fail, without this advance justification, which allowed him to risk hurting others, the price of a hurt is beyond his purchasing power."

"Bravo, Jim, that was really wonderful! Perhaps you will let me detonate the fuse yet, that will explode into a magnificent new world. Another way of saying what you just said is this. From a superficial understanding it might still appear that man would take advantage of not being blamed and punished to risk hurting others as a solution to his problems, but this is a mathematical impossibility when he knows that blame and punishment are required for advance justification (the challenge of the laws absolves his conscience with threats of an eye for an eye and a tooth for a tooth, which is payment in full for the risks he takes). And when he knows that others will never blame or punish him for what they are compelled to excuse — but also that the other factors truly responsible for the dissatisfaction which engendered the consideration of hurting them as a possible solution, will be permanently removed as a consequence of following our slide rule in all of its ramifications — he will be given no opportunity to ever again strike another blow of hurt."

"What are you trying to do, Larry, show me up as an amateur reasoner or speaker? If you want competition, brother, I'll get somebody who will put you to shame."

"Who is that?"

"The one I think is the greatest of them all."

"Well, stop beating around the bush, and tell me who."

"Edward Gibbon, who else? The author of The Decline and Fall of the Roman Empire. Well, do you agree or disagree, and by the way, did you ever read it?"

"Ever read it? You must be kidding! I nearly died at his feet; he charmed me so much with his words. I must have read it at least 7 times, and I do agree with you, Jim, that Gibbon is a master at putting words together in a form that can't help but arouse one's admiration, and one of the most fantastic thinkers, so please don't put me in competition with that man."

"Then don't try to put me down by showing that you can express the same or similar thought in a way that might be judged superior."

"I'm sorry, Jim, I didn't mean to offend you. Will you accept my humble apology?"

"No apologies are necessary, Larry, just continue, okay? And since when are you humble?"

"Do you understand now, Jim, how everybody will be guaranteed his income, and how no one will be considered displaced until all his money is either invested or spent towards his displaced income?"

"I understand that; I can see how everything would function very smoothly, and I think it is marvelous that everybody could receive this security, but I don't understand and can't imagine how this New Earth will be financed to everyone's satisfaction. However, I know that I don't know what you know, so I'm ready to listen to your explanation."

It's really very simple. Once a week, the total expenses to run the earth will be published in the newspaper and announced on the air, and at the same time you will see and hear what percent of your income will be required to meet this expense."

"Do you mean that regardless of how much money a person makes, he will pay the same percentage as someone earning a hundred times less?"

"Can you think of another way that doesn't blame an individual for his earnings? If you say that one man should pay 90% of his income, and another only 20%, isn't it obvious that one is being blamed for having too much money? Consequently, there is only one solution. Whatever percentage is required will be paid by each individual. If 1% is required for the week ending such and such, and you earn $100, you will send $1. If you earned one million, you would then send $10,000. If you are receiving a displaced income of $100 per week, and the taxes call for 1%, you would enter $99 in your record book and send a withdrawal slip to the Bureau with your name and address so that this amount could be acknowledged. Can you think of anything simpler?"

"It's so easy it's frightening."

"There is nothing of which to be frightened. Certainly, a person can cheat if he wants to and nobody will ever be the wiser, except himself, but how is it humanly possible for him to desire cheating when his income is guaranteed never to decrease by the people who now want to help him, and when he knows stealing will hurt these friends who will never blame him for this?"

"It's the same story over and over again, Larry. But tell me, how does the Bureau know what percent to tax?"

"Every week, the Bureau in each country will estimate the total income, divide this by the expenses, and then publish this figure as the required taxation. If the tax returns are a little more or less than required, this is a minor thing, and can be adjusted the following week."

"But what about local or state taxes? You can't expect a person in Maryland to pay for a road being built in California unless it is part of a national highway? And what about such things as the satellite and other programs that people resent having to pay for?"

"A good question, Jim. If a group of scientists wishes to build a satellite to the moon, and can get financing for it, more power to them, but no one will ever again have to pay taxes on something that is not for their own benefit."

"Well, what about garbage and trash collections? Many people today have incinerators and garbage disposals; it isn't fair that they should have to share in the cost of the Bureau of Sanitation when they are not using its facilities."

"You are so right, Jim. Each garbage collection team, at the start of the transition, will have a total number of cans they collect, on average, each and every week. When this is divided by their weekly income and the other costs of operation, a figure can be arrived at as to how much it costs a family for one can of trash or garbage. If then someone wishes to discontinue this service, all he has to do is deduct the cost from his local taxes."

"Will you please show me how taxes are decreased other than on this small scale?"

"It is very simple. Once the transition gets under way the people, realizing their income is guaranteed, will start spending like never before. This will cause the opposite of a depression, which will necessitate millions of employers to hire the displaced for various positions, and every time a displaced person takes a job, your taxes decrease."

"Do you mean there is an inverse relation between taxes and consumption?"

"That's right. The more we spend our money, the less do we have to pay. That isn't the way things are today. The more someone earns now, the more he has to pay."

"In other words, Larry, when people aren't making as much profit, that's when taxes will be greater? That doesn't seem right."

"That's only because you didn't look deeply enough. Since prices can never be increased, and since everybody will be spending like never before, and since there will be more labor available than ever before, competition will be unusually keen, and prices must go down. Consequently, it won't take long before millions of people will be saturated with material things, which will definitely slow up production, causing millions of workers to be laid off with their guaranteed salary. However, when you can't spend your money on the material things others need for their employment, what difference does it make to you if they get this amount in taxes? If you spend it they receive it in the form of a salary, and if you don't spend it, they get it in the form of unemployment compensation. How they get it is entirely up to you. If someone is laid off who is accustomed to earning $25,000 a year, and this amount is his guaranteed income, but no matter how hard he tries, he can't spend his weekly portion, he will simply draw from the Bureau only the amount he spends. In other words, if his weekly salary is $500, but all he could spend was $300 that week, then he only receives $300 in unemployment compensation."

"Do you mean everybody is compelled to spend all his money?"

"Of course not. Just as long as you are not drawing unemployment compensation, what you do with your money is your business, but when your income is guaranteed never to stop or decrease, the previous need to save for a rainy day, the day when you might not have an income, has no further value, forcing everybody, even the millionaires, to spend like they never spent before. Money has absolutely no value unless it can be spent or invested."

"Won't there be other expenses of what little government is left, such as roads, highways, schools, which will increase taxes?"

"There will be no more government, and nobody will tell another what to do. Consequently, there will be the greatest investment opportunity ever dreamed of for the millionaires who want to invest. Nothing is stopping them from building schools, superhighways, bridges, firefighting equipment, for the sole purpose of making huge profits... this is their business."

"But supposing they charge more than a great many people can afford, what then?"

"Shame on you, Jim, you should know the answer to that. What someone can't afford, he doesn't buy. Do you realize what these investors will do with atomic energy?"

"I can imagine."

"In a very short time, the smallest income will have a purchasing power unbelievably high, because prices have got to come down."

"Would you clarify that even more than you have?"

"At present, the installment buyer pays a very high price for the things he wants because he doesn't have the money to pay cash, nor does he have the kind of credit that allows the merchant to charge him a smaller rate of interest for a lesser risk. But when his income is guaranteed, and when it is impossible for him to desire hurting others in any way, he will then be in a position to borrow the money to buy what he wants, at a much lower rate of interest."

"But wouldn't this hurt the installment houses when these people start buying from the discount houses and the department stores?"

"Of course not, Jim, because these merchants are also guaranteed their income, so if they can't compete, they will just be forced to go out of business and get into something else. Besides, even if an installment house wanted to stay in business, which he can do under changed conditions, he must give up knocking at people's doors to collect or sell, for this blames them for not paying and not buying."

"Well, how is a creditor supposed to get his money when he doesn't make an effort to collect it?"

"When a debtor fails to pay what he owes on the day it is due, or within the time allowed, the creditor will simply draw what is due him from the Bureau and send a record of this also to his debtor, which means that the people who pay the taxes will be hurt by this additional tax. Since a debtor cannot find any satisfaction in hurting the very people who guaranteed his income, the very people who refuse to blame or punish him for any hurt he does to them, he is given no choice, under these conditions, but to desire paying all his bills when they are due, and desire not to buy anything his income can't afford."

"How does a person go about borrowing money from a bank or other financial institution, under the changed conditions?"

"These places are no different than any other place of business that has something to sell; consequently, if you need a certain amount of money (what you need it for is strictly your business), you simply walk in, look at the rates of interest and the limits that are displayed conveniently (how it is to be paid back), put your name, address and amount you are borrowing on plan number so and so, record the amount you borrowed in your book, and just put this form in a drawer designed for that purpose. It isn't necessary to talk to anyone. When the payments come due, you simply mail a slip to the lender, who will acknowledge receipt of this and deduct what you paid from your book. If you fail to pay the amount due, the owner or owners of this business will draw the amount past due from the Bureau and send a record of this to you and the Bureau. This would increase the taxes of the people, hurting them, but we already went through that, right Jim?"

"This is really fantastic, Larry."

"The rates of interest will be forced to come down because everybody who has money to lend as an investment will not hesitate to do so under these conditions. You might read in the paper, 'Ten thousand dollars available for immediate use for 1 year, at the rate of 3% interest.' Do you realize what this security means for the entire world, Jim?"

"No, I don't."

"Billions of dollars will be available for people who can think in terms of sound investments, think in terms of mathematical relations."

"You mean like mathematicians?"

"Stop being funny, you should know by now what I mean. Supposing a scientist or inventor knows, beyond a shadow of doubt, or within a reasonable amount of doubt, that if he had X number of dollars, he could make a fortune for himself. He then approaches an insurance company that is also sold on the idea and is willing to insure this venture against any losses that would hurt the people by increasing their taxes."

"Supposing he is absolutely certain it cannot fail."

"Then he doesn't need the insurance company. Anyway, when he obtains this insurance, the premium to be included in the cost of operation, all he has to do is look for a bank or other company that advertises the amount of money he needs for his project, and simply borrows it. This will allow the greatest economic growth imaginable."

"Does this mean that everything henceforth will be a cash transaction?"

"That's exactly right. If you want to buy a refrigerator, television, house, food, or what have you, but you do not have a sufficient amount of cash, you either borrow the money from the business selling the merchandise to pay for it, or else you borrow it from another source. If you want a car, and it sells for $2500, you either borrow the money from some financial institution at a specific rate of interest and time limit, or you borrow it from the people who manufacture and sell the cars. Your choice, obviously, is in the direction of least interest and better terms. If a small businessman doesn't have this extra money to lend for the purpose of making an additional profit on the sale of his own merchandise, then the people who want what he sells must borrow the money to pay for it from another source."

"Gosh, Larry! This will displace many more people who keep records of accounts receivable, but what about the retailer who buys from the wholesaler and manufacturer; does he also pay cash?"

"Yes, he does."

"But supposing he doesn't sell the merchandise he buys, and then can't pay back the money he borrowed to pay for his inventory, what then?"

"There is no difference between this and any other loan. If he thinks there is a risk and that he might hurt the people who will have to pay for his losses, he will be compelled to find an insurance company to guarantee this loss at such and such a premium, because he can't stand the thought of hurting those who refuse to hurt him under any conditions. Henceforth, all carelessness and an "I don't care" attitude will be permanently removed. However, many manufacturers will insure the wholesaler and retailer against being stuck with merchandise that isn't selling."

"These insurance companies are really going to have a ball, Larry."

"And how! So will everybody who has money to lend, and the risk for the insurance companies will be so small that they will make a tremendous profit, while the money lenders will take no risk whatsoever."

"Supposing the insurance companies bite off more than they can chew?"

"Then the people will have to pay so nobody gets hurt."

"But the people will get hurt."

"Jim, you should know this by now if you are going to be my fuse. The insurance companies, knowing that they would hurt the people should they bite off more than they can chew, and also knowing that they would never be blamed for this hurt, will be compelled to restrict themselves within limits they can handle or else get other insurance companies to insure them."

"Are there other ways insurance companies will make money?"

"Yes. Life insurance will continue to be bigger than ever before. If a breadwinner dies without adequate coverage, he will force the people to continue his salary, less what it costs him to live, until his children are grown. If his wife is not employed and capable of working to help earn this guaranteed income, she will prefer to get some kind of a job to avoid hurting the people who have to support her and her children. Naturally, she doesn't have to get a job unless she wants to, and nobody will ever blame or criticize her decision not to get one. But when she realizes that not doing what she is capable of results in serious harm to the very people who refuse to hurt her under any conditions whatsoever, then she is given no choice if capable of doing some kind of work. Now, if her husband doesn't want her to work after his death, can afford the luxury of sufficient insurance coverage, and doesn't want the people to be burdened with an expense he can prevent, then he is given no choice but to take out the necessary insurance to cover this. He will also desire to be insured in case of an automobile accident, airplane crash, fire (no theft, right, Jim?)

"Right, Larry."

"And he will desire to carry insurance to cover anything that might end up costing the people money, such as an inadequate income and savings to pay for hospitalization. If, after doing everything in his power to prevent the people from being hurt by his neglect and carelessness, they should still be hurt by having to pay bills that he incurred, then at least he will know that it was definitely not his responsibility. But not to be blamed by the very people he hurts when he knows it is his responsibility is an unbearable form of punishment, which compels him to do everything in his power to prevent this situation from arising."

"This whole thing is fantastic, Larry; simply fantastic!"

"I agree, Jim! There is no denying what it can accomplish!"

"What about professional gambling, like the horse races, are these gamblers also guaranteed their income?"

"Certainly. They are running a legitimate business in which they are trying to make a profit, but if there exists a slight possibility that they cannot pay off, they too will have to find an insurance company to accept the risk of their losses, simply because they will not find satisfaction in burdening the people who guarantee their income with increased taxation."

"But look how many people get hurt by gambling. Some people gamble away their entire paycheck in pinball machines, on ball games, etc., and doesn't this hurt their families?"

"Jim, you're not thinking again. When a wife does not receive the money she needs for herself and her children, she will be seriously hurt. Since it cannot satisfy you to hurt them when you know they will never blame or punish you for this, you are given no alternative but to restrict your gambling within a degree that you can afford."

"It never fails to work, does it, Larry?"

"Never, Jim. It is a mathematical, invariable law that brooks no opposition."

"What about the nickels, dimes, quarters, half-dollars, silver dollars used to operate pinball and slot machines, and what about the other kind of coin-operated machines?"

"It should be obvious that any kind of equipment designed to prevent a person from stealing is displaced. As for the coins necessary to operate a pinball or slot machine, these can still be used. Someone desiring to do a little gambling, which is his business, goes over and buys the amount of chips he wants, and deducts this from his cash reserve. The machine either pays off in similar chips or registers what has been won. Then he cashes in his chips by adding what they are worth to his cash reserve. Gambling will become bigger and better than ever before, while nobody will be hurt in any way."

"Can't a gambler fix these machines in such a way that he takes less of a risk?"

"Supposing he can, how long would you keep playing a machine that only causes you to lose?"

"Not very long. Couldn't a player cheat the machine?"

"Jim, how many times must you be told that nobody has to go to such great lengths to steal anymore, if he wants to. This will be the easiest thing in the world to do."

"That's what you say, Larry. Under these new conditions, it becomes mathematically impossible to steal."

"Bravo! Wonderful! Great! I think the fuse has finally been ignited. Three cheers for Jimmy!"

"You better cut it out, Larry, or I'll get Gibbon. Seriously, though, how do the people who work on fixed salaries get an increase other than by prices coming down?"

"All businesspeople must guard against the possibility of slack periods, either by protecting their guaranteed income with a surplus to be drawn upon when necessary or else by taking out insurance. When they are satisfied that they have sufficiently protected their guaranteed income, then everything else above this and other expenses is a profit. Since money has no value above this point unless it is spent or invested, it becomes something that an employer prefers giving in bonuses to his employees, when he is satisfied with his income. However, even if he didn't give them bonuses, the very fact that his income is also guaranteed forces him to spend or invest, and this must bring prices down, especially when all employed labor at the start of the transition cannot be given a raise in salaries. Consequently, the value of a dollar must increase. But if an employer has more money than he needs and wishes to share his profits with his employees — since it is impossible to give more of a bonus to one than another without blame — if there are 100 dollars to be distributed to 100 employees, each would receive... "

"Let me figure it out, Larry... Is it $1?"

"Exactly right. I always knew you were a mathematician."

"But if an employer does everything in his power to protect his own guaranteed income, mustn't employees do the same, should they get laid off or displaced?"

"Yes, if they don't want to hurt the people who will have to pay their income."

"Won't all this insurance make someone, as the expression goes, 'insurance poor?'"

"Not at all. Most insurance companies will come out with package deals, and out of absolute necessity, the premiums will be unusually low because there will be very little risk. Automobile accidents will be virtually wiped out, so how much do you think the premium would be to cover what is left?"

"Hardly anything."

"That's why package deals will have to come into existence, something that covers all the needs of a family. In fact, the insurance actuaries will discover the risks to be so small, regardless of what they insure, that the dividends to the policyholder will offer a very good investment."

"According to what you're saying, Larry, even when people die, and even when they get laid off or displaced, they still won't be hurting others if they take out the necessary insurance coverage. Also, if I'm correct, the millions of people who have very large displaced incomes at the start of the transition, and who, even when they get other jobs, will still require drawing the difference in unemployment compensation, will reduce taxes considerably when they die and their families grow up."

"That's right, Jim. Within a relatively short period of time, there will be hardly any taxes at all; that is, there will be a surplus of cash and nothing on which to spend it, and it is this surplus that will be used in paying taxes. There will be no more politicians, and everybody, just about, will be working for private industry. If the whole world is employed in private enterprise, there is no need for unemployment compensation or taxation. And if a great part of the world is not employed because many people have enough of everything, what good is your money, which passes from one to the other in unemployment compensation? Taxes are only necessary, under the new conditions, when people are not working, but how is it humanly possible for them not to work when guaranteeing their accustomed income forces them to spend, to invest, and to look for employment if not employed? However, there will come a time when production is forced to slow down because consumption is being satisfied, but how much taxes have to be paid is determined by spending. If we don't spend, people get laid off, and our taxes increase to pay this unemployment compensation. If we do spend, we keep them employed and lessen our taxes. Now, are we given a choice when our income is guaranteed?"

"But supposing there aren't enough jobs to go around?"

"We can't blame the displaced for that, can we, Jim? So obviously, we will have to continue supporting them until they do find a job. But remember, it isn't necessary to find a job that pays the kind of income they are accustomed to getting simply because we will pay the difference, so they don't get financially hurt. Consequently, with this expanding economy, just about everybody will find some kind of employment."

"But supposing there still aren't enough jobs for millions of people?"

"Then these people themselves, without having anyone employ them, can get together, hire the brains to build a useful project, borrow the money to buy the necessary materials, and supply the labor themselves. They could build, for example, a huge recreation center for dancing, dining, bowling, billiards, swimming, etc., where parties and banquets could be held. Each person in the community would be entitled to use it, without any discrimination."

"But Larry, how is it possible to discriminate when this is a hurt for which the person discriminating would never be blamed?"

"Didn't I say, 'without any discrimination?'"

"But wouldn't this compete with other bowling alleys, pool rooms, swimming centers, banquet halls, etc."

"Certainly it would. So would the building of an ocean liner for public use (taking turns to use it for a vacation) compete with other ocean liners, but competition can't hurt anybody when one's income is guaranteed never to stop or decrease as long as one lives, while forcing prices to go only in one direction... down."

"You seem to have an answer for everything, Larry, but I think I have a question that's going to stump you. What about the people who are in the business of selling dope? This is not like someone robbing a bank. The bank robber is forced to give up his profession because he can't get the necessary satisfaction anymore. But the dope peddler is needed very badly by the addict, so how is it possible for him to give it up without hurting the addict?"

"Are you ready for the answer, Jim?"

"Don't tell me I pulled another boo-boo."

"No more than usual. You just jumped to the conclusion that I couldn't solve this problem, but actually, the answer is very simple. The man selling dope is running a legitimate business since he is not hurting anyone."

"But isn't it true that dope is bad for the body?"

"Even if it is bad, is anyone forcing the drug addict to puncture himself full of holes? Is someone forcing a man to gamble away his entire salary? Is anyone forcing a yogi to sit on a flagpole and stare at his navel for years? These people do this because it gives them a certain satisfaction. If the yogi falls off and breaks his neck, the only thing we can do is bury him, and if the dope addict kills himself, we will bury him too, but it is not our place to tell him what to do. The most the sellers can do is make it known that there is a danger of becoming addicted to the drug, and if someone still wants to use it, more power to him. However, if he can't support this habit on his income, and is forced to write bad checks, I mean bad slips of paper, then he will be hurting the people by forcing them to pay for his dope. But when he fully realizes that no one will ever blame him for his habit; that no one will ever criticize him for hurting those who must pay his bill; that no one will ever punish him for stealing; that no one will ever question him no matter what he does to others and himself, he will be given no choice but to break this habit of his own free will, because it can never give him any satisfaction not to. Consequently, the sale of dope will be forced to go out of business. What would you say if I told you that smoking and drinking of alcoholic beverages are also on their way out, as well as prostitution, premarital promiscuity, adultery, and divorce?"

"I can't say I don't believe it's possible, because I don't know what you know, is that right, Larry?"

"That's very true, Jim."

"Consequently, the most I can say is, how does this come about?"

"I won't go into an explanation now, Jim, because there are still a few things I would like to clear up regarding the economic system."

"It seems to me (I know I'm jumping to a conclusion, but I can't help myself), there would have to be some kind of restriction on pornographic literature, pictures, and television shows, especially since you can't keep children from watching."

"This will be answered when the sexes are discussed, as well as when children are discussed. Can you wait until then?"

"How long is that?"

"Tomorrow perhaps, if we keep moving at this pace."

"Say, Larry, what about Russia and other communist countries? They don't have the same kind of system we have, and you keep talking about competition, insurance, etc."

"It makes no difference because the same guarantee holds true. This is what I want to clear up."

"But supposing Russia needs a hundred thousand tons of wheat, and can't get it because the United States or some other country beats her out in competition for one of her surpluses, what is she supposed to do?"

"At the start of the transition, each person in Russia is guaranteed his accustomed income, which includes the amount of wheat necessary to satisfy this guarantee. Consequently, if Russia is bested in competition and cannot get this wheat, we, the rest of the nations in the world, must supply her with the cash, something more flexible than the surplus of a particular item, to buy what she needs from other nations. She will place an order for this wheat, draw the money for it from the International Bureau of Internal Revenue by sending a slip of paper which will be acknowledged, and then pay for it by sending a slip of paper to the company or companies from which she ordered this wheat. Then the people, all over the world, will pay a percentage of their income to cover the cost. It is very simple."

"In other words, all the people within a nation guarantee each person against having his accustomed income stopped or decreased, and all the nations guarantee each country against the same thing."

"Excellent, Jim! I couldn't have expressed it better myself."

"Supposing someone in Russia wants to go into some kind of business for himself, can he do this?"

"Certainly. But remember, if he quits the job at which he is presently employed (this applies to all countries), he would be hurting the people who depend on his labor or services. Consequently, he must either find a replacement for his job or start this new business after hours. Furthermore, if he finds a replacement and should later go out of business, his guaranteed salary always reverts back to the start of the transition."

"How do the Russian people get a share of the profits?"

"By an equal distribution of the profits above the cost of expenses. Russia will sell its surpluses for cash and will distribute this equally (that is, the profits) among all its people. There will be no Iron Curtain, and every country will be welcome to come in and display what they have for sale. Those who can afford these things will buy. Little by little by little this gigantic corporation called Russia will be broken up into smaller businesses because it is the nature of man to move in the direction of greater satisfaction, and if someone sees an opportunity of becoming wealthy without hurting anyone (this, of course, is a necessary condition), this is his business, and how is it possible to hurt anyone when the income of every person is guaranteed never to stop or decrease as long as he lives and when it is known there will be no blame or punishment for this hurt?

"Communism, and the dream of socialism, came into existence out of mathematical necessity as a reaction to injustice, but once the injustice is removed, communism and the dream of socialism have no further value."

"But isn't it true that a world in which everybody gets an equal income is more just?"

"How can it be just when this limits man's freedom, destroys initiative, and stifles incentive? A just world is one in which an individual is allowed to move in any direction he sees is better for himself, without others judging what is right for him. This was impossible before, because man often found it desirable to hurt others to accomplish his ends. But now, with the discovery of what it means that man's will is not free, it becomes mathematically impossible to hurt others, allowing him to move in any direction he wishes to go of his own free will. How was it humanly possible to believe in determinism, when this necessitated that man stop judging what was right when so many things he did were wrong? But now it is impossible to do anything wrong, which only means 'impossible to hurt someone,' so for the very first time, man can stop judging what is right for others."

"I see what you mean by what you called a mathematical line of demarcation. But tell me, Larry, how does this affect religion and the medical profession?"

"The clergy will be completely displaced, it's that simple."

"Do you mean they will have to take off their robes and gowns and get a job in the secular world?"

"Of course not, Jim. Nobody is going to tell these people what to do. If they wish to wear their robes and gowns for the rest of their lives, as soldiers and generals can continue to wear their uniforms, this is their business, not yours or mine. If they don't wish to go to work, this is also their business. Our business is simply not to hurt them in any way; consequently, we shall guarantee their income just as long as they live. However, if they could take some kind of work, then they would not hurt us, but under no conditions will we ever blame or punish them, no matter how much they hurt us by not taking a job, because we will know it is God's will. But they will know it is not God's will since they will also know that they don't have to hurt us this way unless they want to, for over this, they have mathematical control. Therefore, when they, as well as all others, fully realize that we will never blame or punish them no matter how much they hurt us, they will be given no alternative but to forgo the contemplation of what they know we must excuse and they cannot justify."

"You would think, Larry, that the clergy would be very happy over this news that all evil is soon to be removed from our lives and that God is a definite reality."

"No more so than the government. It takes a good while for certain people to adjust to the knowledge of how truly ignorant they have always been of the solution to man's problems. But once it sinks in — and it won't take too long — then everybody will be singing songs of happiness and thanking God from the bottom of their heart."

"Now don't tell me the medical profession also gets displaced, because you'd have to do some fancy, mathematical legerdemain to accomplish that?"

"No Jim, doctors, nurses, and hospitals do not get displaced, but they will be affected so tremendously that within a very short time, nearly 90 percent of the need for their services will be done away with."

"I still can't believe it. How does it come about?"

"How about a break first, Jim? I could go for a milkshake, what about you?"

"I'll probably get something to eat. Let's go."

# RECAPITULATION

The first step in the solution to the economic and all other problems of human relations is to teach mankind what it means that will is not free, which is nothing other than the knowledge that no one, henceforth (once the transition officially begins), will be blamed, punished, or even questioned, regardless of how much he hurts others. Each person will be given a golden opportunity to steal and cheat all he wants, if he wants to, under the changed conditions, without the slightest fear of being held responsible, because we know that he is compelled to do everything he does. But he knows he is not compelled to hurt others unless he wants to, for over this he has mathematical control, and when it fully dawns on him that he will be excused by all of us for doing what he knows he can never justify, he is given no choice whatsoever.

The second step, therefore, is to remove all forms of advance blame, notwithstanding how many people get displaced. But since this would deprive them of their accustomed income, which would be a serious hurt, and since we cannot desire to hurt them this way when we know they will never retaliate, and since it is within our power not to hurt them, it is obvious that their entire income must be guaranteed. Furthermore, since telling others what to do blames them for doing otherwise, it is also obvious that these displaced people are completely free to do what they want without any fear of criticism. However, knowing that we will never blame them, no matter how much a reduction in taxes would increase our own income, they are given no alternative but to do everything in their power to get some kind of employment.

The next step is to guarantee each person that his income, whatever it is at the start of the transition, will never decrease or stop unless he voluntarily quits a job, and to allow those receiving an inadequate amount to increase their income according to their subsistence requirements; but only these people must judge what this increase should be. The guarantee must be based upon net income, after taxes. Consequently, if the week's taxes reduce one's income below his guarantee, then he will either supply the difference from his savings, or, if he hasn't any, he will just not be able to send in the required amount, and this will show up as a tax deficit the following week. By the same reasoning, if the week's taxes increase one's income above his guarantee, then he is making a profit. At first glance, it appears that guaranteeing each individual his accustomed income would overburden the taxpayer, but this is not true because spending is forced to expand the economy beyond man's wildest dreams, which creates a tremendous vacuum for new labor. As everybody gets employed, taxes must decrease. And spending, as a result of this increase in purchasing power, creates greater profits than can now be envisioned. Since competition will become keener than ever, without hurting anyone, and since prices can never be increased because all justification to do so has been removed by the guarantee, prices will be forced to come down, while the purchasing power of the poorest will be forced to rise at an enormous rate of speed.

Remember, once this security is offered to all mankind, there is no further need to save for a rainy day, although insurance coverage must be taken into consideration so as not to hurt those who will never blame. Furthermore, since a displaced person is only guaranteed his income when he becomes completely displaced, that is, when he has exhausted all his own rainy day resources, he is compelled to utilize all reserve cash because not to do so would be stealing, which forces all money to come out in the open and be spent or invested, again reducing taxes and prices.

I fully realize how involved this solution is to the economic problem, and how easy it is to laugh at it and criticize when it is not understood, but because the basic principle is completely undeniable to those who understand it, I am prepared to go before any group of qualified economists, if necessary, for additional clarification and discussion. If any reader (after reading the rest of the chapters and then the entire book a second time) does not completely grasp the principles involved that compel us to move in this direction, please do not hesitate to write or call, as it is about time we took the bull gently by the horns in view of the fact that the solution is now just a matter of time.

# CHAPTER 5 — THE MEDICAL PROFESSION

"Well, Larry, I still don't believe you are going to obviate the need for all but 10% of our doctors."

"It is a very interesting subject, but before I demonstrate this, let me show you how confused the medical profession is regarding the sense organs. This stems from Aristotle."

"Do you have absolute, undeniable proof that they are confused?"

"Beyond a shadow of doubt."

"But I always thought the medical profession was a scientific organization, and that the brain was thoroughly understood."

"A doctor does the best he can, Jim, with the knowledge he has, but how much accurate knowledge does he have... do you know?"

"No, I don't know."

"Do you think he knows?"

"I think he thinks he knows, but I don't know if he knows. How much does he know, Larry?"

"He knows as much about the human body as a theologian knows about God."

"Are you blaming them for anything? Your voice sounds as if you resent them for something or other."

"How can I blame them when I know their will is not free, that they can't help doing what they do? I get the same feeling around a doctor as I do when I'm near a theologian. The hair stands up on my arms. This always happens when I'm around somebody who doesn't know but thinks he does."

"But doesn't this mean that you know that they don't know?"

"That's right."

"Can you prove it?"

"I certainly can."

"Well, show me then. I'm definitely interested in learning the truth, as most people are, except when the truth reveals our unconscious ignorance, right?"

"Right, Jim. Now to demonstrate this... Look, here comes Doctor Jones. Let's call him over for just one question."

"Hey, Doctor Jones, it's Jimmy and Larry. Can we disturb you for a couple of minutes?"

"What is it, fellows, anything I can do for you?"

"Larry, here, wants to ask you one question because he thinks you're qualified to answer it, all right?"

"I'll do my best."

"Is it true that man has five senses?"

"Are you referring to this talk about a sixth sense?"

"No, I am not."

"Well, you can't be serious about that question, because everybody knows man has five senses. This is an established fact."

"Thank you very much, Doctor, you have been very helpful."

"I don't see where, but you're certainly welcome."

"Now tell me, Jim, is it possible to convince a doctor that this knowledge is fallacious in some way?"

"You can't be serious, Larry. You're not going to tell me that man doesn't have five senses, are you?"

"That's right, Jim, man doesn't have five senses. Now, supposing I stood up in one of our universities and announced: 'Gentlemen, I am prepared to prove that man does not have five senses,' wouldn't all the professors laugh and say: 'Are you serious or are you being funny? We all know that man does have them, for this is an established fact.' Well, isn't this your thinking on the subject?"

"Yes, it is, but even if man doesn't have five senses, he still has taste, touch, smell, hearing, and sight, isn't that correct?"

"That's right."

"So what difference does it make what we call them as a group; this isn't going to make me not have this hearing, touch, smell, taste, and sight, right?"

"That's true, Jim. What we think about our sense organs is certainly not going to change what we are, just as our thoughts about the shape of the earth and the will of man couldn't change these things either. However, if man doesn't really have five senses, isn't it obvious that just as long as we think he does, we will be prevented from discovering those things that depend on this knowledge for their discovery? Consequently, it does make a difference what we call them. Furthermore, just think of all the false knowledge that might exist in the world from believing that man has five senses when he really doesn't have."

"Larry, I'm convinced you're over my head, but I'll do my best to follow your reasoning. Where do you dig up these things, anyway?"

"I told you. I've got a keen smeller, and when I'm around certain people, the hair stands up on my arms."

"Just around doctors and theologians?"

"No. Two other groups affected me the same way. I couldn't even get near a politician without looking like a cat ready to fight, and the professors of philosophy, psychology, and psychiatry irritated me no end. But now that I know why they disturbed me, and know that they can't help being unconsciously ignorant, I'm not affected by their presence."

"Larry, are you sure you're not from another planet?"

"Didn't I tell you? I'm really from Mars. I came here to avenge my brother, who was nailed to a cross a few years ago. I'm going to take over where he left off."

"You're quite a jokester, Larry."

"I'm not joking, Jim. And if I'm not careful, the resentful ignorance of these people will nail me to a cross, and they would do it in the name of justice and truth. However, it appears that they will not be given the opportunity because the very moment the will of God is perceived and understood, man is given no alternative as to what direction he must travel, which is away from nailing me and my brothers to any more crosses."

"Please, Larry, no more digressions. I'm anxious to hear about the senses."

"Okay, Jim, let's get on with it. Now tell me, did it ever occur to you that many of the so-called truths we have literally accepted come to us in the form of words that do not accurately symbolize what exists, making our problem that much more difficult since this has denied us the ability to see reality for what it really is?"

"I suppose this is true, but I've never given it much thought."

"You see, Jim, there are thousands upon thousands of differences existing in the external world, but when words do not describe accurately, we are then seeing a distorted version of what exists, as with 'free will.' The reason we have a word for the sun and a word for the moon is simply because these two bodies are different, and the reason we have a planet named Earth, one named Saturn, Venus, and my hometown is only because these are not one and the same planet. However, the reason we do not call the moon a planet is because we learned it does not function like one. An apple, pear, orange, peach and potato tell us of differences in substance that exist in the world, but we certainly could not call them five fruits since this word excludes the potato, which is not grown in the same manner as is described by the word fruit. The reason we say man has taste, touch, smell, sight, and hearing is because these describe individual differences that exist, but when we say that these five are senses, we are assuming they function alike, which is a wholly inaccurate observation since the eyes do not function like the other four."

"Is that really true, Larry? I never thought much about the senses."

"It's true, Jim. Let us now analyze exactly why this is so, if for no other reason than to show how utterly confused those who teach and guide us are.

The word sense, in this dictionary, is defined as — 'Any receptor, or group of receptors, specialized to receive and transmit external stimuli, as of sight, taste, smell, etc.' But this is a wholly fallacious observation where the eyes are concerned because they do not receive and transmit since nothing from the external world strikes the optic nerve as stimuli do upon the organs of hearing, taste, touch, and smell, which receive and transmit sense experiences."

"Excuse the interruption, but I just thought of something. Didn't you say just a while ago that if the bank didn't receive a payment on time, it would simply draw this amount from the Bureau?"

"What in the hell are you bringing this up now, when we are discussing the sense organs?"

"It just dawned on me that you made a mistake, and that you are not perfect after all in your reasoning. You distinctly said that before any person can draw unemployment compensation, or his guaranteed income, he must exhaust his own surplus or money that is not invested, right?"

"That's perfectly correct."

"Well, supposing someone doesn't make his payment on time, and the banks, although having a surplus, draw this money from the Bureau; isn't that wrong?"

"The banks couldn't do it without hurting the people who must pay for it."

"But you distinctly said they would do it."

"Did I say whether or not they had a surplus?"

"No, you didn't."

"Well, supposing all they had was just enough to pay the salaries of their employees, then wouldn't they have to draw this difference to get their guarantee?"

"Yes, that's true."

"You see, Jim, it shouldn't be necessary to analyze every minute detail when the extension of this discovery is completely mathematical. Once it is made clear that no one is considered displaced until he has exhausted all of his own cash, either by investing or spending it, it is taken for granted that he has conformed to this condition. Remember, everybody can cheat and steal if he wants to, but is it possible to want to under these conditions?"

"The other question, Larry. How do the remaining government workers get an increase in their income, other than by a reduction in prices, when there is no employer to give them a share of his profits if he wants to give it?"

"A good question, Jim, although I thought I answered it. The Post Office, Fire Department, Sanitation Department, Water Department, etc., even the public schools, will receive so much money for their services, which will go to cover salaries and other expenses. If they make a profit, it will be divided equally among all those working, but only after carrying a sufficient surplus to cover the possibility of taking a loss. If they took their profits without allowing for this loss, then when they fell beneath what they need, and are forced to draw upon unemployment compensation, they would hurt those who guarantee their income."

"Do you mean that the rest of the government would be like a private corporation, working on a profit or loss?"

"That's exactly what I mean. If the head of the Post Office finds that business is falling off, and to meet expenses, this necessitates laying off some workers, he will simply lay them off. And if business picks up again to where he needs additional help, he will simply advertise for it. However, if he feels this slump is just temporary and has the reserve to carry their salaries, then he doesn't have to lay anybody off. This will apply to the head of each department, but in conjunction with the overall expenses and profit."

"Do you mean that the head of each department has the right to fire someone if he wants to?"

"If he wants to, yes. But how is it possible to want to when this would have to necessitate someone doing something wrong, which word only means 'hurt somebody else'? Once it is mathematically impossible to hurt another, there is no way anybody can do something wrong. Right, Jim?"

"You win again, Larry. But I didn't think you made it clear about the balance of the government becoming a private, self-sustaining corporation. And supposing, for example, the Bureau of Sanitation is forced to go out of business because of advanced technology, what then?"

"These various departments could also become displaced by competitors selling the same service at a much cheaper rate, or a superior service at the same rate. We will guarantee each person his income; we will not guarantee his job or business."

"There are probably other details you left out, Larry."

"For Christ's sake, Jim, give me a little room to breathe, will you? I'm not a machine, you know. Do you mean to imply that we have such fools in the world that when this knowledge of what it means that man's will is not free is released, they still won't be able to carry the ball unless they are led by the hand every step of the way? No, Jim, I don't think that at all. Once this is released, watch how quickly science, the perception and extension of mathematical, undeniable relations, takes over."

"I hope you're right, Larry. I would love to see the kind of world you've described so far become a reality. Well, let's hear further about the senses."

"Now Jim, it can be easily demonstrated at the birth of a child that the eyes are not a sense organ when it can be seen that no object is capable of getting a reaction from them because absolutely nothing is impinging on the optic nerve, although any number of sounds, tastes, touches or smells can get an immediate reaction because the nerve endings are being struck by something external. The very fact that an infant at birth cannot focus the eyes to see, which has never been adequately explained, is another reason why they cannot be included as one of the senses, simply because the four senses are in full working order. Furthermore, and quite revealing (this can be scientifically tested), if this infant, immediately after birth, was placed in a soundproof room with the eyelids removed, and kept alive for 50 years or longer — if possible for that length of time — on a steady flow of intravenous glucose, without allowing any stimuli to strike the other 4 organs of sense, this baby, child, young and old man would never be able to see any objects existing in that room no matter how much in motion or colorful they might be because the conditions necessary for sight have been removed, and there is absolutely nothing that travels from an object to the optic nerve that causes it."

"Doesn't light travel to the optic nerve?"

"Certainly."

"And doesn't it cause the pupils to react?"

"It does."

"And isn't light the cause of sight?"

"No, it isn't. It is a condition of sight, as other things are a condition of hearing. If there were no light, we couldn't see, and if there was nothing to carry the sound waves to our ears, we couldn't hear. However, if a lion roared, a newborn baby would hear the sound and react because this impinges on the eardrum and is then transmitted to the brain, and the same holds true for anything that makes direct contact with an afferent nerve ending; but this is far from the case with the eyes because there is no similar afferent nerve ending in this organ, which I will explain in a moment.

Consequently, to include them as one of the senses when this describes stimuli from the outside world making contact with a nerve ending, is completely erroneous, and equivalent to calling a potato, apple, peach, pear, and orange, five fruits.

Sight takes place for the first time, Jim, when sense experience (hearing, taste, touch, and smell — these are doorways in) awakens the brain, which then focuses the eyes so that the child can look through them, efferently, at what exists around him. The eyes are the windows of the brain, through which experience is gained not by what comes in as a result of striking the optic nerve, but by what is looked at in relation to sense experience. The brain records various sounds, tastes, touches, and smells in relation to the objects from which these experiences are derived and then looks through the eyes to see these things that have become familiar as a result of the relation. If a newborn infant were not permitted to have any sense experiences, the brain would never desire to focus the eyes to look through them at the external world, no matter how much light was present. Consequently, even though the lids were removed, and even though many colorful objects were placed in front of the baby, the child could never see because the brain is not looking. But when sense experience awakens the brain, then the child focuses the eyes to look through them at what exists. This is somewhat equivalent to a baby sleeping with his eyes wide open who does not awaken when objects are placed in front of him, although a loud noise, which strikes the eardrum, can easily do the job. Under no conditions can the eyes be called a sense organ unless, as in Aristotle's case, it was the result of an inaccurate observation that was never corrected."

"Well, I still say, what difference does it make whether we have four senses and a pair of eyes instead of five senses? I certainly don't feel any different, and I still see you just as before."

"Once it is understood that something existing in the external world makes contact with the brain through the four senses, but that the brain contacts the various objects by peering through the eyes, it makes one helluva difference, and many things can be clarified.

The brain is a very complex piece of machinery that not only acts as a tape recorder through our ears, and a camera through our eyes, but also, and this was never understood, as a movie projector. Consequently, since the eyes are the binoculars of the brain, all words that are placed in front of this telescope, words containing every conceivable kind of relation, are projected as slides onto the screen of the outside world, and if these words do not accurately symbolize, as with 'five senses,' man will actually think he sees what has absolutely no existence, and if words correctly describe, then he will be made conscious of differences and relations that have no meaning for those who do not know the words. To understand this better, let us observe a baby learning these symbols.

It is obvious that as a child looks out through his eyes, he sees various animals and people in motion, but he is not conscious of differences. He may be drawn to play with one animal in preference to another, as with toys, or may prefer one person to another, but insofar as the child is concerned, all he sees are a bunch of objects. However, as the baby's eyes are focused on one of our canine friends, let us repeat rapidly in his ear the word 'dog,' stopping when his eyes wander. Soon this relation is formed, which allows the brain to take a picture of the relation, not the object, and when he sees the animal, he is then in a position to project the word."

"Say, Larry, what has all this got to do with doctors?"

"Nothing, except that they teach that man has five senses, as religion teaches that man has free will, and this teaching has prevented the discovery of knowledge hidden behind this unconscious ignorance. I'll touch on the medical profession shortly, so don't get impatient. Now, before long, the child learns words like cat, cow, bird, tree, flower, television, sun, moon, apple, orange, bee, bug, knife, fork, spoon, chair, clothes, hat, shoes, etc., which make him conscious of specific and general differences that definitely exist. Each word becomes linked with those differences in substance, as with the names of people — Mary, John, Oscar, Monroe, etc. In other words, as he learns these names and words, his brain takes a picture of the objects symbolized, and when he sees these differences again, he projects the word or name, but the brain will not take any picture until a relation is formed. Consequently, these differences that exist in the external world, which are not identifiable through taste, touch, smell, or sounds that are not names, are identifiable only because they are related to words, names, or slides that we project for recognition. If we should lose certain names or words, we have amnesia, because when we see these ordinarily familiar differences, we are unable to project the words or names necessary for recognition. This gives conclusive evidence as to why an animal cannot identify too well with its eyes. In fact, if a vicious dog, accustomed to attacking any person who should open the backyard gate at night, were to have two senses, hearing and smell, temporarily disconnected — and assuming that no relation was developed as to the way in which an individual walked — he would actually have amnesia, and even though he saw with his eyes his master come through the gate, he would have no way of recognizing him and would attack. A dog identifies mostly through sound and smell, and what he sees is in relation to these, just as we identify most of the differences that exist through words and names. If the negative plate on which the relation is formed is temporarily disconnected, in man's case, the words or names, in the dog's case, the sounds and smells, both have a case of amnesia. This reveals that colorblindness is not always an inherited characteristic but a case of not learning words properly. It also reveals that a tremendous number of people wear glasses without having any need for them at all."

"The optometrists and opticians aren't going to like you, Larry."

"What difference does it make to them when their income will be guaranteed never to decrease or stop?"

"But Larry, that doesn't begin until all mankind learns what it means that man's will is not free, and until then, statements like these could affect their income."

"Should I not tell the truth, then? Aren't these medical men interested in the truth?"

"If it is really true, but are you sure it is true? After all, you are not an optometrist; you did not study what these doctors did, so why should your statement be true if they say it is false? In fact, the other day a doctor was called in by my mother for my brother, and when he prescribed some medicine, I blurted out, 'Jack doesn't really need that stuff, Mom.'"

"You jumped to a conclusion, didn't you, Jim?"

"Yes, I did, but I feel that most of it is just a waste of money."

"But who are you to feel this way? Did you have medical training?"

"That's exactly what I started to tell you. When the doctor heard my remark, he said, 'My boy, you... are... not... a... doctor,' as if the fact that he is determines the difference between truth and fiction."

"Well, don't worry about the doctors, Jim; let's just continue with an analysis of the eyes. Now once it is established as a mathematical fact that the eyes are not a sense organ, that the brain looks through them at what exists, then it is obvious that desire is equivalent to the batteries in a flashlight; the more the batteries, the brighter the light; the stronger the desire, the better will a person be able to see what he wants to see. Consequently, an optometrist does not have a mathematical standard to determine the need for glasses. Some children have absolutely no interest in school, which decreases their desire to see what's going on. It's true that some children can't see the blackboard and the writing as clearly as others, and it is also true that the eyes themselves set conditions that limit their vision no matter how strong the desire is to see what is going on. . ."

"Now wait just a minute, Larry. If there are physical conditions that limit vision, isn't this a justifiable reason for a doctor to prescribe glasses?"

"Of course not. If one child sees better by being closer to the blackboard, and another sees better by being farther away, then it is obvious that the children should be arranged in that order."

"But supposing one child can't get back far enough, or another close enough, what then?"

"Then and then only is it necessary to prescribe glasses. However, the distance at which a child sees best is often conditioned by his desire, which is affected by many things. In most cases, children go to elementary and high school with a certain amount of reluctance, just as boys go into the army. This is something they must do; there is no choice. The primary point being made is that there is no mathematical standard to justify glasses, which means that a person's vision can vary to a degree from day to day. I know of a case where a child was having difficulty seeing the blackboard, but when the teacher announced that the class was going to take a bus trip — and she wrote the name of the place to be visited on the blackboard — the child's interest became so great that he had no trouble reading the small print. Even if a child's vision is slightly impaired, he may still be able to function well without glasses. Prescribing the full optical prescription might provide significantly clearer vision but could potentially contribute to worsening nearsightedness over time. In addition, once a person becomes dependent on glasses, the muscles of the eyes actually become weaker, and when the spectacles are removed, even the strongest desire cannot develop those weakened muscles, which makes it necessary to continue using glasses. Just like any other muscle, the eyes benefit from exercise. Interestingly, people who wear glasses may feel that others could benefit from wearing them also and will use the same standard to test whether they need glasses that was used by their doctor to test them. 'Can you read that sentence at that distance?' And when they say 'no,' they proceed to advise them to get glasses because they believe this is an accurate standard. Again, this is not to say that glasses are never needed but should only be prescribed when the eyes cannot adjust to the distance that the patient finds <u>necessary</u> to see clearly."

"Say, Larry, something just came to me. I know there will soon be no more army and therefore no more compulsory draft, but what about elementary and high school, aren't we going to have to compel our children to get an education?"

"The world is in for quite a surprise where education is concerned, Jim, but let's not get ahead of ourselves. Remember, I can't put everything down at one time. Right now, I'm interested in continuing where I left off regarding colorblindness. If someone gets confused between certain shades of blue and green, it is only because the relation between colors was never accurately photographed. This is equivalent to getting confused between certain types of leaves and trees, only because these differences were not accurately photographed in relation. Once a particular leaf is given a specific name, and the leaf resembling this to a degree, but still slightly different, is given a different name, then when the relation is accurately photographed, the person learning the words will never mistake one for the other.

Supposing we were to teach a child that blue is green and green is blue, then place him in surroundings where his identification of colors would be tested. Can you imagine how quickly he would be called colorblind? This child would argue that the green is blue and the blue is green, while the other children, brought up differently, would reverse the argument. This is equivalent to looking at an object through a colored piece of glass, which changes the appearance of the object when a different color is used. But once these children are made to understand that they are both referring to the same bit of substance when the different words are used, then there can be no argument between them. However, in the course of their development, they learn other kinds of words that form inaccurate relations, not only because a judgment of personal value is given external reality by the symbol itself, but also because the logic of unconscious syllogistic reasoning confirms the apparent validity of inaccurate observations."

"Now just hold it, Larry. Don't go slinging those words around me because I just don't know what you're talking about... 'The logic of unconscious syllogistic reasoning.' What in the hell is that?"

"Have you forgotten already, Jim? Didn't I explain this once before regarding two sentences by Durant? This is exactly what doctors do, or anybody, for that matter, who wants to prove he is right. Aristotle did not see that man has five senses; he assumed this by fallacious reasoning. We never see that someone is colorblind; we assume this. Seeing that a person has difficulty identifying certain colors, we set this up as a major premise from which to reason, not realizing that our perception contains a fallacious assumption, just as the word doctor presupposes the qualifications to treat and heal, while the word charlatan or quack assumes the opposite. Advertisers use this kind of reasoning when they tell us that such and such a product is good because the medical profession endorses it, and the medicine man from days gone by also used it when he assumed that his incantation exorcized the spirit of illness."

"But it isn't an assumption when the spirit of illness flies away, is it, Larry?"

"No, Jim, but it is an assumption when the medicine man believes that his incantation was the cause, right?"

"You are so very right."

"However, let me try to clarify the origin of this kind of thinking. Sometime in the course of our development an individual discovered that he liked certain differences better than others because they tasted, smelled, felt, sounded or looked better to him, and then he developed words to communicate why he liked these differences, and when expressing himself, in a limited fashion, all he could say was, 'I like that girl better than all others because the shape of her nose, her legs, her bust, her features in general, appeal to me more. I also like that man better because he has gone to the 100th grade in school, has read a tremendous number of books that I like, can work out the kind of mathematical problems I like, etc.' Then he decided to symbolize what was first a personal judgment into an external reality by calling the first group of differences 'beautiful' and the second group 'educated' or 'intelligent.' Now, did you see what just happened, Jim?"

"Yeah, I saw. You just showed me how a few words came into existence; so what?"

"But these words do not symbolize anything externally real and are in the same category as 'heaven and hell.'"

"Now wait a minute, Larry. I know that heaven is just a figment of the imagination, but 'beauty, education, intelligence, etc., these are real... aren't they?"

"Are you asking or telling me?"

"I'm asking, Larry. Let's not go through that again."

"There is obviously a difference between the shape and features of individuals, as there is a difference between what some people prefer to do, but by having the words beautiful, educated, intelligent, etc. as slides in a movie projector through which the brain will look at the external world, a fallacious value is placed upon certain specific differences only because of the words, nothing else, which is then confirmed as a part of the real world since man will swear that he sees beautiful women, educated, and intelligent people with his eyes; but in actual reality all he sees are different shapes, different features, different books and different actions. This so-called beautiful girl is not striking his optic nerve, which then allows him to see her beauty, but instead he projects the word onto these differences and then photographs a fallacious relation. The brain records all relations, whether true or false, and since it was undeniable that man had five senses which were connected in some way with the external world, that is, they receive and transmit external stimuli, it was so easy for Aristotle to get confused and put a closure on further investigation by including the eyes, which he did only because he never understood their true function. But how was it possible for him to understand that the brain is also like a movie projector, and that words are like slides in this, when these items had not yet been invented to develop the words necessary for an adequate understanding?"

"Now just a minute, Larry. You just said that 'a fallacious value is placed upon certain specific differences only because of the words, nothing else,' is that correct?"

"Right."

"Well, is it a fallacious value when certain differences are admired and respected more by the majority of the world? When a person applies for a job, is it a fallacious value when his education gets him a better job and a bigger salary? Is it a fallacious value when... pardon the fallacious expression... a beautiful girl attracts a millionaire who desires to marry her because of her beauty? I'd say these values are pretty real, regardless of whether we call these differences by one name or another, right?"

"Not exactly, Jim. Of course, certain things need clarification."

"I should say so. I know some nuts, goofballs, idiots, uneducated, unintelligent morons, and if they aren't just plain stupid, I don't know who is. Besides, I saw a girl the other day, and she was simply hideous, just as ugly as she could be. Now, be perfectly honest with me, Larry, if I own a business and need a man with a particular type of education, isn't this individual of greater value to me and to others who are in a similar position as myself?"

"Naturally, no one can argue with that."

"Well, isn't a particular value that is desired by more than one person an external value, something, in other words, externally real?"

"Of course not."

"Now wait a minute. If one thousand males have to choose between two females and the entire thousand pick one in preference to the other, do you mean to say that the differences that attracted them are not a part of the external world?"

"Of course these differences are a part of the external world, just as the difference between the moon and the sun is a part of the external world, and just as the difference between a cat and a rat is externally real, but this has nothing to do with value. Would you rather have a cat or a rat for a pet?"

"A cat, naturally. Whoever heard of having a rat for a pet?"

"I don't know about that, Jim. I know a fellow who had a cute little pussy for a pet, and she turned into a rat. Shortly after that, I heard she became a dirty dog."

"You're right, Larry. She was not only a rat and a dirty dog, but later I heard she became a prostitute. But what has all this got to do with external values?"

"In reality, Jim, there is no such thing as an external value. If you are drawn to hire an individual because he meets certain requirements, or if he judges for himself, as will happen in the new world, that he qualifies, this only means that he is more valuable to you; and if one thousand people think the same way, this doesn't mean that the differences they prefer have external value, although the differences are externally real. Value is nothing other than a word to describe what you want or like."

"Do you mean that 'one man's meat is another man's poison,' or that 'beauty is in the eyes of the beholder?'"

"There is quite a difference between both expressions simply because meat and poison are external realities, but beauty has no external reality whatsoever. I may not like certain types of meat, but I don't create the meat with the word to symbolize its existence, whereas the word beauty does this by placing a greater value on certain specific differences that undeniably exist as part of the external world, when value has existence only for the internal world, that is, for what you like and desire. For example, if I call one shaped nose, aquiline, and another, straight, then I am accurately symbolizing an external difference, but if I say a straight nose is beautiful, and an aquiline nose is ugly, then I am projecting, through my eyes, an internal value that has no external existence, onto a screen of differences that are externally undeniable. Consequently, when any words are used that contain an internal value, something that you recognize as having more value for you, which are then projected as a part of the external world, they then make it appear that this value exists outside of you because you see it with your eyes. In other words, Jim, if the thousand men prefer one girl to the other, it isn't because one is beautiful and the other ugly, but only because certain specific differences are desired. If one thousand men prefer one type of individual for a job rather than another, it isn't because the one is educated and the other is not, but only because certain specific differences are desired."

"You're doing very good, Larry, but could you clarify this a little more?"

"I think so. If a young child, while looking at one type individual, heard over and over again, 'Look how beautiful!' with an enhancing inflection, and at another type, 'Look how ugly!' with a detracting inflection (although the one word implies the existence of the other), it wouldn't take long before this child would be conditioned to desire associating with the first while avoiding the other, and as he would get older you wouldn't be able to convince him that an ugly or beautiful, educated or uneducated, intelligent or stupid person does not exist as a definite part of the real world, because he sees these differences with his eyes. But remember, these words not only describe differences; they create external values when there are no such things. If two boys approached two girls, having never been conditioned with words like beautiful and ugly, educated and uneducated, they might be attracted, without envy, each to the other; but when their head is filled with fallacious standards of value concealed in words, it is obvious that they will prefer the one that conforms more closely to this standard of perfection or beauty, because this meets with greater approval and less criticism."

"But Larry, isn't this approval by others an external value?"

"Of course not. Your approval of what I do has a value for me, but unless I want this, it has no value for me. If I don't like criticism, I will conform to a standard that avoids what I don't like, but this is a relation between myself and what exists outside of me. However, it is absolutely true that just as long as others judge you more beautiful or valuable when your physiognomy conforms to an accepted standard, more educated or valuable when you learn or do certain things, there is ample justification, as I just mentioned, to change yourself to suit them, which is the reason many people have nose operations, squeeze their teeth together, develop a huge vocabulary, walk, talk, and act in definite ways. But what would happen, Jim, if we lived in an atmosphere where there were no values imposed as standards by the unconscious or conscious judgment of others?"

"It would make a tremendous difference."

"Supposing our girls, presently called ugly, were placed on a planet where no such word existed, there would be absolutely nothing to prevent them from living a normal life because the males there would never judge them in terms of ugliness, for no such thing exists except as a projection of our realistic imagination. But here on earth, these girls are handicapped from the day of their birth, not only because they may have an aquiline nose, their teeth apart or bucked, etc. — which does not conform to the standards of beauty — but also because they may never have graduated high school or college. They are constantly judged, not in any personal or direct manner, but in a way we cannot so easily correct because we see them through a kaleidoscope of words that transform them realistically into what they are not. Every other word we use stratifies external differences, which cannot be denied, into fallacious standards and values that appear realistic only because they are confirmed with our eyes and our unconscious syllogistic reasoning, which employs words as realities. The unhappiness resulting from these words is manifold and manifest in the very fact that people develop a complex of inferiority, but much good also resulted by permitting or driving those with this feeling of being inferior to make every effort possible to get rid of something that gave them no satisfaction."

"That may be true, Larry, but what about the people who unfortunately could never raise themselves beyond this adverse criticism, who were compelled to live out their lives while being judged an inferior production of the human species, as many Whites consider the Blacks, and many Jews the Gentiles, and many Gentiles the Jews, and many Catholics the Protestants, and the Protestants the Catholics, and so on? Didn't the Germans consider the Nordic stock superior?"

"You will soon see, Jim, through the extension of mathematical relations, how this kind of hurt will be compelled to end, but remember, I can't put everything down at one time."

"I think I already see how, Larry. To criticize and ridicule is a hurt, and when the critic fully realizes that he will not be blamed or punished, criticized or ridiculed in return for this hurt, then he will lose his desire to do what he knows others must excuse and he cannot justify. In other words, if Black people walk into a restaurant and the owner refuses to serve them, which is certainly his business, they would simply walk out. But this man knows that he definitely hurt these people by judging them not good enough to eat in his place, and when he fully realizes that this hurt to them would never be retaliated upon, never criticized or blamed, because he knows that they must excuse this hurt since they know he can't help himself — because his will is not free — then he is given no alternative but to show no discrimination because he knows he doesn't have to hurt them this way unless he wants to, and it is impossible for him to want to under these conditions."

"Wonderful, Jim! For a minute I thought you were me. But let's go a step further. The reason the restaurateur was discriminating in the first place, when he certainly could use this increase in his business, is because he knew that others, who did not want the Blacks in the restaurant where they ate, would criticize him by not continuing to eat there. But when he knows that they will not criticize him because this is a hurt for which they know he will never blame them, then they are given no alternative."

"You know, Larry, the whole thing becomes crystal clear now. The reason White parents object so strenuously to the thought of their daughter marrying a B is only because of the criticism and ridicule that generally follow in its wake, but when there is no possibility of this, it makes absolutely no difference to the parents just as long as their daughter is happy."

"But let's not get ahead of ourselves, Jim. Some people are so prejudiced that if they thought I was going to create a world in which such a marriage could occur, they might not desire to read my book when it is completed."

"What do you care about these ignorant people, Larry?"

"I do care, Jim. Their prejudices are normal and natural, and they came about out of God's will. But they are not required anymore, and God has asked me, that is, he has commanded me to remove them."

"But what about the medical profession as a whole? How do you go about getting rid of 90% of the illness in the world?"

"It's like this, Jim. When a student of medicine studies certain subjects at a recognized university and receives a diploma, he is given the right by the school and state to open an office and charge a fee to anyone who consults him for his knowledge. It is taken for granted, because of this diploma, the title of doctor, and the syllogistic reasoning that is always unconsciously at work, that this individual actually acquired the knowledge to treat and heal. But just supposing that he does not have this knowledge, that in spite of all he was taught, he really doesn't know, just thinks he does, then he is in a position to hurt others with impunity since he was told by the school that he is a qualified physician."

"Is there a way of testing the knowledge of a doctor? In most cases, doesn't a patient get well after taking the medicine prescribed, and isn't this proof that the doctor knows what he's doing?"

"There are four possibilities when doctors treat a patient, Jim. He could get better or worse because of the treatment, or he could get better or worse in spite of the treatment. In primitive times, when medicine men used to mumble incantations to exorcize the spirit of illness, the patient used to get well in spite of the treatment, although his belief that they knew what they were doing put his body in a more favorable condition to combat the disturbance, so the patient was partially helped because of the treatment. When he recovered, credit was given to the medicine men, but many times in those days, when the patient did not recover, the doctor was hanged and quartered. But today we have a different kind of problem because the medical profession can kill with impunity, while doctors blame everything but themselves. Montaigne observed this even in his own time. They start out with the assumption that their patient will not get well unless he does what they prescribe, and though in years gone by when they used themselves as guinea pigs to test the reaction of a new drug so that they could be of help to their patient, today they are afraid to find out what would happen if they didn't prescribe 90% of the medicines in constant use. Isn't it possible the patient would get well without the drug, or is this the actual cause of returning health? Furthermore, supposing the drug is actually harmful to the body when taken often enough over the years, and instead of the patient getting better, he gets worse because of it, and then after doctors have nearly killed him, he gets better in spite of it?"

"Do these things actually happen, Larry?"

"I know a case of a very healthy boy who cut his hand on a tin can. Ordinarily, there would have been no excitement, but the mother was up to date on the latest medical information, and she rushed her child to the doctor for the purpose of getting a tetanus shot. That evening, the child came down with a high fever, and again the mother called in her doctor. This time he prescribed something else, and believe it or not, the boy was two weeks getting well. Now the question arises, what would have happened had she not rushed him to the doctor for a tetanus shot?"

"Couldn't he have died, Larry?"

"Certainly, he could have died, just as you can die from various causes, but whether he would have died had the doctor not given him the shot is questionable. Besides, what about the other side of the picture. Was the sickness of the boy due to the medicine or the cut by the tin can?"

"I'm certain I don't know, Larry."

"There is absolutely nothing today, that is up until now, that can stop a doctor from hurting others through his unconscious ignorance, consequently, to make himself believe that he knows, even though he doesn't, he must constantly resort to his title, this syllogistic reasoning concealed in words, as a confirmation of his knowledge, which compels him to say in rebuttal to any layman who disagrees with what he does, 'You are not a doctor,' which means, when translated, 'I know what I'm doing because I am a doctor.' 'Do you mean, Doc, that unless the patient takes this medicine you are prescribing, he will only get worse?' 'This is the risk he would be taking.' 'But is there no risk the other way; are you absolutely certain that he will not only get well but not get worse?' 'Certainly I'm certain, I'm the doctor, right?' Are you beginning to see, Jim, that the fear of getting worse unless you abide by what he prescribes is the lever by which he multiplies this need for his services?"

"But you can't blame him, Larry, because he, like the rest of us, is compelled to earn a living, and if he didn't justify what he did, he would have to go out of practice. He must believe that he knows what he's doing, and most important of all, that he is not making his patient worse. But if he believes he is really helping his patients, when all the while he is only making matters worse, how can you correct it?"

"I'll show you in just a minute, but first I would like to recall something that happened to me personally. A friend of mine had a nervous breakdown and consulted a psychiatrist who made no promises as to the length of time it might take to discover the cause and restore her mental balance.

She went to him for several visits, and then one day came to me for my advice, asking if it was possible for me to help her. I told her that I would treat her on one condition, that she stop seeing all psychiatrists. She agreed and told her psychiatrist the reason she was not going to see him anymore. 'Do you realize what you are doing?' he angrily demanded. 'That man is not a doctor, and you could very easily get worse.' Well, to make a long story short, inside of two weeks she was completely well, and to this day has never had any nervous disorders. But when she paid this psychiatrist a visit to tell him of her good fortune, he was not too happy over it, and above all, was not the least bit interested in discovering what I knew that could make his patients well so quickly, for who likes to lose the source of his income? To be a qualified doctor, it is important to know the actual cause of something before treatment is administered and to be absolutely certain that the body is not fully capable of taking care of this matter itself. It is equally important to understand the dangers to the body in trying to learn of a cause. Some patients have died only because a doctor did more harm in trying to find out what was wrong than what could have been done were they left completely alone. One patient, because the various tests showed nothing as to why he was spitting up blood, was operated on so the surgeon could explore, and died under the knife. Another friend of mine died during a tonsillectomy; he never came out of the anesthesia. And even after a doctor has arrived at a mathematical diagnosis, one which allows no disagreement, it is also important for him to know exactly what to do, not what he thinks should be done. Many operations, apparently successful, have killed the patients months later because of unforeseen complications; and how many doctors give drugs to a child, not because they know that this is best for his health, or even because they know the cause of the illness, but only to allay his fears and those of his parents. Innumerable drugs are prescribed every day without the medical profession having any inkling of what the actual cause of a disturbance is, and the only justification for this lies in the fact that the doctor believes there is really no harm and there may be some good. But are doctors absolutely certain that drugs have no relation to the ill health of the body? Perhaps they are equally certain as governments are that the effort to remove crime and war through threats of retaliation and punishment has no relation to the ill health of society.

Who knows at this point (although you will know soon enough) what the constant use of drugs does to the tissues and organs, and how can doctors be certain that many of our ills are not caused by their efforts to make us well?"

"I don't know, that's for sure."

"The body, Jim, is a balanced equation with tremendous recuperative powers that adjusts itself, in most cases, when it gets out of balance. However, there are times when it is incapable of restoring this balance, and then only is the knowledge of a physician necessary, providing he really knows what to do; otherwise, he could only make matters ten times worse. Now to protect the people from the unconscious ignorance of the doctor, our slide rule demonstrates that when he is not given the right by the school and state to use drugs, perform operations, and give other kinds of treatment, then he must be absolutely honest with himself about how much he really knows regarding the distant and near effects of medicine, operations, tests, etc., simply because it becomes mathematically impossible for him to shift his responsibility to anyone but himself. He knows that his patients are putting every confidence in his knowledge, and that he could very easily take advantage of this for his own remuneration. But when he fully realizes that he might be responsible for people getting worse as a result of his treatment, who will never blame him for this, he is compelled to think like he never thought before; otherwise, he might be placing himself in a position that affords no satisfaction. In the new world, no diplomas will ever be issued because the right to practice medicine on the bodies of people will be granted to anyone who considers himself qualified. Each person will judge his own qualifications, and if he wishes to risk hurting others, who will not blame him, this is his business. If someone wishes to open an office and hang out a shingle (in the new world, that is), no one is going to question him, but the full responsibility of hurting others with his treatments must rest on his own shoulders once the school pulls out the props that allowed him to shift his blame. When a student has learned all that the school is able to teach of genuine knowledge, he will also have drawn a mathematical line of demarcation between this kind of learning and the knowledge that is a matter of opinion. Today, the doctors are so confused that they themselves don't know the difference, and they justify what they do by calling others quacks and by the fallacious argument that they know what is right for a patient because they are members of the medical profession, as if an opinion is any less of an opinion because it comes from a doctor. In fact, the greater the unconscious ignorance, the greater is the danger when it is not controlled. But all will be changed when the transition gets underway. In the future, when you consult a doctor, you will pay the same for his advice whether he prescribes something or just plainly tells you he doesn't know what to do, and honesty will be the best policy. The statement 'I don't know' is not a sign of ignorance when you really don't know, but a sign of honesty. Only fear makes an individual pretend to knowledge he doesn't possess, but doctors were compelled to do this as the lesser of two evils when their income depended on this self-deception and dishonesty. How is it humanly possible to be honest with yourself when this depends on being honest with others, and how is it possible to be honest with others when this results in a hurt to yourself?

"Above all, to thine own self be true, and it shall follow..."

"Shakespeare didn't know what he was talking about, although he thought he knew. However, when a doctor realizes that his income will not decrease or stop by being absolutely honest with his patients, then he can afford the luxury of being absolutely honest with himself. Until then, until the transition gets underway, most doctors will continue to pretend to knowledge they do not possess because they are blamed for not having it the moment they are consulted, since no one wishes to pay them for admitting they don't know. It also gives them great satisfaction to be admired for possessing the knowledge of how to restore a person's health; consequently, your belief that they have this knowledge only makes them keep up the pretense."

"Larry, I'm convinced you don't like doctors."

"You're wrong, Jim, because I know they can't help themselves. Everybody, including you, is compelled to move in the direction of greater satisfaction."

"Is this all you have to say about doctors?"

"For now, yes, but something of interest will be revealed when I discuss children."

"Is there anything else you think I should know about the economic system?"

"I can't think of anything else, offhand."

"I'm getting tired, Larry. How about you? Besides, I'll probably stay up half the night trying to absorb all that you told me."

"I'm exhausted, Jim, but I just want to say one thing in conclusion. The economic system I just described is mathematically possible, but only when all people understand what it means that man's will is not free. Until then, we will be forced to live in our present world as the lesser of two evils. However, once the fuse is lit and this knowledge spreads to those who not only recognize its significance but who also have the influence to lay it before those who can disseminate it even more rapidly, then it won't take long before we will develop this world of unmatched splendor, wherein no one will ever be hurt, and everyone will be wealthy and healthy."

"It sounds like you're talking about A New Earth, Larry."

"I am, Jim, and it is not a dream anymore, but an actual reality within our reach."

"I never thought I would spend my vacation listening to you, but I must confess I'm enjoying every minute of it. See you tomorrow. What's the subject, by the way?"

"Love."

"Great!"

# PART 3

# THE EXTENSION OF THIS DISCOVERY INTO

# THE WORLD OF LOVE

# CHAPTER 6 — PREMARITAL RELATIONS

Once again, Jim found difficulty in falling asleep, but for the first time he realized that Larry had truly made a scientific discovery that would change the entire world. He realized further the tremendous problem facing him and knew that it consisted mostly of this "sound barrier of learned ignorance," because who would take the time to read a book that reveals the end of government, religion, and demonstrates how unconsciously wrong these so-called experts have always been about the ultimate solution to man's problems. He knew that theology wouldn't take the time to read the first chapter because, to religion, the will of man is definitely free, and the subject itself is so far removed from the thinking of politicians that to give it to them would be a complete waste of time. The universities were even worse. Here, instead of being centers of investigation where new knowledge can be thoroughly analyzed for the purpose of extracting the needed mathematical relations to reveal its veracity, the professors use what they have been taught as a standard of truth, from which vantage point they survey the landscape of divergent views for the sole purpose of criticism and disagreement. "Larry was right," he thought to himself, "if he stood up before any one of them and said, 'man does not have five senses and I can prove it,' they wouldn't be the least bit interested in seeing the proof, and the same with free will."

Jim realized that Larry's best hope was to find someone who understood the book sufficiently to start a chain reaction of sales, with the possibility of making money for himself, for then somebody, sooner or later, would recognize the logical validity and soundness of his knowledge and light the fuse.

"How can I be the fuse?" he thought. "I know that everything Larry explained to me is true because it is self-evident and undeniable, but supposing I told my father, "Hey Dad, Larry just made a terrific discovery that will actually change the entire world. It puts an end to all war, crime... 'Is that right, Jimmy? It sounds terrific! Tell your mother about it, son, I don't have time to listen.' "And who would take the time to listen to anything I might say that sounds so utterly fantastic? I do know ten people who I think would understand this knowledge when Larry publishes his book; I'll give them a copy on a trial basis. If they want to return the book, I'll know they didn't understand it, but if they do understand it, they will want to keep it and tell others about it. Poor Larry! He really has a problem." And as Jim turned over to find a better position for dozing off, he suddenly sat up with a start. "That can't be! I'm sure I didn't hear him correctly! He just couldn't have said that all adultery and divorce are coming to an end!" And for the longest time, he couldn't fall asleep, wondering if he had heard correctly. He did manage to get some sleep, but it was already morning when he dozed off. Not wanting to be late, he dashed out of the house to meet Larry at their usual place. When he arrived, Larry could see that something was on his mind.

"Anything wrong, Jim? You look disturbed over something or other?"

"Did you say yesterday that all adultery and divorce are coming to an end?"

"I think I did, but if I didn't, it's definitely true. What's more, so is all premarital sexual intercourse coming to an end."

"Assuming that you do have the knowledge that could accomplish what I'm willing to bet my life you can't, are you also trying to tell me that I'll have to give up that 'good thing' I've had for the past 3 months?"

"What good thing is that, Jim, you never told me about it? You mean you've been keeping secrets from your pal?"

"I sure have been keeping it a secret. I'll never invite another male along when I visit my female friends, ever since Inez took a liking to Johnny and ditched me for him."

"I remember your telling me about it. But Jim, do you think I would do a thing like that to you?"

"You might not, but she might. Anyway, I met her about 3 months ago at a bar. She was sitting at Little Joe's drinking beer and watching television, so I... you know what a flirt I am, Larry... went over and started up a conversation. One thing led to another; she got to feeling pretty good off the beer... I was drinking too; I asked her if it was all right to take her home; she said 'yes,' and to make a long story short, I spent the night with her. Well, Larry, she was by far the best piece I ever had in my entire life, but I didn't know until the following morning that she was married and her husband a traveling salesman who makes trips anywhere from two to four weeks at a clip. Larry, this girl can't get enough. You'd think she never got any at home. And that's not all; she likes to play all kinds of games. You name it, and we've played it. This is what amazes me so much. Here I am on a two-week vacation and spending most of my time with you. Of course, Mary's husband doesn't leave until tonight, which might have a bearing."

"But I thought you were engaged to Sylvia."

"I was, but broke it off shortly after I met Mary. This girl has everything I want in a woman, that is, sexually, and I'm not about to give her up for anybody. In fact, as a last resort, I might even marry her, that is, if she can get a divorce from her husband. And you come up with the statement that all adultery and divorce are coming to an end. Does this mean that I'm supposed to give up Mary, and that she can't get a divorce from her husband?"

"Let's not get ahead of ourselves, Jim. Remember, all mankind must understand what it means that man's will is not free before this knowledge becomes mathematically effective. Until then, there is nothing to prevent what you're doing, except, perhaps, the fear of being shot by her husband — if you are caught."

"I don't care when this knowledge becomes effective, Larry. If I'm still going with Mary at the time, nobody on heaven and earth can make me give her up."

"Supposing she gives you up like Inez did?"

"Not a chance of it. She feels exactly the same about me as I do about her. We've been seriously talking about getting married, but there is one drawback. About two months ago, she asked her husband for a divorce, and the shock nearly gave him a heart attack. He's a big, fat guy, and he had to sit down to take the news. But he wouldn't hear of it, so Mary feels that if she tells him that she loves and wants to marry me, he'll give in. In fact, I'm supposed to call her in about ten minutes to find out if everything is all right. But he's Catholic, so I'm wondering."

"Do they have any children?"

"A boy, 10 and a girl, 13."

"Well, what kind of woman is she? Does she take you home where the kids are?"

"Now, who's jumping to conclusions? Of course not, Larry. Her husband makes a good income, and she has some money in her own right, so she is able to keep an apartment."

"You mean she had this apartment when she met you?"

"That's right. I know what you're thinking, but you are wrong. It's sort of a guest house for many of her friends and relatives who visit them. In fact, the apartment is only a block away from her house. Gee, what time is it? I've got to call her right away to find out if he will agree to our getting married. I'll be right back."

Jim rushed to the nearest telephone, dialed the number, and instead of hearing Mary's voice at the end of the line, it was her husband who answered.

"Is Mary there, please?"

"Are you the nitwit she's talking about marrying? Well, let me tell you something, you dirty rat, you can have that whore I threw out of the house. Both of you are rotten right to the core. She's been committing adultery; she's nothing but a prostitute, and I don't care what she does. But I'll guarantee you one thing: she'll never get a divorce just as long as she lives." And bang went the receiver in Jim's ear.

He returned quite upset, and it was only after several minutes that he was able to talk at all.

"What's wrong, Jim? You look like you've seen a ghost. You are white as a sheet."

"That was her husband who answered. He threw Mary out of the house when she told him about us and still refuses to give her a divorce. Mary must be at the apartment, quite upset. I can't stay here now, Larry. I've got to see how she is. I'll see you tomorrow."

Jim returned the next day, determined that Mary get a divorce from that "fat slob," as she referred to him.

"Well, Larry, I'm not going to discuss my problems. Mary was quite upset, but she's resting comfortably. I know now that I love her dearly, and I'm definitely going to marry her just as soon as she gets a divorce. Nothing in this universe can prevent our marrying unless it is impossible for her to get a divorce, and if he doesn't give in, then we'll just live together as man and wife anyway. However, enough about me, what's your story?"

"As I said before, Jim, I'm going to put a mathematical end to all premarital sexual intercourse, all adultery, and all divorce. Are you ready to hear the solution?"

"If it affects me personally, I don't care to hear it, but since I'm convinced you can't accomplish this, go right ahead and try."

"Now let us understand, Jim, that no problem exists in our relations with each other unless someone is being hurt in a concrete manner. Premarital relations come to a peaceful end not because this is morally wrong and man has decided at last to obey the Ten Commandments, but only because we will be shown how to prevent the heart of our children from being broken and cut out with the knife of unrequited love, making it apparent that those who lose in this game — even though it may be better to have loved and lost than never to have loved at all— are very unhappy individuals."

"Just a minute, Larry. Did you say it isn't morally wrong for a girl to have sexual intercourse before marriage?"

"I did."

"Isn't that a terrible thing to teach children? I can just hear what my mother and father would say to this, and what religion would say."

"Is your memory so short, Jim, that you have already forgotten what I am going to do?"

"What do you mean?"

"I am going to put a mathematical end to all premarital sexual intercourse, so what difference does it make if I say, 'it isn't morally wrong?' What difference does it make if I say it is perfectly all right for an individual to steal, commit murder, declare war, if he wants to do these things, just as long as I can demonstrate how to prevent his desire from arising to do them? Furthermore, suppose the effort to correct these so-called sins is partially responsible for their existence, then isn't it obvious that to say something 'is morally wrong' is wrong, since this ends up engendering the very hurt our moralists try to prevent?"

"It appears that you are right again, but why are we so mixed up? Isn't it obvious that doctors try to make people well, that religion is sincere in preaching against evil and sin, that the government is in earnest about trying to get rid of crime, unemployment, and the threat of war? Do you mean that when a preacher says it is 'morally wrong' to indulge in sexual intercourse before marriage, he isn't sincere?"

"These people are as sincere as it is possible for them to be, but how is it humanly possible for a doctor to want to get rid of sickness on a permanent basis, when he needs it for his ultimate satisfaction? How can the religious be sincerely interested in removing all sin and evil, when they need these things to fight against for their own ultimate satisfaction? How is it possible for the government to be sincerely interested in removing all war and crime on a permanent basis, when politicians need these things to fight against for their ultimate satisfaction? How is it humanly possible for the organizations that fight for peace, for health, for security — those that wage a war against the evils of man — to be sincerely happy about the very removal of the things they need for their ultimate satisfaction?"

"I'm beginning to see what you mean, Larry. In other words, if it gives Billy Graham great satisfaction in making speeches to show man what is wrong with himself, how is it possible for him to be satisfied with the knowledge that his speeches, the very thing that gives him greatest satisfaction, are no longer required?"

"That's right, Jim. Can Will Durant be satisfied to learn that his philosophy will not be read anymore? Can people who have written books on what is right for parents, right for marriage, right for teenagers, right for this and right for that, be satisfied to learn that the knowledge they have been teaching will very soon be permanently displaced, just as the science of Aristotle has been displaced?"

"What about books on philosophy, won't they be written anymore?"

"Of course not. Of what would these philosophers write about?"

"Are you trying to tell me that only your book will exist?"

"Don't be ridiculous, Jim, you know that couldn't be true. Novels will always be written, so will history, geography, textbooks of all kinds. I'm only pointing out that when this knowledge is released and understood, all opinions, conceptions, theories, ideas, and philosophies on the subjects we're discussing have only existed until now because there was nothing to prove them wrong. It is humorous to observe, and mathematically undeniable, that the present attempt to remove sickness and evil from our lives has been like cutting off the heads of a diseased hydra; the more we try to do away with these things, the more they have increased, which indicates the unconscious nature of the true motivating factors. Have I made myself clear, Jim?"

"In other words, Larry, to get back on track, when parents, teachers, and preachers advise a girl that it is wrong for her to do certain things before marriage, they are not sincere in their advice; is that right?"

"Wrong. They are sincere. A doctor is sincere when he tries his best to make a patient well, but it cannot give him satisfaction to learn that someone else can do a much better job than he is able to do, and it certainly cannot satisfy him to learn that he is part of the cause he makes efforts to find. Consequently, his sincerity is extremely limited and can exist only under certain conditions. If a psychiatrist lost all his patients overnight as if by miracle, or if a rabbi lost his congregation, could they possibly be elated over this news, even though the very things they have been trying to accomplish are now brought about in a superior manner? Therefore, their sincerity is not sincerely sincere, and that is why this 'sound barrier of learned ignorance' presents such a problem, because it is this group of learned people that are mostly affected by the transition."

"But if their income is guaranteed never to stop or decrease for just as long as they live, doesn't this make it easier to break through?"

"It certainly does, but the primary thing, of course, is the fact that they will be given no choice, once the fuse is lit."

"I have to smile, Larry. If someone were listening to you, they might think you were planning to hurt them in some way, and here you are putting an end to all forms of hurt. But I think you've bitten off more than you can chew where the relations of the sexes are concerned."

"We'll know that soon enough, right?"

"In our present world, Jim, there are many boys and girls who lose in trying to win a particular person for a mate, but there needn't be any losers when the truth about ourselves is thoroughly understood. Consequently, every person is compelled to desire learning the secret of how to prevent this great hurt to himself, because his very happiness is at stake."

"Did I hear you correctly? If two boys want the same girl, neither will lose because both will have her? If this is true, I envy the girl and feel sorry for the boys."

"This is definitely not true. There will be one boy for one girl (this is God's will, as you will see, giving nobody any free choice in this matter), and they will remain together until death do they part."

"But Larry, there have to be losers when two or more people want the same thing; this is completely mathematical. In a hundred-yard dash, there is one winner, and the rest are losers, and in a contest for one person, somebody has to lose."

"Providing there is a contest, but supposing there is none, what then?"

"No contest? What the hell are you talking about, Larry? There has to be some kind of test. A girl doesn't marry anybody, nor does a boy. You were making sense up to now, but I'm beginning to wonder about the rest you told me."

"Would you like to make a sociable bet?"

"That depends on what you consider sociable."

"You were willing to bet your life before, but your life would not do me any good. How much money do you have in the bank?"

"Two thousand dollars."

"Would you bet me the two thousand that I can't get you to admit that all premarital relations, all adultery, and all divorce are coming to a mathematical end? Think very carefully before answering."

"I'm not going to bet all my money, Larry."

"But if you're so certain about what I can and cannot do, you have nothing to lose and two thousand dollars to gain."

"But I'm not that certain."

"You're like all the rest, Jim. Talk is cheap. Now, will you stop trying to tell me what is impossible, when it is impossible for you to know what is possible, unless you know what I know? Do you know what I know?"

"No, I don't think I do. But Larry, you must be somewhat sympathetic towards me. After all, you are making statements that, unless proven, will make you look like a nut."

"Do you think I'm a nut?"

"I know you're not, but others don't know you like I do, and you have to be careful about making statements that will appear ridiculous to the average person. If you told others what you just told me, they would react the same exact way, so don't blame me for being normal. You're the abnormal one by being gifted with the kind of brain you have. You may have the solution to all our problems, Larry, but you will have to be a little more tolerant of our ignorance."

"I'm sorry I snapped at you. You're right, and I owe you this apology. Henceforth, you can ask any questions you want. Now, the problem that exists before marriage can be better understood when we have an accurate knowledge of the true meaning of love, when examined through undeniable terminology. In actual reality, the word symbolizes a conscious or unconscious desire, in varying degrees, for a sexual contact of some kind, and this is easily proven by the fact that a boy or girl can't fall in love with or be physically attracted to someone, no matter how physically appealing this individual might be considered, if they know in advance that this person was born without sexual organs, which knowledge makes them aware that this freak of nature is incapable of giving or receiving sexual satisfaction."

"I agree with that because I know if Mary didn't have the very things that give me such tremendous satisfaction, I couldn't be drawn to her no matter what her face and figure were like."

"This means that the degree of love before sexual intercourse takes place varies with the extent of possible physical satisfaction."

"In other words, Larry, if I know in advance that there is no possible way I can find sexual satisfaction with a particular person, there is no way I could ever be attracted to her."

"That's exactly right. Consequently, if a boy and girl fall in love at first sight, which only means they are mutually attracted to each other, it is obvious that they would want to legally indulge their sexual appetite (especially when they were taught that indulging before marriage was wrong), because each represents what is desired by the other. But if a boy and girl are in love with someone who does not return this feeling to the same degree, the intensity of their desire to possess the other will depend on how close they are allowed to come to this physical possession."

"Do I understand you to mean that when a boy is attracted to a girl (or vice versa, naturally), the more she shows him that a possibility exists of getting what he wants, the stronger will be his feeling of love?"

"That's right. The more they are encouraged through dating, kissing, petting, hugging, the greater will be this desire to completely possess in marriage, or in sexual intercourse, that which was never consummated."

"But Larry, I know a boy who stopped going with a girl because she actually put his hand right on her breast when he was kissing her. If what you say is true, then this should have made him desire to have a sexual relationship all the more. Besides, the possibility of sexual intercourse didn't make him fall more in love, but less, and doesn't this contradict what you just said?"

"Not at all. In this case, the possibility of sexual satisfaction was reduced by what she did, and instead of arousing his desire by encouraging him, she discouraged his desire by making him think she was a cheap girl. You yourself said, 'The more she shows him that a possibility exists of him getting what he wants, the stronger will be his feeling of love.' But what he wanted was a girl who was good, decent, not cheap, not one who did what she did before marriage, so the possibility of sexual satisfaction was reduced under the conditions. However, the conditions are going to change very shortly. Now the meaning of love after marriage or sexual intercourse takes place is a horse of another color, for the intensity of love depends solely on the degree of passionate satisfaction, which proves conclusively that the greater the sexual satisfaction, the stronger will this feeling of love be, and further demonstrates why there are so many divorces, so much adultery, and so many broken hearts. Most couples remain together after physical satisfaction has sunk to its lowest ebb, not because they are still in love (desire a sexual relation with each other except as a last resort), but only because it is the lesser of two evils when children, money, and adultery are involved."

"Are you trying to tell me that unless a married couple has a passionate relationship with each other, they are not in love?"

"They are in love to the degree of their passion for each other."

"Do you mean that when a couple has grown old together, and there is no sexual desire left, they will not be in love anymore?"

"They will be companions, not lovers. Besides, in the new world, sexual desire will last until they die, less and less as they get older, but never completely extinguished."

"I don't think the medical profession will agree with you, and I can show you some old folks in their nineties that couldn't be aroused for anything."

"But remember, Jim, the conditions are going to change, so you have no basis for comparison."

"In fact, some men and women lose their sexual desire at a very early age. Mary's husband is one of them. Here she is all vibrant and filled with a desire for lovemaking, and he hardly has any desire."

"This may be true, Jim, but if the factors responsible for his loss of desire are removed, then he may be able to supply what his wife needs and wants."

"Not a chance. He could never give her what she wants. I know the type."

"And you are her type, right?"

"That's right, and we're going to get married just as soon as she gets a divorce."

"But supposing the transition gets underway before you have gotten your divorce, and Mary, as a consequence of understanding what it means that man's will is not free, finds greater satisfaction in returning to her husband rather than in marrying you, what then?"

"Forget it, Larry, there isn't a chance of that happening."

"Don't be so sure, Buddy Boy; you've been wrong before. Anyway, to continue, this unhappiness in the relation between boys and girls before marriage has part of its origin in words like handsome or lovely, through which they are compelled, completely beyond control, to look at each other, and it is obvious that if they have an opportunity of winning a beautiful, in preference to an ugly individual, they are given no choice, while the other person is seriously hurt and compelled to live in an unhappy world. This doesn't mean there will not be preferable differences among the sexes, but they will not be conditioned by words. For example, if I desire someone who is labeled beautiful, I am judging her, not in terms of unadulterated physical attraction as she appeals to me (i.e., what I personally like, which doesn't blame anybody for being different), but in accordance with a standard that places all others in a gamut of decreasing value until ugliness is reached, which blames them for being inferior."

"Do you mean that if I select a girl because she is beautiful, I am blaming others for being ugly?"

"That's exactly right, but this doesn't mean you can't select what you want. If you date a particular girl because you like her features, her shape, etc., that's your business, and you do not hurt any other girl by your selection. But if you date her because she is beautiful, then you do hurt other girls because you are calling them ugly."

"In other words, Larry, just so I don't refer to a girl with a name that hurts others by an opposite, detracting, or derogating meaning, then there is nothing wrong with dating whom I please."

"That's right. If a boy had never heard the word 'beautiful,' he would still be attracted more to one type than another, but he would not be influenced by the opinions or judgment of others and would not be hurting them, which is what takes place when a standard of value is congealed in words. Children are scarred so deeply by words like cute, adorable, pretty, precious, lovable, smart, educated, brilliant, a brain, etc., because these words place those who do not receive such compliments in an inferior capacity, that it is no wonder we have so many parental problems. We hurt our children, and then punish them for fighting back. Hold it, Jim, don't ask any questions about kids. I'll treat them separately.

"Now when a boy meets a girl in the world of free will, and they are compelled, as was just described, to look at each other through a tremendous amount of hidden standards, whoever comes closer to what is considered perfection for their sex will have a definite advantage over the other by arousing a greater degree of desire to possess what promises to be sexually satisfying; while the other, recognizing instantly this position of inferiority on the scale of physical perfection, will arouse a lesser degree of desire. A perfect example would be a person considered handsome taking out a girl on a blind date who is judged homely. She sees great value in him, which arouses her desire to charm him. He could very easily make her fall in love by encouraging what he knows she wants, because to her, he shows not only the promise of tremendous physical, but psychological satisfaction as well, since she envisions the compliments and envy of her friends in being able to attract such a handsome man. She is influenced by the opinions and judgment of others, while he, also influenced, will never desire to take her out again for the opposite reasons, unless he can use or abuse her in some inconspicuous manner, since he cannot think of her in terms of marriage."

"In other words, Larry, when words like handsome and beautiful are removed from our vocabulary, it then becomes impossible to bring down the value of another since the opposite words must also take leave, which means that the fear someone ordinarily would have in taking out a particular girl called homely, is removed when criticism and ridicule become mathematically impossible."

"That's right, Jim. If, in our present world, this blind date was closer to an equal value with him, then he would not mind being seen with her and would desire, perhaps, to take her out again; but unless she is considered by him as absolutely equal in value, she will constantly be on the defensive because her desire to possess him will always be more since she considers him of greater value than he considers her. Consequently, a handsome man (or beautiful girl — remember, however, these are fallacious words) is bound to have more than his share of female admirers, and since it is impossible to marry everyone, there are bound to be those who lose and get hurt.

Everyone likes to be admired when this gives such satisfaction, but the moment these so-called more attractive males and females are desired, even before any sexual relation takes place, they discover a lack of desire on their own part to possess what they can have for the asking (that is marriage), which convinces them, in many cases, that they are not in love. This is a very serious problem because these fallacious values actually prevent the blossoming of mutual love and give rise to innumerable arguments after marriage, since this feeling of superiority, in one form or another, always imposes a resentful feeling of inferiority. Consequently, the very moment a girl and a boy see that they are admired a little bit more than it is returned, the other is placed at a disadvantage by being unconsciously or consciously considered inferior, and the more this feeling of love is shown, the more they will be uncertain of their love. Unconsciously they feel this other person would be getting a better deal, and so, since it is difficult to desire the possession of what is already possessed if they want to get married, they keep this other on a string, so to speak, while they search for someone with whom they can fall in love enough to get married, that is, someone who will desire them less in return or consider them inferior to what might be gotten."

"I've experienced everything you just said, and I must agree. I was desperately in love with a girl several years ago who wouldn't marry me, no matter how much she knew I was in love with her. When I finally met another girl who took a liking to me, I was then desired more by the first one only because I wanted her less."

"As a result of all this, Jim, the boys and girls who are insecure have resorted to going steady and becoming engaged, so as to ensure themselves that the person they desire will make this sacrifice to reveal their feelings, which only makes matters worse since this is not any real security; and if after becoming physically close the person they love should leave, then any number of things might be preferred as a consequence of this broken heart or unrequited love. Furthermore, if the girl is the one who is left after developing sexual habits of promiscuity, she will yearn for another sexual experience, which turns a good girl into one considered bad; and if her morality never allowed any promiscuity, even with her steady boyfriend or fiancé, she could very well end up an old maid disillusioned with life. The one group keeps our bachelors happily unmarried, while the sight of the other makes many girls marry on the rebound, which keeps them unhappily married and subject to adultery."

"Do you always analyze things so deeply, Larry?"

"Yes, I do. When boys and girls start dating, most of them are actually too young to accept the responsibilities of marriage, but they still have a normal desire for the opposite sex, which allows them to develop habits of kissing, petting, fooling around in general, and when a girl can be made passionate enough, anything might happen. If she considers herself a good girl, one who adheres to the moral code, she will compel the boy to commit himself to marriage before she allows any privileges, but even then, she might refrain from going to the extreme. Courtship, therefore, is a dangerous interlude for the girl because she could become pregnant if she isn't careful, and what if her fiancé or boyfriend should not marry her after all?"

"Did you read in the paper what happened the other day about that young girl?"

"You mean the one who left a suicide note which read: 'Goodbye Mom; I don't want to live anymore because I'm so ashamed. Harold promised to marry me if I became pregnant, and now he has just become engaged to marry someone else.' Is that the article you mean?"

"Yes."

"No, I didn't read it; somebody told me about it. I heard that the father of the dead girl shot and killed Harold, whose fiancée had a complete nervous breakdown. Do you know how many males rejected the thought of marriage when given what they wanted, and how many relished the thought all the more to guarantee the experience?"

"I come under the latter category, Larry, but why should I desire to marry Mary, while Harold, God rest his soul, did not desire to marry the girl who killed herself?"

"The answer is very simple, Jim. He either fell in love with someone else because she offered greater promise of sexual and psychological satisfaction (the reaction of others to his mate), or he indulged with her and discovered, by comparison, that there was no way he could ever marry the other girl. Then there are two other possible reasons. He could have desired to marry her for her money or for what she could offer him in the way of social and financial benefits. Many men will only get married when they can't have, any other way, what promises to be a wonderful relationship. Consequently, there were girls who lost the boys they wanted for their husbands by not giving them enough to whet their appetite, and there were other girls who lost their men by giving them too much, which made the boys lose their desire to possess what was now theirs without all the responsibility. In either case, they were hurt. Because of all this, very few marriages of a first mutual love ever take place, and courtship has become a game to try and make the other person fall. Furthermore, children are taught that they should play hard to get."

"I know one girl who played so hard to get, nobody ever got her, and as far as I know, she still only uses it as a pea shooter after 50 years."

"They are also taught not to rush into marriage because they might end up with someone who is really no good, has no character, no intelligence, a poor education, absolutely nothing with which to make them happy, and the parents were right, in the world of free will, because there were many things that could go wrong."

"But you're going to change all this, right, Larry?"

"One hundred percent right, Jimmy Boy."

"Instead of beating around the bush, Larry, can you sum up what exactly the problem is, other than the fact that you plan to do away with all premarital sexual intercourse?"

"Very easily. The ultimate problem of love before marriage obviously revolves around one point — how to compel a boy and girl, of their own free will, to fall mutually in love and marry their very first date, or, to express it differently, how to prevent the boys and girls, on their first date, from having an unbalanced equation of sexual desire. How to keep their desire constantly balanced after marriage will be the problem I will solve next."

"You must be kidding, Larry; you just couldn't be serious. You are going to force a boy to fall sufficiently in love with his first date, and she with him, so that both will want to get married just as soon as possible. If you can do this, brother, I'll know you're from another planet."

"Would you like to bet that two grand?"

"Yeah, you're goddam right I'll bet it! I'll draw the money out of the bank, and we'll post."

"Don't you trust me, Jim?"

"Where money is concerned, I trust nobody. The other day, a friend of mine was playing nine-ball up in Harry's poolroom for ten dollars a game. I noticed he kept marking up a button every time he won, but no money passed hands. This was unusual for him, so I called him aside to ask what was going on. 'This guy,' he whispered, 'is a big-time gambler, and if I get him stuck, he'll go for a thousand dollars.' 'But I don't see any money passing hands.' 'That's nothing, he's good as gold; he's never welched on a bet yet. I already have him stuck for $320.' I couldn't stay to see the outcome of the match, but I bumped into my friend several months later. 'Say, Ed, whatever happened with your nine-ball game? Did you beat him for a thousand?' 'I beat him for 2 thousand, but that low-down bastard, that no good son of a bitch armed me for everything. I never did get paid.' You see, Larry, you never know about people where money is concerned."

"But Jim, if I know that you will never blame me should I arm you, no matter how much this hurts you; that you would never desire to retaliate or punch me in the nose; never desire to do the same to me because you know that I can't help cheating you this way, then I would be compelled to relinquish any desire not to pay you, simply because it can never satisfy me to be excused for doing what I know, at this moment, that I don't have to do unless I want to, and how can I want to when this would give me no satisfaction under the conditions?"

"You win, Larry. No post is necessary."

"Are you sure you want to make the bet, Jim?"

"I definitely do. There's just no way you can perform that miracle."

"Well, Jim, I can't make the bet with you after all."

"Now who's chicken?"

"If I made that bet, I'd be stealing your money."

"Are you really that certain, Larry?"

"Just as positive as I am that two plus two equals four."

"Well, show me; seeing is believing."

"Now watch very closely, Jim, because the hand is quicker than the eye, and our magic elixir is sometimes difficult to follow. However, when a boy and girl reach the age of sex or nubility in the new world, with the knowledge of what it means that man's will is not free, they know that it is mathematically impossible for any person to desire hurting them when it is known in advance that they will never blame, criticize, or punish this hurt, regardless of what is done. Consequently, when a girl falls in love, whether it is returned or not (this is the key to the problem, which must be worked backwards so you can understand the solution), she is completely unafraid to offer her body to the person she wants for her husband, because she knows, just as certain as two plus two equal four, that it is absolutely impossible for him to desire risking pregnancy, with or without contraception, unless he desires her for his wife. She knows that he knows if he made her pregnant, ruined her life, broke her heart by developing a sexual habit only to leave and never return, she and no one would ever blame him for doing what he was compelled to do; but he also knows he is not compelled to break her heart, ruin her life, make her pregnant, leave and never return, unless he wants to, for over this he has mathematical control. And when it fully dawns on him that she will never hold him responsible for this terrible hurt, which he knows would be his responsibility — and which he also knows he can prevent if he wants to — it becomes mathematically impossible for him to derive any satisfaction from deflowering her under these conditions since there is no way it can be justified or excused, unless he wants her for his wife. Could you deflower a girl under these conditions, Jim?"

"No, I couldn't, Larry, and I agree with you so far. But this still isn't proof of what you said you are going to do."

"I'm well aware of that, but watch our slide rule very closely. Now when a boy discovers, through these mathematical relations, that a girl is perfectly willing to go the extreme once he has won her love, he recognizes that there is no advantage, in fact a complete waste of time, to make a girl fall in love unless he sees the possibility of loving her; otherwise, he will be forced, of his own free will, to turn down her generosity, since it is not a source of satisfaction to take the risk of hurting this person by ruining her life when he knows in advance that she and no one will ever blame, criticize, or punish him for doing what he knows they must excuse and he cannot justify. This knowledge completely revolutionizes dating or courtship."

"In other words, Larry, if the first statement is correct, and he can't desire to hurt her by taking advantage of her body when it is offered, then the second statement must be correct because there can be no advantage in putting himself in the position of the first statement, in a position that would make him desire to refuse her body when it was offered."

"Excellent, Jim. You even made it clearer for me. Now, let's proceed to statement number three. Since the meaning of love, before copulation takes place, is the possibility of sexual satisfaction, how can a boy desire to take out a girl who does not appeal to him in these terms when he knows, well in advance, that he will be compelled to refuse her body when it is offered? To pay her flattering compliments and hand her a line only makes matters worse if he really doesn't want her for his wife, because this will only encourage her to offer him the very thing he will be compelled to refuse, since it cannot satisfy him even a little to hurt her when he knows she will never blame him. By the same reasoning, how can a girl accept a date with a boy who does not appeal to her in terms of sexual intercourse when she will be compelled to refuse his body when it is offered?"

"But Larry, supposing he is not interested in marriage, just in having some sexual fun, and supposing she is not interested in marriage, just in having some sexual fun, what then, can't they get together and have some fun without hurting each other? Remember, there is such a thing as contraception, and there are ways of making love where there is no possibility of getting pregnant. Supposing I meet a girl that appeals to me, and I say to her, without beating around the bush, 'Say, honey, you appeal to me, do I appeal to you?' If she says 'yes,' then I say, 'How about it, would you like to go to bed with me just to have some sexual fun... without the thought of marriage?' Now, if she agrees and we make love in a manner that ensures against pregnancy, how is it possible for either of us to get hurt? Besides, supposing I don't satisfy her, she might really be glad to get rid of me, right?"

"Your reasoning is logical, Jim, but not mathematical. Supposing you satisfy this girl (remember, she is a virgin, has never had any sexual contact before) to such a degree that she can't wait until your next meeting, wouldn't this hurt her if you never came back?"

"But there are a hundred guys that can give her the same satisfaction."

"Are there a hundred girls that can satisfy you like Mary does?"

"Probably, but I'm not interested in looking for anybody else."

"Would it hurt if Mary left you for somebody else?"

"Yes, but only because I found tremendous satisfaction when indulging with her."

"Well, supposing this girl who appealed to you physically at the very start, made love to you, or you to her, in a manner that gave equal satisfaction with Mary, would you desire a repeat performance?"

"Yes, I would, very much."

"Wouldn't it hurt you if you couldn't satisfy this desire?"

"Yes, I suppose it would."

"Not suppose; wouldn't it hurt you if you couldn't satisfy your desire to make love to Mary?"

"Definitely."

"Then this girl, at that moment of equal satisfaction, represents Mary. Now, assuming that you found even greater satisfaction with her than with Mary, is it possible for you not to be hurt if you desire her and she does not desire you?"

"I would be hurt if I couldn't satisfy this desire for a repeat performance."

"Consequently, the only way you could have some sexual fun with a girl and neither of you get hurt, is if you could make love and not have any fun, because the very moment either one of you enjoys the relation, you would be hurt if denied a repeat performance."

"In other words, Larry, I set up an equation that was mathematically impossible."

"Besides, neither the boy nor the girl, on their first date, has had any sexual experience whatsoever, which means they will have no basis for comparison; consequently, the thrill and excitement of physical contact will make them desire tremendously the person who now represents this ecstatic feeling."

"You keep talking about this first date. Well, supposing a boy takes a girl out on a date, doesn't kiss her, doesn't touch her, but finds her to be boring, and also discovers certain things about her he doesn't like, why can't he just never ask her out again?"

"All you are saying, Jim (I'll repeat this perhaps for the third time) is 'if it is mathematically impossible for something to happen, what would you do if it is done?' There is absolutely no way this situation could arise because the moment she accepts a date, you will automatically know that you appeal to her, and the very moment you ask her, she will automatically know your feelings. Consequently, when two people are drawn together, and the girl knows as a mathematical certainty that you could never do anything to satisfy her passion unless you are prepared to give a repeat performance — because this would hurt her for which you know you would never be blamed — she is completely unafraid to offer her body to you for the purpose of your having a most wonderful time, and also unafraid to make sexual advances that arouse your passion."

"But Larry, I told you about that boy who left his girlfriend because she put his hand on her breast while he was kissing her."

"Yes, you did, but that could never happen when he knows this would be a terrible hurt to her for which he would never be blamed. Consequently, if he doesn't like for a girl to do this, and since this possibility will always exist in the new world, let him just not take out any girls. However, Jim, this boy placed this girl in a category of being cheap, and in the world of free will, she might have had dates with other boys and might have done the same thing with them, but in the new world, it will be a mathematical impossibility because we're talking about a first date. Besides, there are facts about the sexual relation itself which will clarify any questions that might now be on your mind. Remember, if a boy asks a girl out who doesn't appeal to him in terms of marriage, but he appeals to her, then she is given the power to test his true feelings immediately by offering her body on the altar of love; and he is compelled to refuse this offering because it cannot satisfy him to hurt her so deeply when he knows, well in advance, that not only she, but everyone alive, will never blame, criticize, or punish him in any way for hurting her. By the same reasoning, he is in a position to test her true feelings. If she should encourage him by developing a habit for her, one way or another, then she would hurt him terribly if she left, which she cannot desire to do. Consequently, they are given no choice under these conditions but to search out, well in advance and regardless of the standards that presently prevail regarding physical attraction, an individual who appears to offer this possibility of sexual satisfaction, which means that when a boy asks for a date he is actually proposing, actually telling the girl he will not reject her desire to make love to him, and when she accepts, which indicates her feelings, they are literally engaged to be married."

"Hold it, Larry. Do you mean that if I see a girl sitting at a bar, and assuming she has never been out before, she is automatically my fiancée if I ask her for a date and she accepts?"

"That's right. From that moment on, you two will never be able to leave each other for someone else, not because anybody is preventing you from leaving, but only because you will never desire to leave. Remember, if she doesn't appeal to you, there is no advantage in asking for a date, no advantage in paying her compliments, because if you appeal to her, she is going to offer the very thing you will be compelled to refuse, unless you really want her. But if she does appeal to you, and you to her, in other words, if you ask her for a date and she accepts, then here is what must happen.

She knows, when accepting this date, that your love for her will increase only by arousing your passion and satisfying your sexual desire, and you know that her love for you will increase for the same reason. Consequently, you are given no choice, and when in a fond embrace your hand begins to wander; instead of checking this motion as a girl was compelled to do to feel clean and decent, she only encourages you all the more as you encourage her. Obviously, both of you will become very passionate and desire to go to the extreme, but she will desire this very much without the slightest fear that you will ever hurt her by leaving. And the very moment you indulge, with or without contraception, you sincerely pledge your love and are married for life — until death do you part — simply because you will fall more and more in love with each passing day when other changes come about. Remember, Jim, a boy and girl do not need permission from anybody to get married, nor do they require an exchange of rings or a marriage ceremony. In our present world, a couple can get married without having sexual intercourse and can have the latter without the former, but in the new world, it will be impossible to have one without the other because they are one and the same."

"In spite of all that you just said, Larry, it's hard for me to adjust to the fact that I can't ask anybody out I want."

"But you can, Jim, that's just the point. No one is telling you who to take out and who not to. What stops you from asking out a girl who doesn't appeal to you sufficiently for marriage is simply the fact that it is mathematically impossible for you to have a sexual relation with her and then leave, unless you want to hurt her, and it is impossible to want to when you know, well in advance, that she will never blame you for this hurt. What makes this whole change so serious is the fact that a boy knows he is not under any obligation to remain, that he is free to have a good time, leave and never come back no matter how much he hurts a girl or she hurts him. Remember, this works two ways, which makes it mathematically impossible for them to desire even getting close to such a situation, unless they really want to get married. Consequently, they can find no pleasure in arousing the desire of someone who does not appeal to them enough for marriage, for this would only create an awkward situation. Knowing that the first girl he asks for a date, should she accept, would lead to kissing, petting, and what he cannot do unless ready for marriage, he has no choice but to ask out, to ask her hand in marriage, the only girl that offers this possibility of sexual satisfaction, the girl that appeals to him enough."

"But supposing he finds one that appeals to him enough, but he doesn't appeal to her enough."

"Then she will just refuse him a date because she knows that he, under this condition, could be hurt, and it cannot satisfy her to do this when she knows he will never blame her. Furthermore, knowing that her parents will never blame him should he make her pregnant, and knowing that all the people will assume the expenses of raising his child (taxes would be increased to cover the cost which would hurt those who pay), he is compelled to prefer preparing himself, well in advance, so that his decision to ask her for a date (or ask her hand in marriage — same difference) will not hurt others, for he cannot derive even a little bit of satisfaction when he knows they must excuse what he cannot justify."

"Larry, I must take my hat off to you. This is simply fantastic. And you definitely saved me $2000. But if someone does not understand these relations, they would have to disagree because it is so different from the way we have been taught, even though the desired end is what the moralists have been unsuccessfully trying to bring about.

"That is correct, Jim. These boys and girls are prevented from desiring the very things for which blame and punishment, moral judgment, and criticism were previously necessary. Under these conditions there is no possibility for unrequited love to develop, no chance for a girl to be swept off her feet and lose her virginity out of wedlock, no chance to sin (this should satisfy the clergy very much; can't you see their smiles of satisfaction?), no chance for a boy and girl to hurt each other in any way, because all the factors truly responsible for premarital promiscuity, which led to the heartbreak of unrequited love, are removed. A boy and girl will have no choice in this matter of marriage as it will be their only source of sexual satisfaction, and the girls will have no opportunity of becoming 'bad.' This mating, with or without contraception — which takes place the moment it is mutually desired — is the holiest of all unions because it is steeped in a feeling of mutual respect and love, a perfectly balanced equation at this moment in their lives, and no one need have any fear for this couple because love will ripen to maturity after marriage, never before, and everything in the past that gave rise to adultery and divorce will be precluded, as you will see."

"But what about romance, Larry, about the excitement of wining and dining a girl to sweep her off her feet? How many times have you, yourself (you Casanova), taken a girl out in the moonlight, whispered sweet nothings into her ear, and made her like you very much for the sole purpose of making love to her? Isn't this a tremendous source of pleasure that would be lost?"

"If you had your choice, Jim, right at this minute, to go out in the moonlight with someone who appeals to you very much, and do all the things you mentioned, or go home to Mary and make extremely passionate love, which would you prefer?"

"You haven't given me much of a choice."

"In other words, Jim, romance is for the sole purpose of leading up to this extreme passionate lovemaking and is only a waste of time when a boy and girl can have what they really and truly want without all this waste. Even when Mary commits adultery with you, what is this but a desire to have this extreme sexual satisfaction she does not have with her husband."

"But couldn't that happen in the new world, that a boy or girl get tired of the other, and if it does, what then?"

"This is a mathematical impossibility, as you will soon see. Now tell me, my fine feathered friend, what is more important, that a boy and girl get a license to indulge their sexual appetite, have a religious ceremony, the blessing of a theologian, exchange rings, or that they fall mutually in love and live happily ever after?"

"That they live happily ever after, naturally."

"What is more important to the parents, the health and happiness of their children or conforming to a moral code that prevents the very thing they want, which means, in other words, conforming to a moral code that has lost all significance when the transition gets underway?"

"Obviously, the health and happiness of their children."

"What is more important to the clergy, that they have sermons and the confessional should these boys and girls sin, or that people act in a manner to each other that makes the services of the clergy no more necessary?"

"That people act in a manner toward each other that makes the services of the clergy no more necessary, naturally."

"If you were given a choice of marrying under our present conditions, with the certain knowledge that you are sure to find a great measure of unhappiness, perhaps be made a cuckold, as was Mary's husband, and end up getting a divorce, or given an opportunity not to marry the individual as you know marriage, with all the attendant ceremonies of obligation, but instead of unhappiness the greatest joy imaginable would be your lot all through life, are you really given a choice?"

"Are you kidding, Larry? Of course, I wouldn't be given a choice."

"Wouldn't it be an insult to man's intelligence to criticize and blame a marriage celebrating half a century of genuine happiness, a marriage in which there was never a thought of another sexual partner, where there was never an argument, where sexual passion never decreased during the potent years, just because this young boy and girl decided to get married without the ceremony and blessing of a rabbi or priest, without the exchange of rings, without a license or right granted by others?"

"Yes, I agree. It would be an insult to man's intelligence."

"Criticizing such happiness because this couple didn't conform to the prevailing customs and standards that constantly judge what is right for others, although absolutely necessary under the existing conditions (not only because millions of people derive their livelihood from the marriage ceremony and from teaching what is right and wrong but also because there is great satisfaction in the criticism itself as this elevates the critic to a feeling of superiority), is equivalent to criticizing a hand of bridge played perfectly because the cards were not cut by the person on the dealer's right, the custom that now prevails in some circles."

"But how is it possible for a person to desire criticizing this when it is the very happiness he wants?"

"Remember, Jim, the priests would be denied their accustomed satisfaction of marrying a couple; they would be denied the opportunity to advise a couple as to what is better for themselves. In other words, they would be denied the very things that gave meaning to their existence."

"But Larry, it would be impossible for them to complain under these conditions, right?"

"That's right, Jim. The problem is really breaking through this sound barrier of learned ignorance. We have developed a very bad, though necessary, habit of putting the cart before the horse, the result of this barrier, and our great need to earn a living. Consequently, we have assumed that certain things are required as a means to an end we have found preferable. We have come to believe that a cooperative society, without using the force that presently exists in communism and without doing away with competition, is impossible, but this, as was shown, is wholly untrue. Likewise, do our religious and moral leaders reject anything that appears to contravene their standard of righteousness, because it seems that unless a boy and girl are forced into a certain mold, they will take advantage of their freedom only to hurt others as well as themselves. But once again, as was just shown, this is wholly untrue.

"It should be obvious that once these young couples lose the desire for another sexual partner because of a perfect conjugal relationship, within a relatively short period of time only these marriages of a first love will exist, and when a boy and girl can get no sexual outlet except through marriage, they will fall in love with the first person that offers any physical attraction, which, however, will take on new significance as the standards of value, now fallaciously congealed in opinions and words that affect choice (although many other factors have still to be reconciled), lose their influence while being replaced with personal feelings that are not affected by the judgment of others. Therefore, the basis for a sound marriage in the new world will be this physical attraction and satisfaction both experience in the presence of each other, not religion or color, although the possibility of marrying someone with a greater purchasing power will still be somewhat of a factor, but not for long, as the poor must, out of necessity, soon become materially wealthy. However, physical attraction will always be the main event, and from this foundation the greatest happiness imaginable will be in store for our posterity — which is only ourselves, as you will soon have mathematically verified."

"That I have to see! You are going to prove that I, me, Jim, am going to be born again after I die, right?"

"I didn't say that, Jim. I said that our posterity is only ourselves, which I am prepared to prove in a mathematical manner. When you die, Jim, you are dead, but there is something we have never understood, which will be very comforting when it is properly explained."

"Do you mean there is nothing to fear in death?"

"That's right."

"Do you also mean there is nothing to cry over when a loved one is lost?"

"Don't be ridiculous, Jim. I cried my eyes out when I lost my father, and tears still dim my eyes when I think of him."

"Then I'm confused about what you mean."

"The whole world is confused, so don't feel too bad. I'll explain everything shortly. Incidentally, it is humorous to observe how certain things take a turnabout as a consequence of knowing what it means that man's will is not free. In our present world, the advantage always goes to the one who makes the other fall in love, for then it is possible to take or leave this person. But now the boys and girls will recognize that there is no advantage in making someone fall in love unless it can be returned, which makes the sexes do everything in their power to reveal their true feelings, as the desire to go to the extreme, which is marriage, depends not only on being loved, but on loving.

Free will engendered the suave, smooth-mannered, expertly controlled habits of the conquering male who ensnared with his captivating style many an unsuspecting female. It allowed one girl to keep on a string, for an indefinite time, many boys who sought her hand in marriage and who ended up, in many cases, not marrying anyone because she found it difficult to desire possessing what was already hers if she wanted them. It also gave birth to jealousy, which arises from a feeling of ownership that tacitly blames and judges what is right for someone else while giving unconscious justification to do that for which one has already been accused. This feeling originates in going steady, then grows in intensity from getting engaged to marriage as it now exists. The first two are a down payment on this right to absolutely possess another individual, and the latter is complete ownership."

"But Larry, when two people are married until death do they part, isn't this complete ownership?"

"Of course not, and I will explain this after we have had some lunch. At present, "I want you" is the meaning of love before this possession takes place, "I almost have you" is the next phase, and "I've got you at last" is the death of love. Why do you think so many jokes are made about marriage if not because it is a sadly humorous situation, as you know it, in spite of religion? However, it will be changed in a manner marvelous to behold, while jealousy is removed from the world because no one will ever again have the desire to seek another sexual partner. Seeing what is truly better for himself for the very first time, not with opinions but mathematical laws, man is given no alternative unless he prefers what he doesn't want, which is an absolute impossibility.

After we eat, Jim, you will be given an opportunity to observe a newly married couple under the changed conditions, as they face life together knowing that they will never be blamed or criticized for anything they desire to do, no matter how much it hurts another, which naturally prevents the hurt. However, there is a tendency to abuse this law by trying to get someone to give up a desire that does not hurt anybody, by making it appear it is a form of hurt, for which there will be no blame. People unconsciously do this when they ask favors for which they refuse to blame the person for not doing what was asked."

"You mean like a father saying to his daughter, 'Honey, would you mind going downstairs to get daddy a glass of ice water?' 'Not now, Daddy,' his daughter hurriedly replies, 'Later.' 'That's all right, dear, you don't have to get dad that ice water now, if you don't want to, no matter how thirsty he is.'"

"That's a good example, Jim. The father makes it appear that she is hurting him, for which he will not blame her in any way, although he already blamed her by asking the favor. Therefore, she is made to feel guilty and reluctantly says, 'All right, Daddy, I'll get it for you now.' This happens very much in marriage as it exists today, but in a more subtle form."

"Before we discuss marriage, let's get something to eat. What do you say, Larry?"

"Let's go."

# CHAPTER 7 — MARRIAGE

After an enjoyable lunch, Jim was impatient to get back to their park bench to hear what Larry had to say about marriage, because he was personally involved with a married woman.

"Now let me understand this, Larry. You are going to demonstrate how this newly married couple, marrying under the conditions you just described, will never be in a position to commit adultery."

"Never desire to commit it, Jim."

"And never desire to get a divorce, is that correct?"

"That's exactly right."

"What about the people already unhappily married, like Mary, who can't stand her husband anymore, and her husband, who doesn't want to let her get a divorce?"

"Let me take care of one thing at a time. First, let me show you how these newlyweds will never desire to leave each other."

"But how can you know this when years hence their feelings might change towards each other?"

"How long would it take a car traveling at 60 miles an hour to travel 93 million miles?"

"Sixty times 24 hours equals 1440 miles, 1440 miles, which represents one day, will divide into 93 million 64,583 days, 365 days will divide into that approximately 176 years."

"But how can you know this, Jim, when the car wouldn't arrive until 176 years later? Supposing the car broke down, had a few flat tires, and maybe the driver wouldn't live that long?"

"We're assuming, Larry, that the car travels at an average speed of 60 miles an hour, so even if there were several flat tires and several drivers had to be changed, it would still take approximately 176 years."

"And you are able to do this, Jim, simply by extending mathematical relations. I am going to do the same thing with this married couple. I am going to set up mathematical conditions that will force them to prefer traveling the full length of their lives together, without ever desiring to commit adultery or get a divorce, and they will be given no choice because they will want what they see. Is it possible for a person not to want what he desires? Is it possible for you not to want Mary if you want her?"

"Okay, show me. Seeing is believing."

"Now it is extremely important to understand that when a boy and girl, who have never been out with the opposite sex, consummate their feelings with a complete sexual relation which is marriage, they are going to fall desperately in love and desire each other all the more because this exciting thrill of physical contact is a new experience that has become associated with one particular person to whom they turn for satisfaction."

"Not necessarily, Larry. I know a girl, 17 years of age, who left her husband after the first three weeks of married life. She couldn't have been sexually satisfied. Now, just supposing the cause of her leaving was the fact that her husband wasn't concerned about her reaching a climax, or didn't know too much about this, or didn't understand that a girl might desire several orgasms, and every time they made love, he left her in a state of frustrating disappointment. What is the poor girl supposed to do?"

"This couldn't happen in the new world because the boy would know that this would hurt his wife very much and also know that she would never blame him for her own dissatisfaction. Consequently, he is compelled to desire learning all about what satisfies the average female."

"What about girls who are not average?"

"These, too, even before he gets married. This subject will become part of the high school curriculum, and no one need have any fear that these boys and girls can ever go in the wrong direction. This couple, out of necessity, will fall desperately in love the first few days of their marriage and will look forward with great anticipation to each time they get together, as you look forward to being with Mary."

"I'll see her tonight, Larry, and you're right... I can't wait."

"They will desire the passion and thrill of this relation as often as possible. Soon, each will be absolutely dependent on the other for what the body now craves, and if this were stopped — as happened frequently in the world of free will for various reasons which occasioned the serious consequences of unsatisfied desire — it would be the worst form of torment. Yet there are two individual desires involved, and it is impossible, in the new world, for one person to desire obligating the other not only because this is a form of advance blame, which is a judgment of what is right for someone else, but because it cannot be preferred when it is realized that this would only make matters worse."

"Do you mean that if I'm in the mood for love, or Mary is, it would be wrong for her to expect it of me, or me of her? Isn't the sexual act a marital obligation? Do you mean that when I go to the apartment tonight, all excited and dreaming about what we're going to do, that I can't make love to her?"

"Remember, Jim, you're still living in the world of free will, and since Mary doesn't know anything about this discovery, or what it means that man's will is not free, the knowledge you're about to hear is not applicable in your case. We're still talking about our newlyweds. In their case, at this precise moment in their lives, neither desires to leave or lose the other, and, consequently, they are compelled to prefer learning the mathematical secret of how to arouse the desire of the person they want... to always want them. This doesn't only apply to sex, but in general. Even in our present world we dream, in our love stories, of getting married and living happily ever after, only it has always remained a dream beyond our reach because sooner or later, a first blow is unconsciously struck which justifies some form of retaliation. The problem, therefore, is to teach these couples how to prevent this first blow from being struck, which, if accomplished, gives to marriage the greatest security imaginable, for all adultery and divorce arise only because this blow starts a chain reaction of hurt."

"Isn't your solution the application of your slide rule — 'Thou Shall Not Blame?'"

"Yes, it is, but let's see what actually happens when it is applied. Now this radiant wife, who has been falling more and more in love with her husband as they continue making passionate love to each other on their honeymoon, as they continue looking forward to the warmth and ecstasy of this sexual satisfaction, knows positively that it is absolutely impossible for her husband to ever desire leaving her, despite the fact that she knows he is not under any obligation to remain and is completely free to do anything he wants to do, just as long as <u>he knows</u> she is definitely in love with him (take your time with this, Jim), because she knows that he knows if he left her under these conditions this would break her heart, for which he would never be blamed, as this desire to hurt her so deeply must be considered by others as God's will or a compulsion over which he has no control. But he knows it is not God's will or a compulsion over which he has no control, because he also knows that he doesn't have to break her heart unless he wants to, and he discovers that it is impossible to do the things that would be a hurt to her just as long as he knows she is definitely in love with him. Therefore, this knowledge that he will never be blamed by his wife for deliberately or carelessly hurting her, who loves him dearly, makes it mathematically impossible to ever leave, and this great security is assured the wife just as long as she <u>shows</u> her husband that she truly loves him, for then only can his leaving her for another sexual companion be a source of hurt."

"Do you mean it is possible for the girl to find justification for leaving?"

"It is mathematically impossible, for when he realizes that she would still not leave him no matter how much he hurts her, he is compelled to stay."

"But supposing she stops showing her husband that she loves him?"

"How is that possible when she doesn't want him to leave?"

"But supposing she wants him to leave because he isn't satisfying her anymore?"

"We have just arrived at the other half of the equation. This young husband, so much in love with his wife at this moment in his life, knows also that she will never desire to leave him just as long as she knows he is in love with her. Consequently, since he knows that her desire to leave depends solely on him being out of love with her, which separation would break his own heart for which she cannot be blamed and he can prevent, he is compelled, for his own security and happiness, completely beyond control but of his own free will (stop smiling, Jim), to prefer doing everything in his power to completely satisfy his wife to show that he is not out of love with her, so that this desire to stop showing her husband that she loves him, will never arise in her."

"This is a little confusing. Can you clarify it?"

"It's really very simple. By knowing that his own security with the person he loves depends on her love for him, which he can control by showing his love for her, and by knowing that her security with the person she loves depends on his love for her, which she can control by showing her love for him, they are given no choice but to do everything in their power for each other as that alternative considered better for themselves, because it is the only means by which they can prevent what they do not want. Therefore, once it is understood that sexual satisfaction, in varying degrees, is the true meaning of love, and as was pointed out, when it decreases a marriage deteriorates, it is obvious that the surest way to success in conjugal affairs is to arouse the sexual passion of the other, since this demonstrates in an undeniable manner that you want your partner to be in love with you, which reveals that you don't want another mate since the love of your wife makes this an impossibility. By the same reasoning, as your mate makes efforts to arouse your desire, she reveals that she wants your love, which makes you conscious that she does not want another husband, since your love for her makes this also a mathematical impossibility, as was just shown. Consequently, when a husband and wife realize from the very beginning that the security of their happiness depends on arousing and satisfying the sexual passion of the other, without imposing one ounce of obligation because this is advance blame, they are given no choice as to what is better for themselves since any word or action that decreases the desire to have a passionate relation only reveals a lack of love by tacitly blaming the sexual desire of the other."

"You're a rascal, Larry; that is completely mathematical."

"The entire problem of marriage is solved by obeying our slide rule which gives us no choice to disobey, for then each person is compelled to <u>show</u> the very love required for his own security and happiness, which means that all advance blame, this judging of what is right for the other, must be removed, for then all the factors leading up to adultery and divorce are precluded."

"Do you mean you're going to do the same thing with marriage as you did with the economic system?"

"That's right. I'm going to remove all forms of advance blame."

"Do you mean that a husband and wife can do anything they want without any control, without any restrictions?"

"Jim, where has your mind been? You know they are going to be controlled by a law that brooks no opposition, so how can you say, 'without control?'"

"It just seems like it won't work. Do you mean that if a golf enthusiast wants to leave his wife and kids every day that he is off from work, to play the game from morning to night, that he can do this if he wants to? Do you mean there will be absolutely no standards as to what is proper for the success of a marriage?"

"Only one standard, Jim. Thou Shall Not Blame your partner in any form."

"Would you mind starting with the sexual act itself, Larry? This, to me, is of utmost importance. I've been trying to figure out how a marriage can exist without some form of sexual obligation."

"To understand this, it is necessary that you realize there are two desires involved in a sexual act, not one, and the desire of one partner is no more important than the other, but the moment you, for example, expect something of Mary, or she of you, then both of you are considering your desire of greater value. To make this clear, we shall refer back to the advance blame that is involved in asking favors. If you would like for Mary to rub your back, then you are blaming her in advance for not desiring to do what you want done. Your desire necessitates that Mary desire the same thing, but supposing she doesn't want to rub your back, what then? You have already blamed her for not doing it the moment you asked her to."

"I think I understand that much of it; correct me if I'm wrong. Should Mary desire something at the store, but to satisfy her, it necessitates my driving the car to get what she wants, then I am involved, and therefore she cannot ask me because this blames my not desiring to do what she wants done."

"Excellent, Jim! I couldn't have expressed it better myself."

"Do you mean that a wife or husband can never have desires that involve the other?"

"Only if both of you agree, without any obligation to the same thing."

"But how can Mary get me to drive the car when this necessitates that she ask me, which blames in advance the possibility that I might not desire to; and what can be done if she doesn't drive?"

"Well, if you know as a matter of positive knowledge that Mary will never ask you to do anything for her, and you also know there might be several things she would like to have done, isn't it just common sense that you would simply say, 'Mary, is there anything I can do for you today?' If she needs something at the store and can't drive the car, then, since you have already expressed your desire to do something for her, all she has to say is, 'Yes, Honey, I could use so and so at the drugstore.'"

"But Larry, wouldn't a wife take advantage of her husband if he asked her this every day? She might send him to carry out the garbage, to make the beds, to bathe the kids, to go to the store to pick up a package she forgot to bring home, and, last but not least, she may ask him to make love when he is not the least bit in the mood. Something is not right."

"The only thing that isn't right is the fact that you just didn't think deeply enough. The wife knows, so does the husband, that her security depends on showing her love for him; consequently, it is mathematically impossible to desire taking advantage of his generosity, for this would be a hurt to him. But realizing that he would still do the things she asked, if at all possible, even though this would be an annoyance to him, because she knows he must excuse everything she does, then she is given no choice but to lose her desire to take advantage of him since she knows that she doesn't have to hurt him this way unless she wants to, which means there is no advantage in taking advantage under these conditions. This means that when they ask each other, 'Honey, is there something I can do for you?', it is mathematically impossible for them to request anything they can do for themselves, and impossible to be careless since carelessness would only necessitate that they work harder themselves."

"What do you mean, Larry?"

"In the present world, if a husband carelessly left the evening paper downstairs when he intended to bring it upstairs, he would simply yell

179

either to his wife or child, 'How about bringing up the evening paper?' And if they don't comply with his request, he doesn't hesitate to blame them for not satisfying his desire. But in the new world, when he fully understands that asking favors is advance blame and a sign of ignorance, he would be compelled to think, just before going upstairs, and say to himself: 'Is there something I want to take along when I go to save myself a trip downstairs later to get what I forgot?' The realization that he can't ask favors of others compels him to depend only on himself, not his wife and children. However, his wife, just before going upstairs, might yell up: 'Honey, is there something I can bring you?' But he, knowing that it would be taking advantage to ask her to do what he can do for himself, would simply reply, 'No thank you, Dear.' And she, knowing that this would be his reply, might bring along a pitcher of lemonade or anything else she thinks might make him happy, as he would do for her."

"But Larry, if she knows this would be his reply, why does she bother to ask?"

"In most cases, she doesn't, but you never know when both of them might have the need of the other. Supposing the wife wanted to rearrange the furniture. To ask her husband to push the television across the room blames him for not wanting to, and how does she know whether he might not be physically able to do this? But when he asks her, 'Honey, is there something I can do for you,' she simply replies, 'Do you think you can help me move the television?', and then he either helps her himself or hires someone to do it."

"But supposing a woman doesn't drive the car, and every time her husband asks this question, she sends him on an errand, isn't this taking advantage of his generosity?"

"It certainly is, and she would know it."

"But Larry, what is she supposed to do when she needs things at the store and can't drive the car?"

"She has three possibilities open to her. One, learn to drive. Two, take a cab or bus everywhere, which, of course, is not always so easy to do. Or three, continue to hurt him by taking advantage."

"But how is it possible to continue hurting him when she knows he will never blame her, when she also knows she is not compelled to do it?"

"That's just it, Jim, she can't continue to hurt him this way."

"Well then, doesn't this reduce the possibilities to two? And if he can't afford taxicabs, and she doesn't want to take buses, doesn't this reduce the possibilities to one?"

"That's right."

"Are you trying to tell me that everybody will be able to drive a car in the new world?"

"Yes, for this is the only way a wife and husband can prevent this taking advantage, which is a definite hurt."

"But supposing a wife is a nervous wreck when it comes to driving a car, when then?"

"Is anybody blaming her, Jim, or criticizing her in any way? Isn't it understood, beyond a shadow of doubt, that she is compelled to do what she does because man's will is not free? If she is forced to stay away from driving a car . . ."

"She might even get a certificate from a doctor to prove that she shouldn't drive, right, Larry?"

"Wrong, Jim. I thought you understood what it means that man's will is not free. Isn't it obvious that she doesn't need proof because nobody is blaming her? As I started to say, if she is forced to stay away from driving a car, then she will be forced to impose on her husband to do this driving for her, and it is mathematically impossible for him to blame her for doing what she is compelled to do. Can't you see what is happening, Jim? A mathematical line of demarcation is being drawn between what a person can do and can't do. If a wife discovers that she is hurting her husband by what she does or what she doesn't do, and realizes that he will never blame her in any way for doing what she knows he knows she is compelled to do, then she is forced to abandon the contemplation of any hurt to her husband she can prevent, because it cannot satisfy her to be excused by him for doing what she knows cannot be justified by her."

"But what has all this got to do with the price of eggs or the sexual relation? And what would stop a wife from asking her husband to make love to her, in answer to his question, 'Is there something I can do for you, honey?' This is certainly one thing she cannot do for herself, right, Larry?"

"Right and wrong, Jim. She indeed needs her husband for the purpose of sexual intercourse, but it is wrong to assume that she cannot arouse his desire to make the very love needed for her own satisfaction. Consequently, if she didn't bother to make any effort to arouse him and relied solely on his desire to satisfy her should she ask, she would be taking advantage of his offer to help her by not bothering to do what she can do for herself, which is this effort to arouse him to satisfy her. Therefore, she would never think to say, 'Let's make love,' in answer to his question, 'Is there anything I can do for you, Honey?'"

"I'm still a little confused, Larry. Do you mean that if I am in the mood to make love, I must go over to Mary, start kissing and petting her until she gets passionate enough to get in bed with me, and then..."

"Of course, I don't mean that, Jim. Isn't it obvious that if you approach Mary to kiss her, you are blaming in advance the possibility that she might not want to kiss you at that moment? How can you be certain that she really wants to kiss you? By kissing her, you only express what you want, but how do you know what she wants? And remember, her desire not to kiss you is just as important as your desire to kiss her, that is, if she doesn't feel like kissing at that moment."

"Well, what am I supposed to do, or say, 'Mary, are you in the mood to kiss me?' or 'I'm in the mood to kiss you, Mary, are you in the mood to kiss me?'"

"Of course not, Jim. It is obvious that Mary would do anything to show her love for you, consequently, if you tell her you're in the mood, she would want to kiss you for your satisfaction, even though she is not in the mood; and if you ask her if she is in the mood, what is this but an inverted way of telling her that you are in the mood. In other words, Jim, this would be taking advantage of her love for you."

"Well, supposing instead of kissing her, for this does require that she kiss me back, I just went over and started rubbing her leg, can I do that?"

"Of course not, because this assumes she wants you to do that, which blames her in advance for not having this desire to have her leg rubbed."

"I give up, Larry, what in the hell am I allowed to do in this new world?"

"That's not nice, Jim, especially in view of the fact that what I will show you is only for your own benefit. Wouldn't you like to have this passionate feeling for Mary, and she for you, for as long as you live?"

"This would be heaven on earth, but if the past sets any precedents, I'm still afraid you're talking through your hat. However, it would be wonderful if you could bring this about."

"Not me, Jim, I have nothing to do with it. I'm only obeying a law that forces me to move in this direction because it gives me greater satisfaction. God deserves the credit, not me. Before long, tears will be flowing in abundance, but happy tears, and the whole world will thank God for this wonderful new world. I'm just the son of God, like you, Jim, and all mankind. None of us is given a free choice, you know that."

"You remind me of Spinoza, Larry. He was God intoxicated."

"There's no comparison, Jim, because I'm cold sober."

"Nevertheless, he was excommunicated from the synagogue while being God-intoxicated, which seems to be a contradiction. You would think that a person would be thrown out for being an atheist, but not for being a God-intoxicated man."

"Because I know that God is a reality doesn't intoxicate me, Jim. I know that the sun is also a reality, but when the heat gets unbearable, am I still supposed to jump for joy? Where's the comparison between Spinoza and me? He was a gentle man; I'm not. He refused to blame his sister for stealing what rightfully belonged to him because he was confused and believed she couldn't help herself. He excused her conduct. But if someone tried to take what belonged to me, I'd fight him tooth and nail."

"But Larry, you know that will is not free and that man can't help doing what he does, right?"

"That's right, but this only means that he is compelled to move in the direction of greater satisfaction. If you sock me, I might get greater satisfaction in socking you back. However, once man understands what it means that his will is not free, then this desire to sock me is prevented by your realization that I will never blame you for hurting me. Spinoza's sister had no understanding of this knowledge, nor did the world of that time, although Spinoza himself knew that man's will is not free. Consequently, he allowed others to hurt him with their first blow by turning the other cheek.

I, on the other hand, would never advocate turning the other cheek when someone can get the advantage by not turning it. Until this knowledge is understood, we will be compelled to continue living in the world of free will; otherwise, we would only make matters worse for ourselves. And if Russia should start a war before this knowledge is released, it is only natural that we fight back with everything we've got. To show you how confused the understanding of someone who doesn't grasp these principles is, a local columnist interested in my ideas, so he called them, made the statement that I believe that man should not be blamed for anything he does, which is true only when man knows what it means that his will is not free. If he doesn't know, he is compelled to blame by his very nature. I'm not a saint, Jim, but a scientist of human conduct."

"But didn't you, like Spinoza, study to become a rabbi, and weren't you thrown out of the synagogue?"

"Not me. I reluctantly attended until I was 13 years of age, although, come to think of it, one rabbi just about threw me out when I pulled off the black tape he wrapped around my arms because the blood had stopped circulating. He referred to this ritual as a body of water — 'Lake Tefillin,' or something like that, as if you were never Bar Mitzvahed, eh Jim? My father used to think I was saintly, but I guess he didn't know me too well. No, you've got me confused with someone else. Now, where were we?"

"I was rubbing Mary's arm, I mean leg."

"There is only one solution to the sexual problem, Jim, once all advance blame is removed, for we are given no choice. Consequently, when our young husband is in the mood to make love, he does everything in his power to arouse the desire of his wife, without touching her in any way. Then she knows he is extending an invitation and if she is aroused sufficiently, she will then approach him, or vice versa. If she is having her menstrual period, she will simply tell him, and then he will wait for her to make efforts to arouse him, which extends an invitation. In other words, if Mary understood these principles, along with you, and you went to her apartment this evening, she would wear the kind of clothes or take off the kind that extends an invitation, assuming she is in the mood. If she makes no effort to arouse your desire, then nothing is stopping you from trying to arouse her by wearing the kind of clothes, or taking off the kind, that extends to her an invitation. If, however, she is extending you an invitation, then you are permitted to make physical contact."

"Are there restrictions as to what I can do?"

"Of course not."

"Supposing I want to kiss her body all over?"

"This is your business. However, if Mary desires to do that, this is her business. In the new world, a husband will know what makes his wife extremely passionate, and he will know this by her reaction to what he does; consequently, he will enjoy doing this most of all, whatever it is. By the same reasoning, a wife will know what makes her husband extremely passionate, and she will enjoy doing this most of all. Under these conditions, passion will reach its peak."

"But Larry, it doesn't take too long before a married man and woman lose this excitement of their honeymoon days. After all, most couples sleep together; they always see each other half undressed, and the thrill of bodily contact soon wears off. Isn't this just human nature?"

"But in the new world, a husband and wife will not sleep together, nor will they be careless about how they dress around their partner, for a certain amount of clothes could be mistaken for an invitation."

"Now, Larry, how is it possible for you to say that a husband and wife will not sleep together, when this depends on their desire?"

"It is very easy for me to say it, Jim, because it is true, and it can be demonstrated very simply by extending our slide rule. If you went out and bought a double bed, wouldn't you be judging that Mary's desire is to sleep with you?"

"Yes, but I know she wants to sleep in a double bed with me."

"How do you know this?"

"She expressed it one time when we finished making love."

"That was then, Jim, but how do you know her feelings from moment to moment? She may desire steak one day, meatballs and spaghetti the next, but does that mean she wants this all the time? Can't you see that to buy a double bed without the possibility of having a single bed on which Mary could sleep alone, if desired, blames her for having this desire to sleep alone?"

"I see what you mean. This is the same as approaching people to kiss them when you don't know, from moment to moment, if that is what they want. If I should buy a double bed, without having another bed available as an alternative, I would be forcing Mary to sleep with me, in other words, I would be forcing her to satisfy my desire, without any consideration for her desire."

"That's exactly right, Jim. Consequently, separate beds must be available. Then, after you and Mary are finished making love, each of you will go your separate ways."

"What do you mean by 'our separate way?' Supposing Mary has one bed in this room, and I have the other, can't we just go to our separate beds, or one of us to the other bed? Besides, suppose we fall asleep in each other's arms; many husbands and wives do that, you know."

"Separate ways is just an expression, but when you are finished making love, it is impossible to lie in Mary's arms without blaming the possibility that she may not want this. The only reason this may be desired is if one partner is not completely satisfied; consequently, if you want your partner to linger in your arms instead of allowing you to go to sleep, make sure the person you love is not sexually satisfied. However, when satisfaction is complete, then Mary will desire to sleep in her own bed."

"Supposing in the morning I'm in the mood all over again, and Mary is lying in the next bed dressed in a manner that arouses my desire, am I to accept this as an invitation? How am I to know what is and what is not an invitation?"

"You won't have any problem showing Mary that you are in the mood because you have an indicator that could very easily arouse her desire. As for Mary, she has a pretty good indicator too, and if she is in the mood, she will let you read her indicator, and that will be your invitation. If Mary wakes up to see you looking at her with your indicator turned on, and if she is in the mood, she will accept your invitation. By the same reasoning, if you wake up to see Mary's indicator turned on and staring you in the face, you will know that she is extending an invitation. Under these conditions, it is mathematically impossible for either person to ever take the other for granted, and passion will always be at its peak."

"But what about arguments, Larry, don't they tend to decrease the desire to make love?"

"They certainly do, but it will be impossible to have any in the new world."

"What are you talking about? There has to be some disagreement."

"Why?"

"Well, Mary might want to see a particular picture that I don't want to see. She may think that a child should be brought up this way instead of that. We may disagree on politics, religion, education."

"There won't be any government or religion, Jim, so how can you argue over what won't be in existence? But even if she still got satisfaction in lighting candles, reading the Bible, praying to God, etc., this is entirely her business. You are not going to argue with her if she prefers to do these things; consequently, an argument could only arise if she tried to make you do them, but how can she desire to do this when her action would blame you in advance for not doing them?"

"Couldn't arguments arise over the raising of children?"

"Is it possible for us to argue over whether two plus two equals four?"

"Certainly not, but that's a mathematical fact."

"So will the raising of children be a mathematical fact when I'm through extending our slide rule. In other words, Jim, arguments can only arise over opinions, not facts, and when it is understood that opinions blame divergent views, each person will be compelled to keep his thoughts to himself. If I like spinach, this is my business, but if I say spinach is good, I am expressing an opinion that blames those who have found spinach to be bad, which will only reveal my ignorance that man's will is not free because of the blame involved. Since I don't want to appear ignorant, and I don't want to blame another person for anything, I am given no choice."

"What are the various other forms of advance blame in marriage that contribute to arguments?"

"First is telling your partner what to do."

"But Larry, isn't it necessary at times to tell a wife, or she her husband, what to do to prevent a possible hurt?"

"How is it possible to get hurt in the new world? The necessity to assume this possibility and make an effort to preclude it with a judgment of what is right for the other — which tacitly blames this possibility — has been removed. Furthermore, the assumption of a husband and wife that they could be hurt in some way by each other, adultery or otherwise, actually strikes a first blow by accusing the other of this possibility, and then it doesn't take long before efforts are made to prevent what is not desired by imposing standards of right and wrong, which not only prevents them from showing the love they need for their own sexual satisfaction, but encourages them to justify doing that of which they have already been accused."

"Let that be as it may, Larry, what about the knowledge that parents teach their children, and what about the knowledge that one partner has over and above the other? What about customs and conventions that tell us how we are supposed to conduct ourselves in society?"

"Children will be treated separately, Jim, but what knowledge are you talking about that one partner has over another? Do you mean like an accountant?"

"Well, supposing the husband is an interior decorator, isn't it obvious that he has more knowledge of this subject than his wife, and shouldn't he have a right to tell her how the house should be arranged? Or, as another example, supposing the wife is an expert designer and knows everything about the proper color combinations, shouldn't she be able to tell her husband what color tie and suit go best together? And what about the grammarian who knows everything there is about good sentence structure, good English, and good pronunciation; should he not be able to tell his wife about these things so she can speak and write better? What about the woman who has made a study of good manners, etiquette, etc., shouldn't she be able to teach her husband, brought up on the other side of the tracks, how to conduct himself among cultured people?"

"I hope you aren't serious with all those questions, Jim?"

"Not really, Larry. Let me see if I can answer them myself. Since it is impossible, once the transition gets underway, to judge what is right for someone else, all standards, customs, and conventions are being removed."

"That's true, Jim, but most important is the fact that once all mankind stops criticizing and ridiculing, which must come about because this is a form of hurt, then everything that came into existence to prevent this criticism and ridicule is completely displaced. How is it possible to waste money on an interior decorator when nobody is ever going to criticize or ridicule the appearance of your house, or discuss its appearance in any way whatsoever? Consequently, the knowledge of interior decorating is equivalent to the knowledge of a lawyer or soldier in the new world. Of what value is pronouncing 'yes' instead of 'yeah,' when nobody will criticize or ridicule the latter? Of what value is holding your knife and fork a particular way, or tilting the bowl of soup one way instead of the other, if no one will ever criticize or ridicule the difference?"

"But Larry, isn't it obvious that if you tilt the bowl of soup away from your body, there is less chance of spilling it on your lap, and isn't it better to spread out a napkin just in case? Shouldn't this knowledge be taught, and to teach it don't you have to tell somebody what to do?"

"This is equivalent to teaching a child how to walk. Isn't it obvious that if a man spills soup on his clothes, which he has to pay to have cleaned, he will figure out a way to prevent this? It is not your business if he spills this soup on his clothes, unless you have to pay for the cleaning or clean them yourself. However, in that case, he would know that this is a hurt to you, and since he also knows that you would never blame him for this because you know he can't help himself, when he knows he can help himself, if he wants to . . ."

"It's the same story over again, isn't it, Larry?"

"Yes, it is."

"Will the designers of clothes be displaced?"

"Both boys and girls, before marriage, will prefer wearing the kind of clothes that reveal their charms sufficiently to attract the opposite sex, so there is a certain amount of usefulness in a design being a particular way. After marriage, a husband and wife will be interested in wearing the kind of clothes that continue to arouse sexual desire, so again, there is a usefulness."

"What about the design of cars and the exterior of houses?"

"It is obvious that one type of house and car might appeal to me and not to you, but this is just a question of personal taste. I might like a particular car, but it would be impossible for me to like it more than another for the reason that it would be criticized less, when there is no criticism. I might like my home to be designed on the inside in a particular way, but again, this is just a question of personal taste. Today, however, a house is designed to avoid criticism and ridicule."

"But supposing you would like to design your home one way, and your wife wants to design it another way, what do you do in a case of that sort?"

"It could never come to that because neither would care. Since the husband — even though he might have been an interior decorator — will no longer be concerned about the criticism of others; therefore, he doesn't mind letting his wife fix it up anyway that pleases her, and she, knowing that he will never blame the way she arranges it, will have no fears. The house is her domain, and earning a living will be his. When it comes time to pick out a tie to wear, neither of them will be concerned about color combinations, and any tie will do just as well, or no tie for that matter. What difference does it make what color it is, or whether he wears a tie at all, when nobody will criticize or talk about his apparel?"

"What about compliments? Isn't it obvious that people will do certain things to be complimented and praised? There's an expression that says: 'If you can't say anything nice about somebody, don't say anything at all.' Now, why shouldn't people desire to fix their home in a particular way even though they know there won't be any criticism, when there still could be compliments, praise, and admiration? A man who develops his muscles knows that you aren't going to criticize the person who didn't develop his, but yet it gives him a great deal of satisfaction when you admire, praise, or compliment his achievement. What about this, Larry, couldn't the interior decorator design his home in such a way that people can't help but praise its appearance? Supposing one decorator was also an artist, and painted a mural that drew much admiration, or aren't people supposed to pay each other compliments in the new world?"

"There will always be admiration for specific differences, Jim, but when all words that create external values are removed, then there won't be any possibility of hurting others by placing them, and the things they like, in a position of inferior value. Remember, there is a big difference between saying, 'Your home is lovely,' and saying, 'I like your home very much.' The first implies that other homes are not lovely because they don't partake of this fallacious standard called 'lovely,' while the second is also done away with simply because there is absolutely no value in saying it under the new conditions."

"I don't understand, Larry."

"In the present world of free will, each person was compelled to make efforts to satisfy the likes and dislikes of others because of criticism and ridicule, but when all forms of blame are removed — which prevents him from hurting them with what he does to satisfy himself — then he is only concerned with his own likes and dislikes. Consequently, the value that existed in making it known to others that you also like what they like, so they could like you more, has been removed because it is mathematically impossible for them to like you less when you don't pay these compliments. Besides, you are not being asked if you like one home better than another."

"But supposing someone asked your opinion of the house or something else?"

"Have you forgotten already, Jim? There won't be any more opinions, for this blames a person for thinking differently. Consequently, I could never ask you, 'What do you think of my house?' because I would be blaming you in advance for your opinion. Just supposing you answered by saying, 'I don't like your house.' Would I like your answer? The reason people were concerned about the opinions of someone on various things was to try and conform so that he couldn't criticize, ridicule, or talk about them behind their backs. In the old world (the present time), I would have asked you a return question, 'Why don't you like my house?', and then we would have gotten into some kind of argument."

"This is all very true, Larry, but isn't it worthwhile to employ an interior decorator for the purpose of designing a house in such a manner that others will be forced to say, 'I certainly admire the way you've designed your home.' After all, everybody likes to be admired for something or other, and if there were no admiration, there wouldn't be any incentive to try and become famous. Look at the great effort a pianist will exert in developing his talent for the sole purpose of being applauded by the world. Doesn't he, like someone interested in developing the interior of a house by employing a decorator, hire the services of a piano teacher to help develop his talent?"

"That's true to a degree, Jim, but when it is impossible for a person to be disrespected because of the way he prefers to fix his house, and there is no possibility that anyone will comment, the extra expense will not be worth it unless he prefers the taste of the decorator. Piano teachers will never be displaced, but interior decorators will be virtually wiped out because the same need for them doesn't exist in the new world."

"Larry, I still can't understand how all the little standards that make for harmony in a marriage will also be removed. For example, isn't it nice when a husband and wife have dinner together? Supposing they enjoy the romantic atmosphere of a candle on their table, with soft music playing, and all of a sudden her husband, while in the middle of dinner, decides to go to the other room to watch football on television, a habit he developed. Or supposing he gets a telephone call right in the middle of dinner from one of his friends, who tells him to come right up the poolroom because they got hold of a sucker who thinks he can play, and then, without saying goodbye to his wife, without telling her where he is going, without finishing dinner, just puts on his jacket and walks out. Isn't it obvious there have to be some kind of standards?"

"These very standards, Jim, are the reason for more divorces and more adultery than you can imagine. Besides, they permit a person an opportunity to justify injustice, or to phrase it differently, they permit an unconsciously selfish person to blame another for what exists only in himself. For example, if it gives the husband satisfaction to watch football, is he hurting his wife in any way? Is he asking her to do something for him?"

"No, but she enjoys his company at the dinner table."

"Then her desire necessitates that he sacrifice his, right?"

"But doesn't his desire necessitate that she sacrifice hers?"

"There is quite a difference, Jim, because his desire makes no imposition on her; it doesn't ask that she join him to watch television, nor does it ask that she stop eating. It leaves her completely alone to do what she thinks is better for herself. But to satisfy her desire, in this instance, he must sacrifice something that gives him great pleasure, which is pure and simple selfishness on her part. To put it still another way, to get him to continue eating at that moment, she would have to tell him what to do or ask him to do her a favor, both forms of advance blame."

"But what about her? Wouldn't this hurt her feelings?"

"If this were a genuine hurt, he wouldn't be able to do it because he knows that she would never blame him for what he knows she must excuse, and he would never think of leaving. But it is not a hurt, Jim, any more than it is a hurt if he ate with his hat on. She might say that wearing a hat in the house shows disrespect to her, but in actual reality, she is showing it to him. He is not hurting her by wearing his hat or watching television, and if it gives him satisfaction, just as long as he is not hurting her, this is his business, not hers. This knowledge of what it means that man's will is not free, and I can't repeat it enough, draws an infallible line of demarcation between hurt that is real and hurt that exists only in the imagination. However, if the wife knows that her husband likes to watch a particular show, and it happens to come on at the time she generally serves dinner, her only solution is either to prepare dinner before or after the show, if it means so very much to have dinner with her husband, or else watch television while eating dinner."

"Supposing she wants to watch a different show, and there is only one television in the house, what then?"

"Jim, are you really that thick, or are you pretending to be? Isn't it obvious that the only fair thing to do is flip a coin? But the reason they desire to flip it in the new world is different from that in the old. The wife, who loves her husband and wishes to show this as often as possible, and her husband, who loves her very dearly and wishes to show her as often as possible, insist that the other watch their desired show, which gives them no alternative but to flip a coin."

"But what about him getting up in the middle of dinner to shoot pool without telling her where he is going or when he is coming home? And supposing she was in the mood to invite him to a tasty morsel for dessert, wouldn't this be a disappointment and a hurt?"

"It would be, no doubt, a temporary disappointment, but it would give her great satisfaction to see her husband satisfy every desire he has, just so he doesn't hurt her in any way, while it would satisfy him to see her satisfy every desire she has."

"But Larry, supposing he stays out shooting pool all night while she's at home doing nothing, just waiting for him so she can turn on her indicator?"

"What you are asking is supposing he hurts her by taking advantage in some way, right?"

"That's right."

"But how is it possible for him to take advantage and hurt her, when he knows that she will never blame or punish him for this hurt? But let it be made clear, Jim, that the only way he could possibly hurt her is by not being there to satisfy her sexual desire. If she thinks he might get a call that could take him away, she may prefer wearing a very sexy outfit during dinner for the purpose of arousing his desire, and he may begin anticipating what he's going to do right after dinner. Should a phone call come in then, he might say, 'Ed, I won't be up right away.' After dinner, finding himself also in the mood, he accepts her invitation and they make passionate love. When he's finished, he simply gets dressed and goes out."

"Doesn't he tell her where he is going and what time she can expect him?"

"Only if he thinks somebody might want to contact him. What time he comes home is his business, just so he doesn't hurt her by not being available sufficiently so she can turn on her indicator. Marriage is purely and simply a sexual relation, nothing else. It is the phenomenon, all else is the epiphenomenon, like the light in a fire or the heat from a lamp."

"What about children; isn't marriage for the purpose of raising children?"

"Marriage is purely and simply a sexual relation, nothing else."

"But supposing a girl doesn't want children, or the boy?"

"When he asks her for a date and she accepts, he will say, 'Do you want children?' If her answer is what he doesn't want to hear, then he will be forced to look for somebody else. Remember, it is the girl who must give birth, and it is she who will decide. However, if for some reason a boy doesn't want children, and the girl does, he still will be forced to look for somebody else. But in the new world, both will want children, or perhaps I should say that the ones who will not want them are so few, the number is too small to be written."

"Do I understand you to mean that a husband and wife, in this new earth (as you call it), will be completely free to do anything they want, without any questions asked?"

"Controlled only by the desire that they might hurt their partner, who will never blame them for what they do."

"Supposing the husband likes to do many things with his wife, other than make love, such as dancing, bowling, chess, checkers, picnics, etc.? Does he have to have an indicator for this also?"

"It should be obvious that when the satisfaction of a husband's or wife's desire involves the other, there must be mutual agreement, and if there isn't, there cannot be any blame. The most they can do is extend an invitation to join them in doing certain things. If he wants to see The Hustler, he will simply say, 'Honey, "I'm going to the movies to see The Hustler; would you like to come along?' If she says 'no,' then he proceeds alone. He may say, or she may say, 'I'm in the mood to go dancing tonight, would you care to join me?'"

"But supposing his wife is a lousy dancer, and he doesn't enjoy dancing with her?"

"He will then say, 'I'll see you later, Hon, I'm going out for a while.' Each partner will be given every opportunity to satisfy personal desires, which will make for a most harmonious marriage, and then when they turn on their indicators, extending an invitation, nothing in this world can make them desire not to accept it. If her husband goes out, nothing is stopping her from going out to do what she wants. If small children are involved, they will discover a fair way to distribute the time so no one will be in a position to take advantage."

"But supposing the husband goes out dancing and the girl with whom he's dancing takes a liking to him?"

"If he doesn't ask her for a date, she won't like him too long."

"But supposing she asks him for a date, there's no law against it, right?"

"He will simply turn her down."

"But supposing she has the kind of appeal that is hard to turn down?"

"Isn't it obvious that he would have to hurt both his wife and this girl, who would never blame him for this hurt?"

"That's right, I forgot, he would definitely hurt this girl because he would have to leave her, but how would he hurt his wife?"

"Wouldn't it be a hurt to your wife if you were unable to accept her invitation only because you just got finished making love elsewhere? And this is a concrete hurt, not one that exists in the imagination. Consequently, it cannot satisfy you to see your wife be seriously hurt in this manner, especially when you know she will never blame you for doing what you are compelled to do. But you know you are not compelled to make love to other women unless you want to, and it is impossible to desire hurting your wife in this manner, under these changed conditions. Presently, a husband doesn't care, nor does a wife, because they have hurt each other so many times that it satisfies them to strike back, one way or another. A husband may sexually starve his wife, which he cannot help because the woman he married is not that woman anymore, and she blames him for her desire to have an affair, or she may starve him for the same reason. Remember, everything works two ways."

"Do you mean that Mary may be starving her husband because he has gotten so big and fat that he doesn't appeal to her anymore? Does this also mean that there is something sexually unappealing in fat people?"

"Of course not. But if Mary married him under conditions where he was not fat, and the conditions changed, then actually he is hurting her by presenting an indicator that is uninviting to her taste, which forces her to prefer going to a bar in search of a more appealing indicator."

"Like me, right Larry?"

"Right, Jim. However, if it hadn't been you, it would have been somebody else, because Mary wanted sexual satisfaction. You just happened along at the right time. In the new world, a girl and a boy will do everything in their power to maintain the same physical appearance that first attracted their mate, whatever appearance that is, unless they discover that preference is given in a particular direction."

"Do you mean that if I asked a certain type of girl for a date, and she turned me down, and I asked other girls of that type, and they also turned me down, it would be obvious that I am not their type, which would compel me to ask a different type. Now, if a girl, who is attracted to me, knows that I prefer a different type than herself, and can see a possibility of changing herself more in that direction, she would desire to do it, right?"

"Only if there is no possibility of hurting herself. But this works two ways. However, Jim, when all words that create external values are removed from our vocabulary because they hurt others by placing them in an inferior position..."

"You're not serious. You mean words like 'beautiful,' 'lovely,' 'adorable,' 'precious,' 'cute,' are going to be removed, permanently?"

"Many many more than that will become obsolete. Just as soon as they are removed, the differences that exist will be reduced, where sex is concerned, to an absolute minimum because we all have sexual organs that give satisfaction. Believe it or not, Jim, within a very short time, the difference between one girl and another couldn't pass through the eye of a needle."

"What about intermarriages between the Blacks and the Whites?"

"This is a personal matter and concerns no one but the boy and girl. If a Black boy asks a White girl for a date, this is his business; and if she accepts, this is her business. By the same reasoning, a White girl could ask a Black boy, or a Black girl could ask a White boy. God is teaching all of us to mind our own business. Under these changed conditions, it is mathematically impossible for arguments to arise in the life of a married couple, and impossible for sexual desire to decrease."

"But supposing a man is much older than the girl, wouldn't it decrease more for him and less for her as they get older; and if that did occur, wouldn't he be hurting her by not being in a position to accept her invitation no matter how hard she tries to arouse his desire?"

"This is very true, and that is why a man will never desire to ask a girl for a date if there is a wide discrepancy in their ages, because he foresees that he might hurt her later on in their lives. Therefore, you would never see a man in his fifties, as you see today, marrying a girl in her teens, because there can be no satisfaction whatsoever in hurting another when it is known there will be no blame."

"But supposing a girl who knows she appeals to a certain rich widower, asks him to marry her?"

"She wouldn't ask."

"Why?"

"Because she would know that he would turn her down, since he doesn't want to hurt her."

"By the way, Larry, you distinctly said that to ask favors is a form of advance blame, and yet when a boy asks a girl for a date, isn't he blaming the possibility that he might be refused, and isn't he disappointed when he is turned down? And what about the married men who go to dances, or women who are asked for a date by them?"

"Because they don't want to hurt anybody, all married couples will continue to wear an identifying symbol, such as a wedding ring, which means that a married person, unless he has his wife with him at these dances, will not be doing much dancing, because these dances, believe it or not, are strictly for the purpose of boys and girls meeting each other. They are looking for a mate, not for a dancing partner."

"But what about the other thing I mentioned? I've got you now, there's no way out of this. A boy must blame the girl in advance if he asks her for a date, right?"

"Wrong. The same conditions exist between a couple before marriage as after. If a boy sees a girl that he likes, he must, in some way, indicate to her what he wants, and then it is up to her to accept or decline the invitation. In other words, if on the beach a girl sees a boy who appeals, she will simply sit down beside him and let him devour all she wants to show (bathing suits will be sexier than ever, in fact, hardly anything will be covered by those who are looking for a mate), and when he sees this tempting invitation, he will either get up and walk away if she is not his type, or else he will take her in his arms and kiss her right away, knowing that he has just selected her for his wife."

"Supposing he sees a girl that he likes, what then?"

"Are you being serious?"

"Cut it out, Larry, can't you see I'm only kidding. I know that he would sit next to this girl and let her get a good look at his muscles."

"Or at his muscle, Jim."

"But supposing it's the wintertime, what then?"

"There will be all kinds of dances, get-togethers, etc., and the clothes these young people will wear would shock the modesty of the people today. But remember, Jim, nothing can go wrong under the changed conditions. Consequently, if a girl sees a boy she likes, she will stand near him and flirt; then it is up to him, and if he sees a girl he likes, he stands next to her and flirts. When an invitation is accepted, they will find a little cozy love nest and have a ball, but they will be married for life, until death do they part. You see, Jim, this is similar to the conditions that make it unnecessary for a bank to check on the credit of an individual before lending him money. The person borrowing knows the bank wants to lend money, and as long as he knows he can pay it back, plus the interest, the bank extends an open invitation to everyone who wishes to use its services. Once the boy extends to the girl an invitation, or vice versa, they know the other is prepared to give what is desired — passionate lovemaking and a partner until death do they part. If the boy wasn't prepared for this, which includes his financial support, he would never have flirted."

"But supposing she doesn't want any children, how does she communicate this?"

"She just doesn't accept his invitation. But then she would have to turn down all invitations because what a boy wants is her body, and he is willing to take all that comes along with it, including children."

"But just supposing he doesn't want any children?"

"Then the person who doesn't would have to wear a sign that says: 'No kids,' and if one sign sees another sign, then it is possible they might be able to get together. But everyone will want children."

"Boy, Larry, you have all the answers, don't you?"

"That's easy, Jim, when God gives them to me."

"What about the handling of money; who does that?"

"The person who earns it. However, after a husband — assuming that he is the breadwinner — takes out all that he needs for the rent, gas and electric, telephone, water bill, other bills, and what he wants for his own expenses and pleasures, he will give the rest to his wife for food, clothes, and whatever she wants to do with it. There is no possibility for arguments to arise over money because neither will desire to hurt the other when there will be no blame for this hurt, and they will be compelled to buy only what they can afford. As for taxes, this will be paid every week, as described. All he does is enter the amount of his paycheck in his record book, less what he wants for himself. He doesn't actually hand his wife anything; she just consults the book."

"This appears to be a wonderful life you've described."

"It really is, Jim, and it must come about once all mankind understands what it means that man's will is not free because it actually benefits everyone, without exception."

"Can't we speed things up?"

"No, Jim, we can't. We are moving at a mathematical rate, which includes our efforts to speed things up."

"But what about marriage as it exists today? What about all the adultery and premarital relations, the heartache of unrequited love; how do you go about solving these problems?"

"Do you mean, how do I go about getting Mary to return to her husband?"

"Hey, take it easy, Larry, are you my pal or aren't you? Besides, if she returned to her husband, all three of us would be miserable. By the way, I know Mary would love to read your manuscript as much as you have written. How about borrowing it? I'll take real good care of it."

"Okay, Jim."

"Are we all finished for the day, no more talk about marriage?"

"There is more to be discussed, but I'm kind of tired. Tomorrow I'm leaving for Atlantic City for two weeks, and then I have to go to Boston on business for two weeks, so I'll see you in about a month."

"Okay, I'll see you when you get back, but first give me that manuscript."

"I've got a copy in my car. Wait, I'll get it."

"Thanks a lot, Larry."

"You're welcome, Jim."

# CHAPTER 8 — THE TRANSFORMATION

Jim didn't want to tell Larry that he had an ulterior motive in borrowing the manuscript. He felt he could persuade Mary's husband to give her a divorce once Jerry understood that she could not be blamed for falling in love with somebody else. He planned to get her to read the book first, and then, in some manner, try to get her husband to read it.

That evening, after making love, Mary stayed up till the wee hours reading the manuscript, and like Jim, she began to see the possibility of getting Jerry to give her a divorce, providing she could get him to read the book. She had such a vehement argument just the other day that she didn't know how he would receive her. But she was determined to get him to read this book and decided to go down the street and give it a try.

As she left the apartment, she was happy with this wonderful news that man is not to blame, and said to herself, 'My problem is solved at last, the very moment he reads and understands this book, for then he will never blame me for wanting to marry Jim, and never stand in the way any more of my getting a divorce. She was so happy with the thought that she can at last set herself completely free from the man she now refers to as a "big, fat, sloppy, nagging husband," who every day, when home, would say, "Mary, where are you going, where have you been, why didn't you call, why didn't you come home last night; do this, don't do that, get me this, get me that," that she began to sing, "Happy days are here again, da. . da da. . dada . . da da. . da da." She was still humming when her husband answered the knock at the door."

"What do you want, you rotten whore, and what are you so happy about? You might as well forget about that divorce because I'll never let you marry that gigolo, that wife stealer. If you think for one minute that you can ruin my life, make me miserable, you lousy prostitute, and then expect me to help you find happiness, you have another thought coming. When I die, that's when you'll get your freedom, you dirty bitch, so don't bother coming over to see if I have changed my mind. You think I ever loved you? I hate your rotten guts. Now get out of here before I call the police to arrest you for dirtying up the sidewalk."

"Wait a minute, Jerry, don't close the door. I didn't come over to ask that you give me a divorce because I know it is useless. I brought something for you to read that I thought you'd find very interesting because you are a religious person who believes very much in God. Isn't that right, Jerry?"

"You know I am a devout Catholic, Mary. Don't I go to church every Sunday when I'm home, and didn't I always ask you to join me and the children? But you never did because you preferred going out with your friends from early morning to late at night. How the neighbors used to talk."

"Well, Jerry, what's done is done, and you don't have to live with me anymore. Anyway, this author has positive proof that God is a reality. We don't even have to believe or have faith in him anymore. He is going to reveal himself by performing a miracle. This author demonstrates in this manuscript how God comes down from heaven in the form of a mathematical revelation and puts an end to all evil in the world. This author further proves that no one is to blame for anything because man's will is not free, which makes God responsible for everything."

"God is responsible!!? What in the hell are you talking about? Do you mean that God is to blame for your committing adultery, for my not wanting to give you a divorce because it is against my religion, and also because you're a no-good rat? He is to blame for my hating your rotten guts, is that what you mean?"

"Not exactly that way, Jerry, but that's right. It's all here in this book. It's easy to understand, too. The theme is sort of a game for two people; I won't blame you if you don't blame me. I won't blame you for not wanting to give me a divorce and for calling me all those nasty names, and you won't blame me for wanting one. You know, tit for tat."

"Is that what the book is all about? After ruining my life, you don't want me to blame you because God is responsible, and now I should let you get off the hook, right? Isn't that what you want? No wonder you like the author, but you're both nuts. You can take that manuscript and stick it up you know where. God is all goodness, and you, a rat born of the devil, want to blame our Lord for your sins, for giving your body to anybody."

"But wait, Jerry, don't close the door yet. I'm not blaming God, actually, because I didn't have to do these things that hurt you so much if I didn't want to, but God made me want to. You see, there was a purpose to all the evil, and therefore, you shouldn't blame me for committing adultery and wanting to marry someone I love very much. I wouldn't blame you for committing adultery and leaving me, because I know that God is truly responsible, and I don't even blame you for calling me all those names, because I know your will is not free. I know you can't help doing anything you do."

"Where in the hell did that author pick up all that crap! The Catholic religion teaches that man's will is definitely free. He must be a real goofball, that guy; but he's perfectly right about one thing. I am definitely not to blame because you are to blame. That's right; you didn't have to eat my heart out like you did, hurt me to the core, hurt the children by becoming a cheap slut, ruin our lives. And I further agree that you did it only because you wanted to do it, and now I'm going to get even."

"But Jerry, I don't think you quite understand what I'm trying to explain. I'm truly sorry about all that happened. I could not help falling in love with Jim; it was just one of those things."

"Yes, I know the very thing you're talking about, and I'm not blaming you either, but I can't help myself because God is making me make you suffer like you made me suffer. Now get out of here along with that other goofball."

"Wait one more minute, Jerry. Please don't close the door yet! Maybe I'm not explaining this book right, but some scientist said it is a fantastic, mathematical revelation, direct from the horse's mouth, God himself."

"Shame on you, Mary! How can you talk like that about our Lord... 'The horse's mouth.' You will be punished for such disrespect."

"Don't take me so literally, Jerry. Anyway, this book is supposed to make everybody happy — once they understand its significance. Maybe it is a little over my head, but it did make me happy. However, it can't hurt you to read it, and since you are unhappy, maybe it will do the trick. Besides, you certainly don't have to agree with the guy if you don't want to, right?"

"Are you concerned for my happiness, Mary? Is that why you want me to read this book? I'm sure you have some ulterior motive, and more than likely, it is another attempt to convince me that I should give you a divorce. But I'll look it over anyway, not that it will change my mind. I agree, it probably was slightly over your head because you never were too intelligent, and you never did get much of an education. In fact, you never even finished high school, let alone go to college. My father, God rest his soul, used to tell me you were absolutely nothing, except that you were good looking and that I would be making a big mistake, especially after my little sister beat you in a game of chess in twenty minutes. He could never see what I saw in you, and now I really wonder what possessed me to marry someone like you. Goodbye, Idiot! Thanks for the book, but please don't bother me again about a divorce."

But despite his last words, Mary had accomplished her purpose, which was to arouse his interest enough to read the book, and she felt absolutely certain that he would never stand in the way of a divorce once he understood that it wasn't right to blame her for wanting one. She then went back to the apartment to tell Jim.

As she walked in, she noticed that he was wearing a translucent robe and that he was deliberately letting her see glimpses of his penis. She knew that he was in the mood and was extending her an invitation. He was pretending to be asleep on the sofa. So, Mary went into the other room, got undressed except for a half-slip with nothing underneath, and then tiptoed back in. Then she sat across the room on a chair, opened up her legs so Jim couldn't help but see, and yelled, "Jim, it's me, Mary; I'm back." And when he looked over, his blood began to boil. When they finished making love, both of them thought how wonderful this would be if it could last forever.' Just before starting, though, Mary managed to tell him that Jerry would read the book.

Larry finally returned after 5 weeks and arranged to meet Jim at their usual place.

"Well, Jim, where's my manuscript?"

"The truth is, Larry, I really borrowed it so Mary could read it and then give it to her husband to read. I felt that if he understood the principles, he wouldn't stand in her way of getting a divorce."

"Well, where is the manuscript?"

"Mary called him up about a week after she left it, and he said he wasn't ready to return it, that he was studying it very thoroughly."

"What's the address? I'll get it myself."

"I'll take you there, it's only a block away from our apartment. You can have dinner with us. How about it? Besides, you never did meet Mary, and I told her all about you. She's anxious to meet the author."

"I won't be able to stay for dinner, Jim, but I'll come in for a few minutes. I am very anxious to get my manuscript back."

"Well, let's go right now."

Jim drove Larry over and actually waited one-half hour before he came out with the manuscript.

"I'm sorry for keeping you waiting, Jim, but Jerry wanted to talk about the book. Now I'm ready to meet Mary."

Inside the apartment, after being introduced, Larry told them he had some good news.

"What's the good news, Larry? Did you find enough money to publish your book?"

"I wish I did. The good news is that Jerry has consented to a divorce on one condition."

"Did you hear that, Mary? It worked! He's going to give you a divorce! But what is the condition?"

"He wants Mary to live in the same house with him for a two-week period; after that, she is perfectly free to leave and marry you, Jim."

"That sounds reasonable enough to me, Mary. How about you?"

"I don't know if I can take him for two weeks longer, but I'll try. When does he want to start?"

"August 1st, he gets a two-week vacation, that's three weeks from tomorrow. If that's satisfactory, I'll tell him."

"Well then, tell him, Larry. Mary and I are both willing."

Everything was arranged, and on August 1$^{st}$, Mary said goodbye to Jim for two weeks. She approached her house rather awkwardly because she remembered the last time, and the terrible names he called her still rang in her ears. She really dreaded these two weeks but made up her mind to stick it out. When Jerry answered the door, never in a million years did she expect to see such a complete transformation.

After finishing the book and realizing that his wife was henceforth free to leave him under the new conditions, if she really wanted to, Jerry decided to get back in the shape he used to be when he first met Mary, solely for the purpose of attracting the kind of female that appealed to him. But before exerting himself in this direction, he thought he would give his marriage one more try, according to the principles he had just learned, which required that she understand them too. Realizing that it was only fair to Mary to get back in shape, he went on a blitz diet, lifted heavy weights, and did a number of things to reduce his weight. When Mary saw him, it was like a ghost out of the past, because this man who stood in front of her resembled very strongly the man, many years ago, she fell in love with and married.

"Hi, Mary," he said very cheerfully. "Let me take your suitcase."

They had always slept in a double bed, but Jerry had arranged a room completely for her. He also hired a housekeeper to do the cooking and cleaning so Mary would have nothing to do. The kids were away at camp and wouldn't be home for two weeks. Jerry had thought of everything.

That evening, after the housekeeper had left, Jerry asked Mary if there was anything he could do for her, but she simply said, "No thank you." She decided to put Jerry to a little test because she knew that the condition was to stay in the house with him for two weeks, so a little later she remarked, "I'm going out for a while, do you mind?"

"I want you to know, Mary, that I read and loved that book. It is exactly what you said, a mathematical revelation. Consequently, you don't have to ask my permission for anything you want to do, nor do you have to account for your actions."

Mary walked down to the drugstore, got herself a sundae, and then returned. Jerry, in the meantime, doing what he wanted to do, put on the sexiest, translucent robe that couldn't help but make any normal girl feel a twinge of excitement. But Mary just went up to her room and didn't come downstairs again until the following morning. This went on for four days. On the fifth day, he was really hurting. He was so hungry for a sexual relation that he was wondering if he could stay away from Mary for the entire two weeks, that is, if she continued to turn down his invitation. But that evening, she was also beginning to feel the pressure. As usual, he had put on his sexy outfit, only this time he stretched out on the sofa and began to squirm in a manner that made her feel a little warm, but she felt kind of funny. She wanted to make love in the worst way, but she wanted the kind of love that Jim made to her. The thought of how unsatisfied she always was with her husband was not an encouragement. Furthermore, she enjoyed kissing Jim's body all over. She knew this made him very hot. But she didn't know how her husband would react if she did this to him. He might start calling her names again, might call her perverted. She also knew what a pleasure it was when she and Jim turned around and kissed each other's indicator, and how extremely passionate it made them. Her husband might throw a fit. "But his body certainly does look appealing," she thought to herself, "and here it is five days and we haven't had any arguments. I'm sure in the mood. Besides, what Jim doesn't know won't hurt him. However, I still can't go over to him, but maybe I'll put on some other kind of clothes to see if he would accept my invitation."

"So she went upstairs, and Jerry, for the moment, thought he had lost her again. But in a few minutes, his eyes nearly popped out of his head, for Mary came in wearing the same kind of outfit that a stripteaser wears, only this one allowed him to see her indicator pretty clearly. She sat down in a chair opposite him, and he was drawn as if by a magnet. As he approached her, she began to tingle all over.

He started to kiss her toes, then her ankles (she couldn't believe this was her husband), and little by little, he kept going up her leg. Before long, she began to kiss his body and his indicator. Soon they were making passionate love, and when it was all over, they actually wept in each other's arms.

For the very first time, she realized there was absolutely no difference whatsoever between making love with Jim and her husband when the conditions were changed. At the end of two weeks, they had made love so many times it was like their honeymoon all over again, only much better. She also realized that if she left her husband now, this would really be a terrible hurt to him, for which he would never blame her, since he would have to excuse what she was compelled to do. But she knew that she was not compelled to make love to her husband, unless she wanted to, and she wanted to because she saw first, that he wanted her back, second, that he was not the same man as before, and third, that her life with him henceforth, with both of them knowing what it means that man's will is not free, could only go in one direction, towards the greatest happiness imaginable. Furthermore, and not to be overlooked, Mary missed her children, and now she was back with them as a family.

She called Jim on the phone, but though it hurt him to hear the news, he knew that Mary was doing this of her own free will; that she wanted to go back with her husband and that he, Jerry, had priority. Jim also knew that he couldn't blame anybody because it was God's will and because he also knew that Mary had no choice. However, though he was quite upset, he was also bursting with questions to ask Larry, and the next day they met at their usual place.

"Did you hear what happened, Larry?"

"No, I didn't, Jim, but I can imagine. Mary went back with her husband, right?"

"How did you know?"

"Because the difference between you and her husband, when certain things are changed, couldn't pass through the eye of a needle. Therefore, since she already has two children with Jerry, once this difference is removed, she would have no choice."

"What did you talk about when you went to pick up your manuscript?"

"He just told me he thought the book was wonderful, and that he always considered sex in a different light because things were judged as perverted and wrong to do. After reading the book, however, he realized that 'perverted' is a word without meaning because it blames an individual for doing what he wants to do, and what he wants to do, in this case, hurts nobody. Further realizing that he was not the same man Mary had fallen in love with and married, because he had put on so much weight, and that their lives together would be very happy under the changed conditions, he

208

asked me if I thought I could get Mary to come home for two weeks. It was my idea to tell you and Mary that he would consent to a divorce if you complied with the one condition."

"But why did you side with him instead of with me?"

"I didn't side with him over you, Jim. When I was leaving and knowing that he wouldn't ask any favors of me, I asked him if there was anything I could do for him. It was then that he asked me if I thought I could get Mary to come home for two weeks."

"But why did you say he would consent to a divorce if she came home for two weeks, when he didn't say that?"

"The moment he understood the book, he knew that he was already divorced if she wanted to leave; therefore, his only chance to keep her was to prove that under changed conditions, there was no difference between the two of you. In actual reality, had you understood the principles yourself, you would have known that just as soon as Jerry grasped what it meant that his will is not free, Mary was automatically divorced if she wanted to leave, because Jerry would never have blamed her. I wanted to prove to myself that the difference between one man and another is insignificant, once certain changes come about, and prove also that love is purely sexual satisfaction, nothing else. I then decided to help Jerry by getting Mary to come home for two weeks."

"But this hurt me, Larry."

"Not really, Jim. Just as you met Mary in a bar, so you will meet a dozen like her who are waiting to satisfy your sexual desire. And if the girl is unmarried, you will never lose her, once she is taught what it means that man's will is not free."

"But supposing she had never gone home?"

"Then she would have missed her children terribly and, despite sexual satisfaction, she would not have been completely happy. However, since this change came about in her husband, as well as herself, she now has with him what she had with you, plus her children. In most marriages today, Jim, there is not this passion in lovemaking that exists in adultery; consequently, a husband or wife is drawn to this difference. Also, the type of lovemaking that exists in adultery, because of this passion, doesn't often take place in marriage. Men and women have classified certain things as perverted, degrading, cheap, done only by whores, and as a result, this kind of excitement, which their wives or husbands cannot give them because they are above it, becomes illicitly attractive. With the knowledge of what it means that man's will is not free, all people are compelled to become, with their partner, this cheap, degrading, perverted individual. But remember, these are only words that will soon become obsolete, and these actions, since they hurt no one and are a motion in the direction of greater satisfaction, are done in obedience to God's will — that force that gives us no choice. Furthermore, in the old world, the subconscious mind of man was filled with feelings of guilt over words, nothing else."

"Will these principles do away with all adultery at the start of the transition, as well as all divorce?"

"When the transition gets underway, in other words, when the knowledge we have been discussing is thoroughly understood by all mankind, every husband and wife will be standing on this moment of time called here, making preparation, so to speak, to move to the next spot called there. Consequently, if two people have not been thinking about a divorce — although they may be committing adultery and having arguments — this knowledge, when thoroughly understood, will mathematically prevent any more concrete hurt in their relations with each other by the realization that they are completely free to do anything desired, without any fear of blame, which means that when those concerned try to get back into the kind of shape they were in that first attracted their mate, and then when they make efforts to arouse the love of the other only by extending an invitation as was explained — without any obligation attached — then this desire for love will be aroused. At the same time, they will realize that their partner will be seriously hurt if this sexual desire is not satisfied. Therefore, when all the other factors contributing to arguments are removed, which eliminates all justification for hurting each other through sex; and when they see that passion has again been restored in their marriage, they will not be able to find satisfaction in continuing with adultery because they will realize that this would be a serious hurt to the very person who now refuses to blame or criticize them for anything that is done.

As for the husbands and wives who are thinking about or trying to get a divorce, they will be completely free to do whatever they think is better for themselves, knowing, of course, that no one will ever blame their decision, no matter how much hurt is involved. However, the problem of hurt is only sexual where the wife or husband is concerned in the new world, because the wife, should her husband leave her for another and not give her the amount of income she is accustomed to receiving, will simply draw the difference from the Bureau, which means that the husband will be prevented from doing it because he knows this would hurt the people by increasing their taxes, for which he also knows he would never be blamed. Since it cannot satisfy him to hurt anybody when there can be no justification, he would have to have the kind of job or business that would allow him to support two families, for this is the only way he could possibly leave with a clear conscience when money is involved."

"In other words, Larry, you're saying that if any of those considering a divorce when the transition gets under way will allow their partner ample time to get back in the kind of shape that first attracted them, as with Jerry, and then live together for a period of two weeks under the changed conditions (no blame), all the money in the world couldn't make them prefer another partner?"

"That's right, Jim, but you must remember that some couples prefer their partner according to the way they have changed over the years. If Mary had preferred Jerry's weight to the way he used to be, and this was not detrimental to his health, he would have no reason to change back."

"I'm beginning to see the whole picture now. With every income guaranteed never to decrease or stop, no wife or husband can find justification to leave because of money. Therefore, the only justification can come as a result of sexual dissatisfaction, which is occasioned by various arguments and other things. But when these are removed, nobody is given any choice whatsoever."

"That's right, Jim. You see, in our present world, the husband and wife blame each other for any hurt in their marriage because they are unconscious of who or what is really to blame. By revealing this knowledge that man's will is not free, which releases the corollary that no person is to blame, every individual becomes conscious that he alone is responsible for any hurt done to himself.

You are beginning to see the infinite wisdom that governs this universe of human relations through invariable laws when you remember that the acts of government are removed only because they are not needed at this stage of our development. By removing all forms of advance blame, this judging of what is right for others, which was necessary under the previous conditions (I've projected us into the future already, Jim), we are mathematically prevented from doing those very things for which government came into existence. There is no law that can compel a man to live with and support a woman if he makes up his mind that anything else is better. Consequently, when financial burdens increase along with a terrible feeling of insecurity, the slightest spark could set off a tremendous explosion of arguments that reduces sexual desire, which then gives ample justification to commit adultery and shirk the responsibilities that were transferred to the government, friends, relatives, and religion. The government doesn't come to an end because it is a form of blame, but only because it is a useless, costly appendage when the truth, which our philosophers have been searching for since the earliest of eras, is mathematically revealed. The services of a rabbi and priest during a marriage ceremony don't come to an end because these include the inculcation of a couple's obligations to each other, which is a form of advance blame, but only because the boy and girl, at this stage of development, are getting married in a superior manner, which renders this service obsolete. Of what value is having a law to compel a man to pay alimony, when he, of his own free will, can never desire a divorce?"

"It's really fantastic, Larry!"

"Think further about this immense wisdom. At the very time that God reveals what love actually is — nothing other than a desire for sexual satisfaction (as if we didn't know) which would allow a man or woman to fall in love with any number of people who could satisfy this passion — He prevents the possibility of having more than one sexual partner all through life."

"All I can say, Larry, is that this whole thing is simply fantastic. Have you covered everything there is to be covered on marriage and premarital relations? You did say you were going to tell me something about pornography."

"Pornography I'll discuss where children are concerned. As for marriage, it shouldn't be necessary to analyze every minute detail, as this slide rule is applicable no matter what a person's problem is. If a wife and husband want their partner never to leave them for another sexual playmate, this is within their power, provided they <u>show</u> their love, which only means the absolute giving up of judging what is right for the other. This demonstrates a complete respect for their partner's desires while preventing any desire to hurt or take advantage of another. Remember, Jim, if the satisfaction of your desire requires your partner to do what she does not desire, then you are selfishly asking the sacrifice of her desire not to do what you want done, even though your partner is reluctantly willing. However, when she fully realizes that there are many things you can absolutely not do for yourself, and that you will never ask a favor, she will desire to do for you the things you cannot do for yourself. Just constantly bear in mind should you meet another Mary who, of course, must also understand these principles in order for them to work, any time you tell her what to do you are mathematically at fault by judging what is right for her. But remember also that it is impossible to desire to tell her what to do when there is no chance that she could do anything wrong. This tacit blame of judging what is right for others decreases the desire to make love by striking the first blow, while it justifies, in the world of free will, a retaliatory measure not desired. It has an inverse relation to sexual passion; the more you judge how your partner should be, the less her desire will be to make love, giving you no choice as to what is better for yourself. Consequently, if you have followed these undeniable principles, you re compelled to admit that before very long all premarital sexual intercourse, all adultery, and all divorce are coming to an end."

"I have to agree, Larry. Isn't the loss of my girlfriend substantial proof?"

"That is only one small part of the tremendous transition soon to take place. These changes, yours included, must come about because it is the mathematical direction man's motion is compelled to take when he thoroughly understands what it means that his will is not free."

"What is the next subject on the agenda?"

"Parents and children."

"I'll bet you will have your hands filled with those little devils."

"I'm going to make them into little angels."

"When?"

"Tomorrow, same time and place, okay?"

"Good enough, Larry. See you then."

# PART 4

# THE EXTENSION OF THIS DISCOVERY INTO

# THE LIFE OF A FAMILY AND THE

## ACCUMULATION OF KNOWLEDGE

# SEYMOUR LESSANS

# CHAPTER 9 — PARENTS AND CHILDREN

That evening, Jim went to the same bar where he first met Mary. He was hungry. And sure enough, there was another girl sitting there drinking beer. Again, he started a conversation, but since she knew nothing about what he had learned, he knew that asking her if he could take her home wouldn't mean that he was asking her hand in marriage. Furthermore, after taking a second look, he saw that she was not the type he wanted for the rest of his life. He realized that if he went home with her and taught her what it meant that man's will is not free, he would never be able to break away without hurting her, assuming that she wanted him. This meant that he could take her home only to have a good time, and the only way he could do that with a clear conscience was to avoid teaching her what he had learned. By the same reasoning, he realized that if he became attached to her, as he did once to Inez, and she left him, there was no way he could prevent it unless she was taught these principles. One way allowed him to hurt her with impunity; the other permitted her to hurt him. He decided against taking her home and went to another bar.

There, he saw a girl who really appealed to him. "But supposing she is married," he thought. As usual, he started up a conversation and, without any qualms, plainly asked her if she was married. "No, I'm not," she said rather coyly.

"Would you care to dance?"

"I wouldn't mind."

After a few drinks and several dances, they sort of took to each other. Both of them were very hungry. But Jim realized that in order to prevent himself from getting hurt, it would be absolutely imperative to teach her the knowledge he had learned. He also knew that if both of them understood the principles, he could never hurt her. So, to make a long story short, he took her to a motel, taught her the principles, and they were married that night. The next day, he broke the news to Larry.

"Hi Jim!"

"Hi Larry! I'm sorry I'm late."

"Why are you apologizing to me, Jim? You know I will never blame anything you do. Isn't it obvious that you couldn't help yourself?"

And for the first time, the true significance of the corollary was beginning to sink in because Jim knew that he didn't have to be late if he didn't want to. He just carelessly neglected to set the alarm clock. "But supposing the alarm didn't go off and I was forced to be late," he thought to himself.

"Jim, are you in a daze this morning? I just said, 'You know I will never blame anything you do.' Isn't it obvious that you couldn't help yourself?"

And then the answer came to him. No matter what made him late, Larry would never blame him. Therefore, if it was the fault of the alarm clock not going off and not because he failed to set it, he knew that it really wasn't his responsibility. So, if Larry was hurt by this delay, it really "was not my fault." Since he knew, subconsciously, that it was his responsibility because he could have set the alarm and been on time, he felt guilty, which made him desire to apologize. But Larry, by making him conscious that no excuses were necessary for doing what everybody knows he was compelled to do, made Jim realize that he would have to change his ways in order to be satisfied with his own actions.

He was about to say, "I'm sorry, Larry, I didn't hear what you said," when he thought better of it.

"I got married last night."

"You what?"

"That's right. I was hungry for the kind of sexual relationship I had with Mary and decided to find myself a wife, not a girlfriend. So, I met Julie at the Ritz, asked her if she was married or single, and then when she told me she was single, after having a few drinks and several dances, I took her to a motel, taught her what it means that man's will is not free after we finished making passionate love, and now we are married for life. Now, let some Jerry come and take her back. In fact, I rented a furnished apartment after using the motel until 11 p.m. and made sure it had twin beds. We checked in at 12:30, made love again, and then went to sleep. At 3 a.m. I heard a noise and woke up. It was Julie. She had gotten up to go to the bathroom. When she came out and saw that I was awake, she sat down on her bed, opened up her legs to extend me an invitation, and boy, I felt that twinge of passion all over again. Talk about being pooped this morning, I can hardly lift my arms. But what I mainly want to bring out is that Julie caught on really quickly to the principles. When I left the apartment to meet you, she didn't ask where I was going or when I would be back, nor did I say anything to her. As I was getting ready to walk out the door, she said, 'Jim, is there anything I can do for you today?' 'Nothing at all, Honey,' I replied. Then I asked her the same thing, and she answered, 'Yes, there is. On the way home, I would appreciate if you could pick up some food so I can prepare dinner.' Then I realized that she was far from the store, had no car, and perhaps no money. This system is really wonderful, Larry, and I can't thank you enough. Ordinarily, I might have considered Julie a cheap girl for letting me pick her up this way, but now I know better."

"Don't thank me, Jim. I only work here in this world, the same as you. If you want to thank the proper party, thank God."

"Well, except for being exhausted, I'm ready to listen again. But I won't stay as long today because I have several things to do. So how about it, Larry, what's what with our little demons?"

"The problem here is slightly different only because every young child cannot understand what it means that man's will is not free. Consequently, under this condition, the parents are compelled to set up standards to prevent others and themselves from being hurt. In other words, they are compelled to live a little longer in the world of free will even after the transition gets underway; otherwise, matters would be worse."

"Can you give me an example of what you mean?"

"Yes, I can. At the same time, I will show you how confused some psychologists are, for which they cannot be blamed. The other day, my brother told me about someone who believed that a child should not be punished for anything. This person was visiting my brother with his young boy, about 4 years old, when the little fellow decided to use a brand-new sofa for a trampoline. 'Whee... Whee... Whee...!' he shouted with glee as he jumped up and down. The father was kind of embarrassed and kept asking the boy to please come down. But he was having too good a time and just ignored his dad's pleading request. Finally, the father couldn't take it any longer and just lifted him off. But the little fellow jumped right back on. Wanting to adhere to what he was taught (no punishment), he told his son that he would buy him something really nice if he came down, and he wouldn't come down until dad told him what this 'really nice' something would be. Now the question arises, Jim, what should the father have done, or did he do what was right?"

"Well, according to you, Larry, the boy shouldn't be blamed for doing what he was compelled to do, right?"

"You know that isn't right, Jim. Under these conditions, the rascals must be prevented from hurting others, one way or another. Since the knowledge that no one will blame or punish him, should he hurt my brother by jumping on the sofa, is not a factor to control his desire, he must be told in advance that should he do anything to hurt someone, directly or indirectly, he will be punished in such and such a manner. Then, if he is willing to suffer the consequences, this is up to him. Under the circumstances, I would simply have said to the boy, 'Jimmy, you are hurting this man's furniture. Now it isn't nice to do that, and I am going to have to stop you if you keep on doing what you're doing.'"

"But supposing he didn't heed this warning, what then?"

"Supposing a bank robber didn't heed the laws that threaten him with imprisonment if he gets caught in the act of trying to hurt others, what would you do, Jim, if you were the judge?"

"I'd punish him according to the letter of the law."

"Well, I would punish the boy in a manner that would compel him to get off the sofa, either by telling him what I would do later, or by doing something on the spot."

"Do you mean you would spank him?"

"If he didn't heed my warning, definitely."

"Then you are actually blaming him, right?"

"I know that he was compelled to react in this manner because of his upbringing, and I can't blame him for his desire to jump on the sofa since, at that moment of time, this is beyond his control. However, even though

I know he is not to blame, it is necessary to prevent him from continuing to hurt somebody else. Therefore, I must punish him as the lesser of two evils. But since I know that the boy is really not to blame, the problem is to prevent his desire to jump on the sofa, and do similar things that hurt others, from ever arising, without any form of advance blame or threats of retaliation."

"In other words, Larry, your slide rule will demonstrate how to prevent a young child, before he knows what it means that man's will is not free, from ever doing those things for which blame and punishment are now necessary as the lesser of two evils."

"Exactly. But our slide rule, where these very young children are concerned, can only have application by our realization that when we blame them even before something is actually done, we are motivating and justifying in advance that for which they are being accused. To put it another way, since it is mathematically impossible to blame a child for being born or for the subsequent needs and desires that develop from his nature in relation to those around him (because it is now a matter of undeniable knowledge that man's will is not free), we are given no alternative but to prevent what we cannot blame and punish anymore. Therefore, our slide rule sets up a mathematical standard to test all knowledge relating to children, by simply saying: 'From the very first day of birth it is important for the parents to determine only what they feel would be a real, not an imaginary hurt to their child and others, for which the baby, now and all through life, cannot be held responsible. But if they are unable to prevent their child from desiring what they feel will be a hurt, either to him or someone else, or unable to prevent him from not wanting what they think will be for his benefit (<u>both without any form of advance blame</u>), it is rather obvious that what they like or dislike for him — and cannot prevent without blame in some form — is something not in any way harmful to the child or others, and exists only as an imaginary fear based upon false knowledge, otherwise they would definitely have the power to prevent this harm without blame in any form.'"

"That was beautiful, Larry, but what does it mean?"

"You don't mean 'beautiful,' Jim, because as of now, between us, that word is obsolete. You meant to say, 'I like the way you expressed that, Larry.' Remember, Jim, there is a world of difference between the two expressions."

"Let me see if I know the difference, Larry. The one creates an external value when there is no such thing, while the other simply describes how I personally felt about your expression. The one places a lesser value on expressions not considered beautiful, which could make me look down on a person who did not talk in a particular manner. For example, I might like the expressions of Gibbon much better than those of Durant, but this doesn't make the one beautiful and the other ugly or not so beautiful. It only means that I, personally, like the way Gibbon writes better than Durant."

"I like the way you expressed that, Jim. In other words, you like the physical appearance of Julie better than other girls, but this doesn't make her beautiful because this would make other girls ugly. However, to clarify what you don't seem to completely understand about the mathematical standard I just set up, let me say this: If, for example, not eating a particular type food is thought to be harmful to a child, then the parents will be compelled to discover a way to prepare it so that he can like it the very first time it is tasted, for persuasion in any form can no more be used as it is a method of blame and an assumption of what is right for this child. But if they cannot prevent him from disliking this food no matter how it is prepared, or from liking rock and roll instead of Beethoven (without any form of advance blame), then it is mathematically obvious that the harm they perceive has existence only as a figment, or improper relation, of their mental development."

"Now wait just a minute, Larry, something doesn't seem to be kosher. If I teach a child to act in a certain way, this is advance blame, right?"

"That's right, you're blaming the child for desiring to act otherwise."

"But if by not teaching the child to act in a certain manner, he gets hurt by being criticized or ridiculed... Excuse me, Larry, for the moment I forgot that all criticism and ridicule are being removed. In other words, you're saying that there is no need to teach children anything anymore because this blames them in advance for acting otherwise, and since the only hurt they could receive is from this criticism, it is prevented by removing this blanket of blame."

"I didn't say that children should not be taught."

"But the moment you teach them anything, aren't they being blamed for not doing it?"

"It depends on the manner in which they are taught and on what they are taught. If I teach a child that two plus two equals four, I am not blaming him for anything, am I?"

"I don't think you are."

"But if I teach a child that spinach is healthy, I am expecting the child to eat spinach, which means that the child's desire is involved here."

"I see. The desire of the child is not involved in teaching him that two plus two equals four, unless he doesn't want to learn; but whenever his desire is involved in what is taught, then he is being blamed in advance."

"That's exactly right, Jim. Now let us see what our slide rule has to say about the many things that currently pass for knowledge, since to teach what is right and wrong, good and bad, presupposes the possession of this knowledge, right?"

"You've already demonstrated that man's will is not free, and that we don't have five senses. What other surprising knowledge are you going to reveal?"

"You'll see soon enough. I shall begin with the birth of a child and try to proceed with some order while letting you see the relation between the great need to earn a living and the development of false knowledge.

"Every year, millions of babies are blamed for being born with a foreskin, and the only proof that this is of no value for the body is the fact that its removal is sanctioned by the medical profession, which lays its arguments not on why this is better or healthier but on who says it is. Therefore, since there is no valid foundation for this operation when all religious and medical justifications have been removed, it is obvious that written and verbal knowledge as to why it is healthier is completely fallacious."

"Have you any idea, Larry, how much money is made every year on the removal of this foreskin?"

"But remember, Jim, these people are not going to be hurt by having their income stopped or reduced, so what do they care now?"

"I can see where they would care a little. Supposing a young doctor has only developed a practice of removing 1,000 foreskins a year, and he was aiming for a record of 10,000. How can he like you for upsetting his opportunity to break a record? Besides, his income could increase in this profession, but may never go up in something else."

"Don't misunderstand me, Jim, these doctors can continue removing the foreskin if they want to, but how is it possible for them to want to when this would only reveal their ignorance, not their knowledge?"

"But how do you really know it isn't healthier, Larry?"

"I just told you, because these doctors are compelled to blame the child for having a foreskin."

"Now wait a minute, Larry, not so fast. Are you trying to tell me that tonsils cannot be removed along with the appendix, nor a leg when gangrene sets in? According to what you just said, a doctor can't do anything because this blames God's handiwork, so to speak. Is that what you mean?"

"Yes and no, Jim. It is obvious that certain things need clarification."

"They certainly do. What are you trying to do, run these doctors out of business altogether?"

"Of course not. Anyway, in order to remove a part of the body, the medical profession must have absolute proof that a person's life is at stake unless it is removed or that his existence will be worse if he continues without the operation. In other words, there must be a mathematical line of demarcation, but there is no such line where the foreskin, the tonsils, and the appendix are concerned."

"But what about when the appendix gets infected, and when the tonsils swell up, isn't this dangerous to life?"

"In some instances, the removal of tonsils and the appendix is absolutely necessary; otherwise, the patient would die, but what about all the other times? How many doctors advocate the removal of these organs only because they are classified as vestigial, which means that Darwin's theory of evolution has been accepted as a fact for the purpose of justifying certain operations."

"Do you mean that we have not evolved from a lower order of species, like the apes?"

"I'm not interested in getting involved in a discussion as to what came first, the chicken or the egg, or in one as to the origin of man. However, just as long as this is a theory, a doctor is not justified in removing an organ by calling it vestigial, for this word states that evolution is a fact, and it is not. A doctor doesn't advocate removing a finger when it becomes infected because he doesn't classify it as vestigial, but when the tonsils get infected, he right away tells the parents that they should come out sooner or later because they do more harm than good, and the same with the appendix. Therefore, since this knowledge is based upon an assumption, a doctor will henceforth treat the appendix and the tonsils as just another part of the body. Should these organs become infected, and the body is incapable of taking care of this matter itself, then a doctor will try to treat the infection and remove the organ only as a last resort."

"Say Larry, little by little, you're putting these doctors out of business. What about obstetricians and pediatricians, don't they render a useful service to mankind?"

"The medical profession has established a tremendous fear in the minds of people that unless a person does as a doctor prescribes, they will only get worse. Consequently, a woman will spend a small fortune for the services of an obstetrician who doesn't really do anything of value except to reduce the pain. However, the pain is magnified so tremendously by fear, as is the case with a dentist, that the average woman is scared to death when she goes into labor. After the baby is born, she is made to think that she is too weak to do anything, and her not doing anything makes her weaker. Then she calls up her pediatrician, who comes out to make up a formula for the baby, as if the mother's milk is not the best formula in the world."

"Now wait a minute, Larry, there is certainly nothing wrong with a mother preferring bottle to breastfeeding, especially since her breasts are involved, right?"

"You're right, Jim, but supposing the doctor doesn't know what he's doing and the baby survives not because of his formula but in spite of it?"

"I don't understand."

"In other words, some babies might require only what the mother herself can give, and if this is not present in the formula of the doctor, then the body of the child must overcome this handicap or else get sick. As an example of what I mean, go get that book by Durant from your car, I'd like to read you something."

"Here it is, Larry."

"Thanks, Jim. He writes: 'In the first three months we were guilty of a grave blunder, for we allowed our child to be used as a laboratory for a newfangled form of desiccated milk. It is a crime which many years of parental solicitude cannot quite clear from our memories. We believe now, with Ben Franklin, that the human race should beware of young doctors and old barbers.' He implies that an old doctor couldn't make the same mistake. Now isn't this a perfect example of a child getting well in spite of the doctor who prescribed what the child's nourishment should be?"

"But that was years ago, Larry. Today, the doctors have greater knowledge of the body."

"You mean they think they have greater knowledge, don't you, Jim?"

"I really don't know what I mean. If I didn't have confidence in the knowledge of a doctor, how could I consult one? Besides, I certainly don't know what to do when I'm sick."

"If it gives you greater satisfaction to call in your doctor, you should definitely do what you think is better for yourself. However, the doctor himself, under the changed conditions, will be compelled to refrain from prescribing anything that he is the least bit uncertain of, because it cannot satisfy him to risk hurting others when there is no way it can be justified, that is, of course, once the schools stop making him think that he does know when he doesn't. In the future, should a doctor be asked if it is perfectly safe to feed a baby with a particular formula, he will be forced to admit his ignorance and say, 'I really don't know, Julie,' simply because he really doesn't know. Each child is different, to a degree, and many require the formula only the mother can generate to prevent colic and various other discomforts, but if she wishes to take whatever risk is involved to avoid breastfeeding her baby, this is her business, although she will have nobody but herself to hold responsible if something goes wrong."

"Why the name Julie, Larry? Is this your subtle way of suggesting that we have a child?"

"What possible difference does it make to me? I could have used any name."

"It just struck me funny because Julie and I both want children. By the way, what does your slide rule have to say about waking a baby for any kind of feeding, breast or bottle?"

"Since we cannot blame the child for anything, it is obvious that all knowledge that tries to teach it is healthier to wake children for a feeding is mathematically wrong."

"What about waking them to administer drugs?"

"Isn't it obvious that if you wake a child or adult for anything at all, you are blaming them for sleeping?"

"But Larry, there are certain times it is absolutely necessary to wake a child. Supposing the house is on fire?"

"Don't be ridiculous, Jim. Isn't it obvious the child doesn't want to burn up in a fire?"

"But isn't it also obvious that the child wants to be healthy and to have this health it is necessary to wake him for a feeding and a regimen of medicine?"

"Do you mean that after all this you are still unable to tell the difference between an assumption and a fact? Do you put waking a child because the house is on fire in the same category as waking him to swallow some medicine? Isn't it possible that sleep is of the utmost importance, much more valuable than the medicine, but there is no value in continuing to sleep when the house is on fire? This is the syllogistic reasoning doctors use when they want to make it appear that they know when they don't. Right now, if you called in a physician who prescribed a regimen of medicine around the clock, and you told him that your friend — the discoverer of certain knowledge that will change the world — told you that sleep was more important than to be awakened for medicine, he would say, 'Who is your friend; is he a doctor?' 'No, he isn't.' Well, there you are, that is your answer. Don't listen to these quacks. They don't know, they think they know. You take this medicine religiously at 4, 8, 12, 4, 8, 12. Set the alarm if you have to.' 'How much do I owe you, Doc?' 'Let me see... I was here last week two times, then there was that injection. The week before I... do you have an adding machine?' 'Right over there, Doc.' 'Thank you... That comes to $30 even.' 'That's pretty reasonable.'"

"Larry, that's not very nice. I really think you have a dislike for doctors."

"That's not true, Jim, because I know they are compelled to do everything they do, and only when the conditions change, when man understands that his will is not free and what this means, will they be able to change. After all, a doctor also has to make a living."

"My mother, Larry, out of a sort of instinct, never did trust the knowledge of a doctor, and one time when I was a child, to teach me a lesson, had one come out to the house when she was perfectly well. I'll never forget this. She pretended she was very sick. The doctor examined her and then prescribed some medicine, which she ordered right away. When the medicine came, she said, 'Now watch, son,' and she poured the whole bottle right down the toilet. 'Why did you do that, Mom?' 'I feel sorry for people who are struggling for a living. That doctor hasn't been doing too well in this neighborhood, neither has the pharmacist, so I thought I'd give them some business.' 'But why did you waste the medicine, Mom?' 'Who wasted it? The doctor and pharmacist have to earn a living, and I helped them in this respect, but I certainly don't have to follow their advice.'"

"My mother went a step further to prove a point. She actually took the medicine prescribed when she was well and threw up all over the place, but actually it wasn't the medicine prescribed. She replaced it with some kind of emetic. Then she turned to me and said, 'You see, Larry, just imagine what would have happened had I taken the medicine when my body was too sick to eject that stuff?'"

"This reminds me of Montaigne, Larry, who said that in trying to make him well, his doctor nearly killed him."

"But that was so long ago, Jim, when medicine was in its infancy. Today, the doctors have so much more knowledge, and they have so many more words to describe our ailments. A cousin of my wife, in his fifties, went to one for a six-month checkup. After giving him a thorough examination, the doctor stopped, looked quizzically at the floor, tapped a pencil on his own forehead, and said... 'I don't know.' 'What don't you know?' said my wife's cousin with a worried look on his face. 'I'm trying to make up my mind whether you have Xyczeghusites or Idykfyjffkskdls.' The poor guy got so frightened by hearing names he couldn't understand that, together with his high blood pressure, he had a heart attack three days later, worrying about it. I learned about this from his sister on the day of the funeral. My father died in a hospital as a result of an experiment. An hour before he took his last breath, I asked the doctor what the condition of my dad was. 'He's doing pretty good, but we're trying a new drug, and we only hope his body can tolerate it.'"

"I'm sorry to hear about your father, Larry."

"Think nothing of it, Jim, for it was God's will, as it was also his will that 6 million Jews get slaughtered. But it is not His will that these things continue, and when the knowledge of what it means that man's will is not free is thoroughly understood by the medical profession, and when the transition gets officially launched, you will see, for the very first time, an honest admission of genuine ignorance."

"Well, what do you say that we return to children. Sometimes these digressions, although somewhat related to the subject, can be rather lengthy."

"In other words, Jim, you are blaming me for this lengthy digression, right?"

"I suppose I am, Larry, but I didn't even realize it. I'm so in the habit of blaming somebody for something. But aren't you blaming me for blaming you?"

"Not really, Jim, because I'm still trying to ignite you as the fuse, and I want to make sure that you fully understand the many ways in which a person can be blamed. Not having too much time because you want to get back to Julie and take care of several things — and yet wishing to hear more about children — you blamed me for not using good judgment as to when I should have ended the digression, which, in reality, is an insult and a hurt to me. But if you were conscious of this hurt and realized that I would never blame you for hurting me this way, you would have bitten your tongue before telling me to get back on the subject."

"I'm beginning to understand, little by little. By the way, when will the subject of education be discussed?"

"When we finish with children."

"And then what follows?"

"Death."

"Is that the end?"

'No, Jim, death is not the end, as you will see."

"You know what I mean, Larry. Is it the end of our discussions?"

"I know what you meant, Jim. Yes, it is the end. Anyway... to get back on track, the first real problem with a child arises when he begins to annoy the parents with his cries and screams, which interrupt many pleasurable activities and moments of relaxation. Since they cannot blame him for what he is compelled to do, there is only one possibility open; they must try to prevent, without any form of blame, this desire to scream and cry from arising. However, should these not be prevented, then the only alternative, as the lesser of two evils, is to blame the child by trying to quiet him in some manner."

"But Larry, doctors say that crying is good for a baby's lungs."

"That may be, Jim, but the noise is bad for my ears; I don't know about you."

"Do you mean that your concern is not for the welfare of the child, but what is better for yourself?"

"In this case, that's right. Who likes to hear screams and cries, to stay up half the night walking or rocking the baby to sleep because every time you put him down, or stop rocking, he starts up all over again. Would you like it, Jim?"

"Not in a million years. But Larry, sometimes you can't stop a child from crying, no matter what you try to do to correct it, let alone prevent it from arising. What do you do then?"

"Let me demonstrate how easy it is to prevent a child from crying at all, except for food. In 99% of cases, except where the formula disagrees with the baby, the child screams only because he is spoiled, which is a word to describe a habit, not good or bad, the parents allow to develop and then blame him for their annoyance. Consequently, if he is fed with the proper nourishment, the mother's formula, kept clean, made comfortable, and is not in pain, the only thing that could make him cry is this desire to be picked up and played with, which develops from being picked up <u>when he cries</u>. So if this is a source of annoyance to have to rock the baby to sleep, pace the floor at odd hours of the night because you can't put him down unless you prefer the screaming, then you had better think twice before picking him up when he cries, even to feed him, which can be done, breast or bottle, without picking him up. This does not mean that a baby should never be picked up and played with, on the contrary, it could be done often depending on your desire, but when he is not crying, providing (and I qualify this because it is not harmful to pick him up when he is crying)... providing you don't want to develop this annoying habit."

"But Larry, what about when grandparents and friends, hearing the baby cry, just take it upon themselves to pick him up?"

"They will understand this could develop into an annoying habit, which would hurt the parents who would never blame them for this. Consequently, they are given no choice but to play with the baby only when he is not crying."

"Supposing people want to pick up the baby when he isn't crying, should they ask permission of the mother first?"

"Jim, where is your head? Isn't this asking a favor, and . . .?"

"That's right, Larry, it is. Well, what happens if Grandma is visiting, for example?"

"The mother, knowing that no one will ever ask permission or take it upon himself to pick up the baby without receiving an OK, will say, 'Mom, would you like to play with the baby and pick him up?' If Grandma doesn't want to, she will simply say, 'No thank you.' If she does, she would say, 'Yes, I would.' You must understand, Jim, that this slide rule is an invariable law that gives no one a free choice — once it is thoroughly understood. But no choice before this was known, too."

"Well, Larry, what's the next problem with our little angels?"

"When they begin to crawl, for if they should knock lamps over, scratch the furniture, or hurt themselves in some manner, we have no one to blame but ourselves. Consequently, we must prevent this hurt without any form of advance blame, but this presents somewhat of a problem because the moment we check a child's desire to knock over a lamp by saying — 'don't,' 'naw naw,' 'mustn't, stop,' it is obvious that we are blaming him for being in a position where this damage could be done; and even if we pick him up every time he is about to do something we'd rather he didn't do, we are still blaming in advance his desire to do it, and his desire will be aroused all the more to do that of which he is accused in advance, giving him motivation with justification. Then when he does it we criticize, blame and punish him for what is our own responsibility. Consequently, we strike the first blow by allowing the child to be in a position to have desires that require checking, and he will get satisfaction in retaliating because he resents our standing in the way of what he wants to do. Therefore, to prevent those desires from arising, those that hurt us by climbing on and knocking over furniture, there is only one possible solution to this problem without advance blame, and that is to keep the children in a playroom, play yard or playpen where he cannot hurt himself in any way, or desire to do the things which previously required the checking of his motion from here to there. We are given no choice when it is impossible to blame in any form.

By the time he walks, he will have learned the difference between play and living quarters without ever being blamed. Then he will never desire to play with his toys in the wrong part of the house without ever having to be told; but by constantly telling him not to do this, don't do that, he will soon desire to do it all the more simply because you are daring or challenging him. Remember, nothing is stopping you from saying, 'don't,' 'stop,' 'naw naw', etc., if you want to, but how is it possible to want to when you know that this will only encourage your children to do the very things you do not want. Once you strike the first blow by allowing certain desires to arise that require checking, then you will be compelled to blame and punish as the lesser of two evils, bringing about a chain reaction of unpleasant experiences while leaving yourself vulnerable to spoiling."

"But Larry, isn't it just about impossible to control the environment to such a degree that these desires cannot arise? I consider Durant a pretty good thinker..."

"Jim, how in the world am I ever going to light you up with this knowledge if you don't grasp these fundamental principles? Isn't asking favors a form of advance blame?"

"Certainly."

"Doesn't an opinion blame in advance the possibility of disagreement? Aren't you blaming me for thinking that Durant is not a good thinker when you say that you think he is?"

"That's right, it is a form of advance blame. I completely forgot. Anyway, Durant says somewhere in his book... let me find it... he agrees with you on a lot of points... here it is... he says, 'First, use the word don't sparingly;' now isn't that what you mean when you say parents shouldn't say, 'stop,' 'don't,' 'naw naw,' etc.?"

"But what does he say next, Jim?"

"That's just the point, Larry, he doesn't seem to agree with you on your method of controlling the environment of the child, because he says next: 'If a child misbehaves, apologize to it; for you have misfed or maltreated it. Don'ts are necessary, but like a doctor with alcoholic prescriptions, and perhaps, like the doctor, he should exhaust his annual allotment on January first, and leave himself a clean slate for the rest of the year.' In other words, Durant says that don'ts are necessary, and I must agree with him."

"Bully for you, Jim, but does agreement make something true? Durant is a typical example of a man who does not know the truth at all, but thinks he knows, for which he cannot be blamed because he, like the rest of us, is moving in the direction of satisfaction. If it wasn't for his mistakes, I would never have made my discovery. However, the reason he says parents should be restricted to a limited number of 'don'ts' is only because it is mathematically impossible, in the world of free will, to eliminate all of them."

"Both of us may be wrong in our agreement, Larry, but it seems to be impossible not to say 'no' to some of the children's desires, regardless of how you control the environment. Just take bedtime alone, I think Durant handles it beautifully... I mean, I like the way he handles it. Let me read this one passage: 'Many a bribe of tender words, and dimpled arms about the neck, has been offered us for permission to "stay up" beyond the year's decreed retiring time. But here we have been quietly and inconspicuously resolute; we will not condescend even to discuss so absurd a proposal; we turn it aside as a criminal idea, and send Ethel up to Morpheus every evening at her usual early hour. Now, though she is a great lady of almost ten years, she still disappears regularly at eight-fifteen, wishes us from the staircase "tight sleep and pleasant dreams," and is all tucked in and set by half-past eight. The law has been broken now and then, as when some genius of the piano was honoring our home; but for the most part, it has been with us a sacred monastic rule, a trifle of surpassing moment in our philosophy.' Now, Larry, what is wrong with the way he handled this?"

"Everything, Jim, once it is known as a matter of knowledge that man's will is not free, and what this means. Isn't he blaming the possibility of his daughter desiring to stay up beyond what he decreed is her retiring time? And when she expresses this desire by asking permission, doesn't he say, 'we will not condescend even to discuss so absurd a proposal?' which means he is showing no respect for her desire."

"But Larry, children have to get up early for school, and they should have a minimum of eight hours' sleep. 'Early to bed and early to rise . . .'"

"Yeah Jim, I've heard it many times before."

"But isn't it true?"

"Of course it isn't true. How much sleep any child requires is determined by their body. Some may desire to sleep ten hours, others eleven, and many more only seven or less. How is it possible for any doctor or philosopher to know what is better, when there is no mathematical standard to determine this?"

"Even if you are right on this point, what if a child should go to bed at 3 in the morning and must get up at 7 for school? Isn't it obvious that he would be exhausted, and shouldn't the parents try to prevent this exhaustion? If Durant didn't set up a 'decreed retiring time,' his daughter, having a lot of fun with visitors, might forget that she has to get up really early for school. Besides, I would like to have a dollar for the number of children that, just because they were exhausted the next day, didn't go to school or were late. By the way — to change the subject for just a moment — I notice that Durant refers to a child with the pronoun 'it,' but you always use 'he,' why is that, and who is right?"

"This is just a matter of personal taste."

"But aren't there rules of good English that prove Durant is correct?"

"Perhaps there are, but the purpose of these rules is to allow an individual to express himself in a manner that is less ambiguous and more clear. There is no ambiguity about the person to whom I am referring when using 'he' instead of 'it.' Besides, how is it possible for anyone to blame me anymore for my not conforming to the rules, when, first, I am not hurting anyone, and second, when it is known that man's will is not free and what this means?"

"Okay Larry, you nonconformist; I'm satisfied with your answer. This change is certainly going to hurt a lot of people by denying them the right to continue criticizing those who are different than themselves."

"You are wrong, Jim, because this is not a genuine hurt. The person hurt is the one criticized, not the critic, by being denied the right to laugh and ridicule. Furthermore, he is not being denied if he wishes to continue, but, of course, we know that he will not be able to. The critic strikes the first blow unless the person criticized has done something to hurt him. If he has not, then the critic cannot possibly have any justification when all blame is removed in advance. You must understand that in the new world, all forms of blame must be removed because man's will is not free. Durant blames his daughter by imposing standards of what he thinks is better for her."

"But shouldn't parents do what they think is better for their children?"

"Definitely, but remember the mathematical standard that was just set up by our slide rule for the purpose of testing the accuracy of what parents think: 'From the very first day of birth it is important for the parents to determine only what they feel would be a real, not imaginary hurt to their child and others, for which the baby, now and all through life, cannot be held responsible. But if they are unable to prevent their child from desiring what they feel will be a hurt, either to him or someone else, or unable to prevent him from not wanting what they think will be for his benefit (both without any form of advance blame), it is rather obvious that what they like or dislike for him, and cannot prevent without blame in any form, is something not in any way harmful to the child or others, and exists only as an imaginary fear based upon false knowledge, otherwise they would definitely have the power to prevent this harm without blame in any form.'"

"Simply beautiful, Larry! I mean... I keep forgetting... I like that very much."

"Consequently, we can test the knowledge of Durant and other parents who think this way or other ways, very simply. By setting up a 'decreed retiring time,' he blames his daughter in advance for her desire to stay up beyond that time. However, this doesn't mean that Durant shouldn't do everything in his power to get her in bed at that hour that is 'a trifle of surpassing moment in his philosophy.' God isn't stopping him from satisfying his desire, but he must do it without blaming her desire. This means that he and his wife must set an example by shutting off the television, he must stop whatever he and his wife are doing, they must turn off all the lights at a very early hour, and then get in bed. However, if she doesn't want to imitate, this is her business, not that of her parents, and if she should desire to go downstairs after they are in bed and turn on the television to watch a later show, there is absolutely nothing they can do about it without blaming her desire. Consequently, this proves that there is no harm whatsoever in a child not going to bed at a specific hour, simply because the parents cannot prevent it without blame."

"But wait a minute, Larry. What if a child gets up late for school, is punished by the teacher, gets behind in his schoolwork, and eventually fails? This certainly is a hurt to the child and to the parents, right?"

"Completely wrong, Jim; must I explain everything?"

"You're blaming me, Larry; I caught you this time. And if you knew that this was a hurt to me, because you are criticizing the fact that I can't catch on as quickly as others, and that I would never blame you for this, you couldn't do it."

"Very true, Jim. However, I knew that I was blaming you and hoping you would detect it. Nevertheless, if a child, regardless of his age, wants to go to school, this is his business, not that of his parents or others. Therefore, he would set the alarm clock at the time he wishes to get up. If he doesn't get to school on time, this is also his business. However, this child will know that by coming in late to class he will interrupt the lesson, even though it is for a fraction of a second, which distracts the teacher and other children. Since he also knows that this annoyance will never be blamed by the teacher or other children, because they know he can't help himself when he knows otherwise, he is given no choice but to get there on time, if he is interested in school."

"But Larry, education is very important, and many children thank their parents in later life for forcing them to get it. If my mother didn't get me out of bed every morning and literally chase me to school, I doubt that I would have finished elementary school. Besides, a person who has a certain amount of education gets a better job. Three of my friends, the other day, were all turned down because they didn't have a high school education. At that moment, I'll bet my bottom dollar they wished their mother had seen to it that they had gotten an education."

"But Jim, you have set up an assumption as a major premise in a syllogistic equation, from which to reason. You are assuming that what the mother wants her children to develop into is impossible without employing force, or perhaps I should say, advance blame. Furthermore, you are assuming that the mother knows what is better for her child to develop into, more so than the child. The very fact that the school system and parents are permitted to blame him, they are not compelled to change their ways. But when they are not permitted to blame, you will behold a fantastic transition, as you will see very shortly."

"Do you mean that children will desire to go to school of their own free will?"

"It will not be of their own free will, naturally, but they will want to go only because they want to go, without anybody influencing or forcing them."

"If that's the case, then parents won't have to worry anymore about forcing their children."

"That's right, Jim, but remember, in order to get children to want what mother knows is truly better for them, it is first necessary to remove the forces that try to prevent the desire of these children from not becoming what mother and the school think is best. It is the same with government and religion, do you recall?"

"I can't think back that far, Larry."

"To render war and crime impossibilities, it is first necessary to remove the forces that try to prevent these evils through threats of retaliation, because this kind of effort unconsciously motivates and justifies the very things these forces are trying to prevent."

"Now I remember you saying that."

"Consequently, though Durant did what he thought was actually better for his daughter under the existing conditions, when the conditions change, and he is permitted to see what is truly better for himself, he is given no choice but to become a part of the change."

"But Larry, even though I understand most of what you said, and I do agree, what about a preschool child desiring to stay up while a party is going on? Supposing I want privacy, and here comes my four-year-old wandering into the room at midnight. Do you mean I can't send her up to bed?"

"Jim, you can do anything you want to do, nobody is going to blame your actions. But if your friends see you do this, they will know that you are truly ignorant of the fact that man's will is not free and what this means. They would look at you with a certain amount of amazement, just as they would should you ask one of them to do you a favor or tell them what to do. At the present time, the opposite is true; they would look at you in amazement if you didn't send her up to bed."

"Well, supposing I am alone in the house, except for my daughter, and she comes in to watch a television show I think she shouldn't see because it is too scary. Can't I send her up then?"

"You can if you want to, but how is it possible to want to when blaming her desires will only bring about a horrible relationship between you? Anytime you stand in the way of a child's desires, you hurt yourself."

"But what about when my daughter's desires hurt me? Isn't she striking the first blow then, and don't I have the right to retaliate?"

"The only way she could hurt you is by standing in the way of your desires."

"Well, isn't her coming in at midnight when I'm watching 'Chiller' a hurt to my desire, since I have to either turn it off or send her upstairs?"

"Why must you send her upstairs? Weren't you watching the show? If it's good enough for you, why isn't it good enough for her?"

"She might get scared half to death."

"I suppose that if you were drinking a highball or a beer, and she wanted to taste it, you would not allow this either, right?"

"Well, it isn't proper for children, especially at such a young age, to drink these things."

"Aren't you assuming that she would drink it? Would you bet your $2000 that if I lined up one hundred small children, who have never been influenced to become more like an adult, that they would drink beer in preference to milk? I wouldn't take your money, Jim. Every one of them would spit it out because they wouldn't like the taste. But when you constantly tell a child you can't have this, that, or something else, because these things are not for children, then you have created in their minds a value that is now being denied. Consequently, they will drink and watch what they really don't enjoy, only because they are trying to discover what this unknown value is. If your daughter sat down beside you to watch something that had a tendency to frighten her, she would simply get up and walk away while wondering what you see in them. However, assuming that this might not be completely true, and you are still worried, then the only thing to do, to be absolutely certain that she may never wake up and come in unexpectedly while these horror stories are on, is to go to a bar to watch your show, or not watch it at all. There is nothing else you can do when you can't blame the child in any form."

"But wouldn't this kind of attitude spoil a child?"

"A spoiled child is one who insists on doing what you don't want him to do, and who gets his way. But how is it mathematically possible to spoil a child, under the changed conditions, when spoiling requires that you stand in the way of his desires first, and when he knows you don't want him to do certain things which will never be done? It's true the child in the new world will get his way, but when you and the child are not hurt, what difference does it make, just as long as you also get your way? No one is stopping you from watching the television, if not at home, elsewhere, so why should you judge that your child should not watch it, if he wants to?"

"But there are so many things children shouldn't be allowed to see."

"Well, who is stopping you from doing your utmost to prevent this? You could eliminate television altogether from your own home, but this won't stop a child from watching television in other homes. You could keep all the doors and windows locked so he doesn't know of any other world to arouse his desire. Can't you see, Jim, that the moment you have to sacrifice what you want to prevent your children's desire, then you begin to wonder about the reliability of the knowledge you learned over the years. Just as long as Durant didn't have to sacrifice hours working on his books, he didn't object to setting up a 'decreed retiring time.' But if he had to go to bed every night at eight thirty, when his desire was to stay up thinking and writing, he would soon find all kinds of flaws with the knowledge that says, 'early to bed and early to rise.' The reason all this so-called knowledge came into existence was to enable parents to satisfy desires they felt couldn't be satisfied any other way. That is why Durant says, 'Don'ts are necessary,' because how else could he manage to stay downstairs while sending Ethel up to Morpheus? But remember, Jim, this kind of attitude was unavoidable under the banner of free will."

"But there have to be some desires that conflict with those of his parents, before a child is taught what it means that man's will is not free. Supposing a four-year-old should ask his father, 'Daddy, will you run me over to Grandma's house? I want to see her.' Now tell me, Larry, how is it possible to satisfy the desire of the child if you don't feel like making the trip?"

"This, Jim, is a horse of another color, since the desire of the child involves your own. When walking in while you're watching television, to watch it also, he is not asking that you do anything, but should he say, 'Daddy, I don't like that show, will you please change it,' then we have a different problem."

"Well, how do you solve it without blaming the desire of the child, and how can you prevent this condition of the environment from arising? According to you, we must not blame children for anything, before or after."

"That's not true, Jim, and you have already forgotten the anecdote about my brother. The little boy who jumped on the sofa also wanted to satisfy his desire, but it was my brother's desire, and the desire of the little boy's father, that he not jump on the sofa. Consequently, under these conditions, since the child has not yet learned what it means that his will is not free, we have a perfect right to refuse the satisfaction of a desire that involves or hurts us. In other words, the child's desire is to see Grandma, not necessarily that Daddy takes him; consequently, it may be possible to get him there without sacrificing your desire not to go. If, however, there is no other way to get him there, and you still don't want to go, which is your privilege, then you must explain to him that you do not want to go because you are doing something you prefer, but also explain that you do not mind him going if transportation can be furnished. Should he insist that you take him, then under no conditions must you give in, because this develops a spoiled child who will make all kinds of demands. But remember, Jim, this only applies when children have needs that involve your desire for their satisfaction."

"What about if you and your child want to watch different television shows, and the set is not on? In other words, nobody is watching a show."

"You simply flip a coin, what else? Your desire because you're older is no more important than his. It is necessary to remember that children do have some desires that definitely require the assistance of their parents for satisfaction. When they know what it means that man's will is not free, then they will be prevented from asking favors. But dad, knowing this, and also knowing that they will never take advantage of his generosity, will ask every now and then if there is anything he can do for them. Then little Jimmy will respond to dad's question, 'Yes, Daddy, there is something I would like you to do for me. I would appreciate being taken over to Grandma's. But until these principles are taught, parents have a perfect right to refuse the satisfaction of any desires that involve their own. All other desires, however, are not their business just as long as no one is being hurt by their children. Have I made myself clear, Jim?"

"Not completely. I know that young children will not imitate too readily certain things that will reflect on the parents when these are not done. For example, suppose my little girl receives a gift from a friend. Isn't it proper to teach her to say, 'Thank you?'"

"Of course not. Do you teach a child to walk or talk?"

"But that's different. It is good manners to say 'thank you' when receiving a gift, and if a child doesn't say it..."

"Mother gets embarrassed as to what the giver must think of her training and her child, and she makes a scene of some sort in an effort to get this customary response, for which the donor patiently waits. Right, Jim?"

"Right."

"But when mother knows that the giver is not going to judge them, not going to criticize or talk against them in any way, because the donor knows he has not been hurt the slightest bit..."

"Wait a minute, Larry, not so fast. Hasn't the giver a right to expect appreciation for what he gives?"

"Of course not. How is it possible to expect a person to act in a certain way without blaming him for acting otherwise? What is the difference between telling your little girl to say 'thank you,' and the giver to expect it?"

"But Larry, isn't it nicer when a child does say 'thank you?'"

"It is human nature, Jim, to thank somebody for rendering a service or giving a gift, and any person would do this normally. However, when a giver expects something in return, then he is not a giver but a salesman; in other words, he wants to be paid. But when you are given a gift for which you know positively there is no obligation attached whatsoever, not even to say 'thank you,' you will desire, of your own free will, to say 'thanks' from the bottom of your heart. And when a child sees and hears with what sincerity his parents thank people for what is given generously, without expecting anything in return, he will soon imitate the very things they have been unsuccessfully trying to force. However, Jim, there is a certain amount of subtle humor here."

"What's that, Larry?"

"When a child, in the world of free will (our present day and age) received a gift, the parents, feeling an unconscious twinge of obligation, shifted the responsibility of meeting it to their children, rather than meet it themselves; but when the obligation is removed, the desire to shift the responsibility disappears, the parents will be sincerely grateful without being under obligation, will express their thanks, and the children will imitate — all with one clean sweep of God's magic elixir, Thou Shall Not Blame, when both parties to an action understand what this means."

"I like that very much, Larry. But I still feel that there are certain situations in which blame is necessary, situations that do not include the imposition of a child's desire on his parents."

"Like what, for instance?"

"Like eating too much candy, cake, and ice cream. Or what about the development of talent? Supposing a very young child shows musical ability, shouldn't the parents influence him to desire what could lead to fame and fortune? Do you mean that parents can't mold him into what they think he would later be grateful for, because this blames him in advance for not desiring, at that moment, what they want? And what about food? Do you mean there is as much value in pickles and candy as in potatoes and meat?

Isn't it fitting for a mother to direct her angels towards what she thinks is better for them?"

"The mathematical standard set up by our slide rule, Jim, takes all this into consideration. Parents are supposed to do everything in their power to get their children to do what is thought to be better. But — and this is our mathematical standard — they must do it without blame in any form. To better illustrate what I mean, hand me that book by Durant."

"Larry... you slipped up... You told me what to do or asked me to do you a favor, one of the two, and both are forms of blame, remember?"

"You're right, Jim. I did the same thing before when I sent you to the car to get it. You might be my fuse yet. Anyway, on page... here it is... 240... he says: 'So with the piano. This is a problem that agitates every home: "Go and do your practice!" It is a silly phrase, for it suggests, most unmistakably, "Piano is a bore, practicing is torture; go and suffer; you deserve it." We tried another plan with Ethel; we merely offered her the opportunity to learn the piano if she wished; we left it to her choice. But for weeks before putting the question we spoke of the glory of music, and of the high privilege of performing or composing it. Then we looked about for a teacher who would begin not with sleepy scales and terrifying finger-exercises, but with simple, ear catching melodies that would set the whole household humming them. We found the teacher, and soon our home rang with tunes played by a chubby finger laboriously. We older ones went about our work singing the melodies that Ethel evoked; she was pleased to note our delight, and felt herself already an artist; at the very outset the piano meant music to her, not noise and pain.'"

"I remember the passage well, Larry. I hope you're not going to tell me that something is wrong with that. He didn't use force and simply aroused her desire to do what he felt was better for her."

"That's the rub, Jim. Not better for her, in reality, but better for him. If he were sincerely interested in what was truly better for her, then he would have allowed her to hear every kind of musical instrument and every type of music for the sole purpose of letting her choose for herself what gave her the greatest satisfaction. But if he did that, then she might select rock and roll in preference to Beethoven, and she might prefer a set of drums to the piano. Consequently, he couldn't risk this possibility, so he limited her environment."

"But Larry, you distinctly said it was perfectly all right to control the environment. You even did it yourself when you placed the crawling baby in the playpen, play yard or playroom. Besides, if the noise of drums and bugles would disrupt his writing, he certainly has a right to prevent this from arising, especially when his desire is involved. Didn't you put the baby in the playpen solely to prevent him from knocking over a lamp or something else, which would hurt you by having to pay for another one?"

"That's true, Jim, all but for one thing. I gave the child the freedom of the playpen, play yard, or playroom, and only kept the kind of toys out that could hurt the child; but Durant did not give his daughter the freedom of the musical world, only a part of it. Therefore, he blames the other part of this world not because of any hurt it might do his daughter, and does not want his daughter to have anything to do with it."

"But let's say he doesn't blame this other world, Larry, just that he likes a certain type of music better than others, certain instruments better than others. Don't you like one type of music in preference to others?"

"I certainly do. I can't stand listening to rock and roll. To me, it sounds like the clanging together of pots and pans. But my three children enjoy it, and my little boy is in love with the Beatles. Now, if I tried to influence them to like what I like, then I would be blaming them in advance for not liking it. When I put the baby in the playpen, I wasn't blaming his desire for one type of toy in preference to another."

"But Larry, in the world of free will (you've got me doing it now), parents were influenced by the criticism and ridicule of friends and relatives, and if Durant belonged to a cultured group that looked down on rock and roll, etc., he would have preferred the piano and certain music to the risk of being looked down upon."

"That's right, Jim, but when this blanket of blame, criticism, and ridicule is removed, when all words that describe nonexisting external values become obsolete, then the only thing that could prevent a man like Durant from desiring that his daughter prefer the piano to the drums would be the pain to himself of having to listen to that all day long. Now, to show you that he actually did blame his daughter for not wanting to learn, he says in the next paragraph: 'Later a plateau in her progress came: she did not want to practice anymore; and we had to gird our lions and fight the demons of passion and custom that bade us command and compel. Instead, I sat down at the piano and practiced the lesson myself; it was within the measure of my ability. Then I invited Ethel to join me and make it a program for four hands. She came, and for a week I practiced with her; when she did not care to come I played her pieces alone. The teacher provided us with simple duets, and we learned them together. (At this very moment she has called up to me, 'Daddy, come down and practice with me!') Rapidly her pleasure in the piano returned. Soon she was playing simplified selections from Beethoven, Mozart, Schumann, Schubert, Handel, Haydn and Bach; we sang these famous strains with gusto, and made her know how grateful we were that she was filling our hearts with song. She came to feel that music was a great boon, worth all the trouble that it involved. 'Now,' she says, after playing the Adieu to the Piano, 'I understand why you're so crazy about Beethoven.'"

"I don't know about you, Larry, but I think Durant did an excellent job in arousing her interest again, without resorting to the demons of passion and custom that make us command and compel."

"You plagiarist, you! I've got a good notion to report you to Durant."

"Seriously, though, Larry, what is so wrong with what he did?"

"In the world of free will, nothing at all. In fact, it was commendable when compared with what other parents did. But when compared with what God instructs through our mathematical revelation, it becomes obsolete. Under the new conditions, Durant has two possibilities: either let his daughter select from among the various types of music and instruments while he lives elsewhere — just in case she chooses drums and bugles — or let her select from among the various types of music and instruments while he lives at home, regardless of what she chooses. In either case, he can't blame her anymore for her desire to be different than what he wants her to be. If she doesn't want to practice, this is her business, not his, and if she wants to play chopsticks instead of Beethoven, this is also her business. Everything he did was to satisfy his desire, not hers. It was psychological trickery that he found preferable."

"But Larry, she is grateful now."

"Gratitude is not in question, Jim, but happiness. If Durant had been my father, I would have developed in any direction he wanted me to go because his psychological techniques were pretty effective. Is it difficult to get a child to eat more by putting such small portions on his plate that he is compelled to keep asking for more, or less by using reverse psychology? When parents do these things, they are concerned with the satisfaction of their own desires, not that of their children. Mother thinks her child is underweight or overweight; therefore, she is interested in restoring the balance for her own satisfaction, at the expense of her children. Durant's daughter might have preferred playing with dolls or soldiers, or doing any number of things, but he resented her not practicing, so he set out methodically to force her to give up what was making her happy — not practicing — to do what made him happy. And no matter how you look at this, it is pure and simple selfishness."

"But Larry, it is a different kind of selfishness. It is true that he desired she give up certain preferences, but he wanted her to develop in a direction that he thought would make her ultimately more happy, and you certainly can't blame him for doing what he thought was better for his daughter and himself."

"That's true, Jim, but God is putting an end to all kinds of selfishness, and he is insisting that everybody henceforth, once the transition gets underway, mind his own business, which includes the kind that previously allowed parents to judge what they thought was better for their children when advance blame is involved."

"You don't mean he is insisting, but that he is showing us a way which gives us no choice but to move in this direction when all the facts are understood."

"I really liked the way you expressed that."

"Thank you, Larry, but I'm still not satisfied. If parents have a talented child, and by developing this, they, as a family, could become wealthy and famous, why shouldn't the parents move in that direction when this is a real, not imaginary value?"

"The answer is very simple, Jim. Only an untalented child needs to be pushed; a truly talented individual, in the new world, that is, will move in the direction of development, especially if the values to himself are recognized, without any form of advance blame being necessary."

"I'm still not satisfied that all advance blame can be removed. What about teaching a child to swim; don't you have to try and prevent him from drowning?"

"Since it is impossible to blame him for his desire, and since a very young child might desire to jump in water that is over his head, or slip and fall, he must be equipped with something so secure around his body that there is no chance of his head going under. However, once he understands the dangers involved and discovers how easy it is to prevent himself from drowning, then he will have no fear of the water. But under no conditions must parents put the child into the water, for this assumes that he wants to go and blames him for not wanting to. With something wrapped around his body while he plays on the sand or grass, then should he decide to go in, there will be nothing to check his desire. Without this, a certain amount of advance blame is necessary. Remember, he will have a normal fear of the water, but when you try to protect him by constantly checking his desire, he will soon lose this normal fear and jump into the water even if it is over his head because he sees you going in and resents your standing in his way. This is equivalent to the boy who went outside on a freezing day without a jacket, and then ate an entire bag of candy, because it gave him great satisfaction to do the very things his mother had been constantly telling him not to do."

"I'm beginning to yield, Larry, but what about this eating of candy? How is it possible to prevent children from desiring these unhealthy foods? Supposing mother prepared a chicken dinner, and the kids fill up on cake, ice cream, and candy. Isn't she allowed to use even a little bit of blame to prevent this?"

"Not the slightest bit. God is very emphatic when He reveals this law. But remember, the understanding of this law only demonstrates how we can at last accomplish the very things we have unsuccessfully been attempting to bring about."

"Well, supposing mother has done everything in her power to prevent this without blame, and the kids still continue to do the things she knows are bad for their health, what then?"

"Then whatever fears she has exist only in her imagination. However, God is not going to allow her to solve this problem without a little assistance, because it may be over her head. Besides, what do you think He hired me for?"

"Are you getting paid a salary, Larry?"

"Strictly commission, and sometimes I'm sorry I took the job. But this guy God is a smart cookie, believe me. He didn't even ask me if I wanted to take the job; he just talked me into it. And you know, I still haven't been paid a goddamned dime. But if I don't get paid soon, I'm definitely quitting. He can get himself another salesman. Have you any idea how tough it is to break through this sound barrier of learned ignorance, Jim?"

"I can imagine."

"These guys, like Durant, are a real stumbling block. They don't know, but what they don't know is taught from one end of the earth to the other, and this knowledge that isn't knowledge is used as a standard to test knowledge that is knowledge, which permits them to tell me that I am wrong when I know that I am right. The man who believes the world is flat tells the man who knows it is round that he doesn't know what he's talking about. The man who believes that man's will is free tells the man who knows it is not free that he doesn't know what he's talking about. For the life of me, Jim, I can't figure out why God hired me when he has so many assistants already. I know several rabbis and priests who would love to have the job, and I don't think they would have charged as high a price for their services. Oh well, let me get back to work.

Now the problem of candy comes in the category of eating and drinking, but this is a mother's domain, and since it is she who has to prepare the meals, her desire must be considered. After all, she isn't running a restaurant. However, in the new world, she will not be able to blame her children for not liking what she cooks, nor will she be able to persuade them in any form for the same reason. Consequently, if she wants her family to eat what she judges to be of greater value, then she must prepare everything in a manner that makes them like what they taste. Under no conditions will she use psychological techniques to get them to eat more or less, for any effort blames their desire to be different, which is their privilege. All she will do is put the food on the table, nothing on their plate, and let them eat the quantity their body desires, without any form of discrimination."

"Supposing they eat nothing?"

"She still leaves them alone because this is their business, not hers. Her business is to prepare what she thinks her family will enjoy, but before long, she will know that certain vegetables, meats, poultry, and fish are preferable to others; also, the approximate amount each will consume. Under these conditions mother will soon know how many meals a day to prepare, and what is the best time to eat; but just as long as she believes that children need three meals a day, that they require so much of this and so much of that, she is given no choice but to force or persuade them to do what she feels is better for their health. However, all this knowledge is proven to be completely false by the use of our slide rule."

"Candy, Larry, what about candy?"

"I'm coming to that, Jim. Now at the dinner table, in our present world, children see that certain foods and drinks are for adults only, which blames their desire to have the same. They also discover that dessert is something special at the end of a meal, usually given as a bonus if the rest of the food is eaten in sufficient quantity, which blames their desire not to eat. Consequently, it doesn't take long before they will desire this dessert wherever and whenever it can be gotten, and they will also discover a yen to become more quickly an adult so they can drink coffee, tea, beer, highballs, lowballs, chew tobacco, and smoke. Many children do these things behind their parents' backs, and their satisfaction is not derived from any great pleasure in drinking and smoking, until a habit is formed, but from the thrill of being a young grown-up.

Many children and adults overeat and get sick only because of this distinction between appetizer, the main course, and dessert, which makes them desire to eat the latter food even though they are filled to the brim. However, there is no possibility of a child desiring to eat cake and candy to other things when there is only so much an individual can eat, unless he gets psychological satisfaction Therefore, if the dessert and appetizer become part of the meal served as a whole at one time, then a child can select what he wants without any psychological impediments, and you will be amazed at how little of cake, candy and ice cream he will eat... if left completely alone to choose for himself. By the same reasoning, he would never prefer tea, coffee, carbonated soda, or alcoholic beverages to milk, providing you don't encourage his desire by denying them or telling him these are for adults. Consequently, it is not necessary to remove what you like from the table for fear a child will get hurt in any way, as his body will not permit the eating and drinking of what is preferred less, providing — it is necessary to qualify — he is left completely alone."

"Did I hear correctly, Larry? You say that cake, candy, ice cream, beer, pickles, coffee, tea, etc. should be put on the table along with the regular course, so that a child can select what he wants, right?"

"That's exactly right, Jim, if the children are already consuming these things, which are a problem. Let them taste and eat anything they want. Without trying to check their desire in any way, shape, or form, in other words, without any psychological impediments, they are compelled, by their very nature, to prefer the food and drinks that give the greatest pleasure and satisfaction. However, if mother prepared a tasteless meal and the children prefer the sweetness of cake and candy to her vegetables, she has no one to blame. Remember, there is just so much a person can eat, and if a child is left alone, he is compelled to fill up on what he prefers, not on what he doesn't prefer. Because mother could always blame her children, she never had to prepare the kind of meal that would make them prefer cookies and candy less. But now she is given no choice unless it gives her satisfaction to see them eat what she doesn't want them to eat. Even a dog will eat what he likes less when what he likes better is not available. Candy and cake will be reduced to such a minimum once a mother realizes what it means that man's will is not free, in other words, once she realizes why it is better for her when all forms of advance blame, this judging of what is right for someone else, is removed, that the candy and cake manufacturers will be virtually wiped out. As for alcoholic beverages, how is it possible for these to survive to any great degree when children will never be made to see any fallacious value in them? If a child should taste a beer, he would spit it out, provided he hasn't already been conditioned, and once he tastes something he doesn't like, he will always remember the experience and wonder how in the world people can actually drink the stuff."

"But Larry, wait until he learns that alcoholic beverages are taken not so much for the taste but for the effect, won't he desire to experiment, and if he likes the feeling, couldn't he become a drinker?"

"Everything that gave rise to the desire to drink is being removed, Jim. Some people drink because they were hurt, and the liquor makes them mean so they can strike back. Others like to assume a different personality, and drinking breaks down barriers otherwise impossible to bridge. But whatever caused the desire, each person will know that should he hurt someone while intoxicated, he will never be blamed or punished, which means that all drinking and driving will come to an end because the risk is too great. How is it humanly possible to stand over someone you just killed and know that no one will ever blame or punish what you know he must excuse and you cannot justify?"

"I hope it never happens to me."

"It won't happen if you don't want it to happen, and how can you want it to happen? There are many factors, Jim, that occasion this desire to drink, but when I discuss education, you will see how the final vestige of hurt is removed from our lives, which means that in order to desire alcohol as a beverage in the new world, it would be necessary to find pleasure in drinking it while isolated on an island. By the way, Jim, are you still concerned about candy?"

"I can't get used to the idea of letting children eat and drink anything they want."

"Well, let me clarify this a little more. Once mother has developed eating habits by preparing the kind of meals her husband and children thoroughly enjoy, she can easily diversify them for specific days depending on how many dinners she is able to prepare, so that Monday, for example, could correspond with chicken, Tuesday with something else, and so on; and she could serve specific side dishes also which could include everything served at one time. Under these conditions, it wouldn't take long before the entire family would look forward to the enjoyment of eating what they know will be served on a particular day, and the children would no more think of eating ice cream, cake, and candy between and after meals as they would think of eating chicken, steak, potatoes, or anything else. It is only by making a child aware of a value which is then denied (I can't repeat this enough) that you stir up his desire to have it. Under these new conditions mother will discover that the food she has to throw out more and more is cake, candy, and ice cream. Furthermore, it will be impossible to overeat in the new world for another reason. The sexes will desire to retain the physical appearance that first attracted their mate. Since these marriages will take place when a boy and girl are very young, and since all psychological impediments to eating will be removed from birth, very few will be carrying excess baggage. However, some boys and girls are naturally heavy, and there is no reason for them to worry in the new world because, to certain people, this is a physical attraction."

"It still seems to me, Larry, that certain foods have greater value, like spinach, carrots, fruits, and other vegetables, as well as whole wheat bread over white."

"There is nothing wrong with thinking anything you want, but until you have mathematical proof, you cannot teach that these are better for a child's body, for this blames the possibility that he might not like them. How do you know what his particular body might require? How do you know what foods are not best for him, what he may be allergic to? By assuming that you know what is better for his body, you could very easily make him seriously sick and never know the cause. Then your fears will call in a doctor who will prescribe medicine that could possibly make matters much more serious. It is for this reason that God says — 'Hands off, don't judge what is right for your child, don't blame him in advance by teaching the value of spinach, carrots, or any other food. Remember, my children, 'one man's meat might be another man's poison.' This doesn't mean, Jim, that a mother shouldn't prepare the kind of food she feels would be better for him, providing she doesn't exclude other kinds from which he can choose; but if she remembers the rule, she will have nothing to fear. Even if he should eat absolutely nothing, leave him alone, for this is his business. More arguments and punishment, in the world of free will, resulted when children dared to stand up to their parents who were constantly trying to force them to do what they didn't want to do, and all because the latter mistakenly believed that mother and father knew best; and in many cases, even when they knew they were wrong, they still persisted in exacting obedience solely for the satisfaction of putting a child in his place so he would honor his mother and father, which started a chain reaction of mutual disrespect. Today, mother serves so many meals the kids do not like because she is constantly blaming them in advance for not eating what she thinks is for their welfare, that they are compelled to prefer filling up on cookies, ice cream and candy because they know this will irritate her, which gives them compensating satisfaction; and when Thanksgiving approaches, the family looks forward to turkey as if this is the only time of the year one can have this kind of dinner. But when she is not allowed to blame the children and her husband for not eating what she prepares, or for filling up on what she prefers they did not eat, then she is given only one alternative, and that is to do a complete study of cooking so that she can satisfy her <u>own desire</u>. Can you imagine, Jim, how happy a family would be if all arguments were removed, once and for all?"

"I think it would be a blessing, Larry. But many of the arguments in a home are between children themselves, and how do you go about preventing that?"

"You understand, of course, that all arguments must cease when children are able to comprehend what it means that man's will is not free; consequently, we are only talking about the very young group."

"Yes, I do know that much, Larry."

"This conflict between children has its origin in the discrimination shown when parents use words like beautiful, darling, sweet, precious, intelligent, smart, etc. for these words absolutely discriminate against the other children who do not evoke these expressions, and then when clothes also bring forth a discriminating response, the one who was hurt will compensate by trying to take away from the other what has become a source of envy. But once these words are removed, once the parents refrain from any outward sign that certain type clothes and physiognomies are of greater value — because in reality they are not — the children will never desire to wear or have what their sisters or brothers have because these differences will not be a source of importance to them until... until they see that others value these differences. What difference would it make to a child what kind of dress you put on her if no one made any comments?"

"Absolutely none, I can see that, Larry."

"And what difference would it make to a child what kind of color and physiognomy he has if no one made any comments?"

"It would make no difference whatever; this I can see is completely mathematical."

"Therefore, the problem is simply to remove the desire to make any comments either up or down, either by praising or blaming these differences."

"Does this mean that all praise will be removed from our lives?"

"Of course not."

"Well, isn't praise the opposite of blame? If I praise you for doing something, am I not blaming you for not doing it?"

"This, Jim, is one of those logical, not mathematical conclusions; consequently, it will require some clarification. First, it is important to understand that all words of praise or compliment that describe a nonexisting value also blame a nonexisting value. In other words, the word beautiful praises something that is nonexisting, so, consequently, the word ugly blames something that is nonexisting."

"But what if I didn't use the word beautiful and just say to a child, 'I like you very much!' Now isn't it obvious that if another child is present, he will observe a difference in my reaction, should I not say the same thing to him?"

"Certainly he would, but for what reason should you say this to one child and not to another?"

"Well, maybe one acts in a way that makes me more proud of him, and, consequently, I can't help but favor him more than the other or show my partiality in some way."

"But supposing these differences are removed, what then?"

"Then it would be mathematically impossible to be partial. But Larry, how is it possible to remove differences that are real? Supposing one child sits down at the piano at the age of 3 and picks out a melody, shouldn't I applaud him and say 'I liked that very much?'"

"But there is a big difference between saying 'I liked that very much' and 'I like you very much,' although both expressions get displaced."

"Even so, Larry, another child hearing me would become envious of his brother being able to do something that causes daddy to react differently.

No matter how you slice it, there is a certain amount of discrimination because the one is being applauded and the other is not. Even if you just pick up one child, at that moment you have discriminated."

"Jim, you're certainly a tough cookie, but you are a hundred percent right. Therefore, it is necessary to avoid all actions that appear to show discrimination and partiality until children are old enough to be taught the principles."

"Do you mean that once they are old enough and are taught, then it is all right to show partiality?"

"Partiality itself is a form of hurt, as is any kind of unjust discrimination. However, my realization that they would never blame me for this hurt prevents my desire to do it. Applauding my 3-year-old for playing a piece on the piano is not showing any unjust discrimination, except, in this instance, that my other young children, who haven't yet been taught what it means that man's will is not free, will feel that I am showing partiality, and believe that I like this child better because of his ability to play the piano. Consequently, this is a real, not imaginary, hurt to them. But once they are taught, they would know instantly that I couldn't possibly desire to hurt them under any condition and would know that my applause is not a sign of partiality. However, applause will come to an end also, which will be explained shortly."

"You just said, Larry, that no praise or compliments can be given to these young children no matter what they do, because it may hurt the other children, right?"

"That's exactly right."

"Well, what about compliments and praise when other children are not around to be hurt?"

"Since it will be impossible for one child to desire teasing or hurting another, it would be perfectly all right, provided your praise is not being used in a manner that blames the opposite for not being done. However, as with applause, the value in paying compliments is being removed."

"How do you know they will never tease or hurt each other, these very young children?"

"Because the desire to do this arises only from a feeling of envy and jealousy towards their brothers and sisters whom they wish to hurt in some manner. When the envy and jealousy are removed, this desire could never arise."

"Do you mean that it is impossible for one child to become envious of the other child's toys and clothes?"

"I already explained about clothes, Jim. These are not a source of fun to a child until he sees that you react in a different manner to a different type of apparel. When your reaction is the same, in other words, when there is no reaction whatsoever, then children could never become envious because of the differences that exist. As for toys, this is something else. However, let me first clarify when praise is blame. To help me do the job, I shall borrow your book again. Durant writes: 'Perhaps, too, we can substitute praise for blame in forming the character of the child,' not realizing that whatever is praised to further this end is an inverted form of blame which justifies not doing what is desired when the praise is not forthcoming. He is only praising to avoid the necessity of blaming. He gives his daughter a monthly salary 'dependent upon her keeping her room tidy, making her own bed, getting up promptly, arriving at school on time, and doing her lessons well,' which obviously blames her for not doing these things; but since he knows that not to give her this allowance would be a form of punishment which he doesn't approve of, because he writes: 'It is remarkable how well behaved a child can be without punishments and without commands' — he is compelled to resort to pride in addition to praise in order to prevent her from desiring not to do that for which she is being paid, so that he doesn't have to stop her salary which would be a form of punishment. 'We suggest to our daughter that she is too proud to let anyone see her untidy or unclean; that she is too proud to run forward for gifts or preferment; too proud to let anyone surpass her considerably in her work.' This is somewhat like a man who starts out by making a small investment in a new venture, only to discover that he now has to invest more money to ensure himself against losing the first. Before long, he realizes that he bit off more than he can chew and ends up getting deeper and deeper in the hole. Then Durant writes: 'Censure craps the soul, and makes the imperfect task forever hateful; praise expands every cell, energizes every organ, and makes even the most difficult undertaking an adventure and a victory,' which plainly tells us that praise is so powerful as a means to an end that he can get a child to do what is not liked, perhaps even hated, to earn the praise. 'Egotism is the lever by which we can move the world,' to do the bidding of others without using force, which only changes the means, not the end. 'Instead of pouncing upon work ill done and heaping up reproaches, we keep an eye alert for things done well and mark it with praise that shall linger sweet in the memory as a call to further accomplishment'... for the purpose of accomplishing what the parents want, not what the child desires. 'If my daughter has to report she has fallen short in arithmetic, we show regret, but we have not the heart to reprove her,'... as if showing regret is not reproof when a child is being paid in praise that blames her for not doing what is expected, which demonstrates how easy it is for a philosopher to get confused with words. 'But when she comes home with news of perfect marks we dance and celebrate, and exhaust our ingenuity to show new joy at each victory.' But supposing he is tired one day and doesn't feel like dancing, what then when he is under this obligation to pay his debts? 'When she has done something that especially delights us we have slipped a dollar into her bank,' and a seal, for a good performance, is given extra fish. And what would he do if his daughter especially, especially, especially delighted him?"

"I was just thinking about that, Larry. It looks like some fathers could run out of cash or praise."

"It is quite obvious, Jim, that she is performing to get paid, whether with praise or cash, just like a man working at a job he doesn't like but stays because of the money he needs to support his family. The only difference between Durant and other fathers is that he resorts to praise, a monthly allowance, and pride to get his daughter to do what he wants done, while they blame and threaten with punishment any failure to do what is expected. He punishes by not giving what is desired, while they punish by giving what is not desired."

"What's that, Larry?"

"I said that Durant punishes his daughter by taking away the praise when he feels she hasn't earned it, as when she had fallen short in arithmetic. He punished her by letting her see that he was disappointed, and punished her even more by implying that, though she was responsible for his disappointment, he wouldn't reprove her, which made her feel guilty and desire never to hurt Dad again this way. But the other fathers are not so subtle, and when a child comes home with poor grades, they say, 'Jesus Christ!! Did mother see your report card yet? I warned you the last time, Jimmy, that if you fall short in arithmetic again, you're really going to get it. Now just for that you can't watch television for three whole weeks, you can't go to the movies for three whole weeks, you can't have candy, cake, or ice cream for three whole weeks, and... get the hell upstairs to your room this minute; and you'd better get that arithmetic correct, or you'll really get what's coming to you.' In other words, Jim, to repeat myself, 'the one punishes by not giving what is desired while the other punishes by giving what is not desired.'"

"You are simply the greatest! I mean, I liked that very much."

"Let me say this, Jim. I'm not criticizing Durant and these other fathers for bringing up their children the way they did because they couldn't help themselves under the circumstances of not knowing what was truly better for every person concerned. Gosh, you should see mine! These parents were constantly impelled by the desire to get a favorable reaction from the people around them. Each father wanted to hear the compliments of his friends."

But you do know what is better for every person concerned, Larry, so why shouldn't your children be little angels?"

"Have you forgotten already? I, too, am still living in the world of free will. The criticism of others is still a part of our society. The school system has not yet been changed, and if I don't adjust to this learned ignorance, my family would be hurt even more. Remember, it takes two to tango, or it takes two people to understand these principles in order for them to be effective."

"Do you mean then that you are like Durant in bringing up your children, or like the other fathers?"

"Neither. I simply tell the children what to expect from others if they act in a certain manner; then I leave it up to their choice."

"Well, supposing your daughter came home with poor grades, is part of what she can expect from others a punishment from you?"

"You must be kidding. Of course not. She knows what society wants. If she doesn't want to give it to them, this is her business."

"But couldn't this hurt her in later years?"

"Certainly, under the present conditions, but she knows this, so the decision is hers to make. If a person has been taught that playing with matches could set his clothes on fire and take his life, and he decides to do it anyway, this is his business, not mine. You see, Jim, the difference between Durant and me under the present conditions is that he tries to protect his daughter by seeing, with his psychological techniques, that she conforms to what society wants in a young lady. I don't care whether my daughter conforms, but I want her to know what the reaction will be to a nonconformist. Then, at least, she can decide what she thinks is better for herself. This, you understand, is only necessary in the world of free will because others hurt us with their reaction. But once man learns the truth about himself, then this criticism and ridicule disappear, and I won't have to teach my children how they can be hurt, only how they could hurt others, for which they will not be blamed."

"You know, with all this talk about praise, I still don't know the primary difference between praise that is allowed and praise that is not allowed."

"It is taken for granted, Jim, you understand that everything is allowed if an individual wants to do something."

"This I know, Larry."

"The answer is very simple. All praise is allowed if it does not blame the person for anything or blame anybody else. Durant was blaming certain desires and actions of his daughter by praising other desires."

"I understand that, and I also understand that calling somebody beautiful is another way of calling someone ugly. But what if a girl should design a dress, just as an artist paints a portrait, and I see that this dress stands out above all other dresses . . ."

"You mean, Jim, stands out for you."

"Of course, for me. Then am I allowed to say to her, 'I think your dress is wonderful?'"

"Of course not. There is no difference between 'wonderful and beautiful.' By using such words, you make it appear that this girl has created something that partakes of a value called 'wonderful' or 'beautiful,' but in actual reality, all that we know as a matter of mathematical knowledge is that you like what she is wearing. Remember, Jim, there are no external values by themselves."

"Aren't food and money values?"

"Certainly."

"Aren't they external?"

"They are."

"Then don't we have external values?"

"This is that logical or syllogistic reasoning, Jim, but it is not mathematical. Everything that exists outside of us is external, but you presupposed that because 'beauty' is a fallacious value that does not exist, and money does exist externally and is liked by all mankind, therefore, money has external value. But actually, money and food, though they exist externally, have value for us only because we want them. However, where the words 'beautiful' and 'wonderful' project our feelings about a particular thing — as if what we like exists that way in the external world for others — the words food and money do not."

"In other words, Larry (correct me if I'm wrong), our values do not exist as part of the external world, yet despite this, because or eyes are not a sense organ, and because our brain is also a movie projector among other things, we are able to record these feelings on slides or words and then project them, through our eyes, onto the screen of the outside world. Then we photograph these feelings, which we now see in relation to certain specific differences, and then when we project the word, thereafter, we actually see, with our eyes, these values as existing outside of us."

"Now, if I were to say at this moment, 'Beautifully expressed,' then I would be actually saying that your words are wonderful because other words are not wonderful. Consequently, since these differences that appeal more to one person than another cannot be made into standards for others because this blames them for liking what he does not like, and since this also hurts them by criticizing their taste, the most I can say about anything that I like... is that I like it. I liked the way you expressed that, Jim."

"Do you mean then that the most a girl would ever hear about her dress is... 'I like it, or I like it very much?'"

"She won't even hear that, nor will you hear what I just said... 'I liked the way you expressed that, Jim."

"Why, because this would blame her for wearing what you don't like?"

"Of course not. What I like doesn't blame somebody for not liking what I like. If I meet a girl who doesn't appeal to me, I am not blaming her because I don't marry her."

"But supposing your wife bought a dress that she likes and you don't like?"

"Why shouldn't I like it when there is no possibility that others will criticize it?"

"Well, don't you feel that certain dresses would arouse your passion more than others?"

"My business is to arouse her desire; what she wears to arouse my desire is her business, not mine. As long as I know that she is happy wearing a particular dress, then I will like what she wears; and how is it possible for her not to be happy in what she wears when no one will ever criticize her taste?"

"Well, supposing she asks you if you like it?"

"How is it possible for her to ask when she knows what my answer will be? This was already discussed, Jim."

"You win, Larry, but tell me something. According to you, there will be no praise, no applause, no great admiration for certain differences, nothing."

"I don't recall saying that. Specific differences will always be admired. However, this will be treated more thoroughly when we discuss education. Can you wait until then?"

"I hate this waiting, but I guess I'll have to. Anyway, what about toys, Larry? How is it possible to avoid arguments between children over toys?"

"Tell me, Jim, if you had four children and put on the dinner table only three baked potatoes, wouldn't you be blaming the desire of one of your children to eat a potato?"

"I certainly would, but if I had four children, I would put four potatoes on the table."

"Would it be possible for you to desire putting unequally sized potatoes on the table, when this also blames the appetite of those who want an equal amount with the others?"

"Not necessarily, Larry. If they all know what it means that man's will is not free, then the child who goes first, not wishing to blame anybody, would take the smallest potato, the next child would select the smallest of the three remaining, and so on."

"That part is true, Jim, that your children would not blame or desire to hurt each other, but wouldn't you be blaming the desire of three children to want this difference they are forced to give away, which certainly would arouse envy if they were hungry enough?"

"Not if I had more potatoes to give them. But if I did not have, then I would be showing discrimination."

"In other words, you certainly could never put enough milk for three glasses only, when there are four children, right?"

"That's perfectly true, I couldn't do that. You don't have to explain to me that any kind of discrimination, especially where children are concerned, is a hurt."

"But even though you and others will admit this, let me show how much unconscious discrimination actually goes on where toys are concerned. If you give a little boy a soldier and a girl a doll, isn't this discrimination? Why shouldn't the boy want to play with the doll, and the girl with the soldier; and should both desire the doll at the same time, what then?"

"You tell me, Larry."

"Supposing we watch daddy try to solve this problem. 'Jimmy, this doll belongs to Diane; dolls are for little girls, not for boys.' 'But I wanna play widda dolly.' 'Diane, you're older than Jimmy, you be a big girl and let Jimmy play with your doll just for a little while.' 'No! Dolly mine: you buy for Diane and dolls not for boys; only goils, Daddy; Jimmy is a boy not a goil.'"

"So what's the solution, Larry?"

"Before children are old enough to understand what it means that man's will is not free, parents must buy the same exact toy for all children. What is given on one birthday to a small child is given to the others, or else you give nothing at all, and the toy must be identical in all details, including the color. If it is a soldier you wish to give to a boy, you must also give the same exact soldier to the girl; and if it is a doll you wish to give to the

262

girl, you will give the same exact doll to the boy. However, when children understand these principles, when they know they will never be blamed for hurting others (they will learn this before they start school), they will be given the same exact money as a gift, and with it they can buy what they want. This applies to adults as well. All gifts, in the new world, will consist of money."

"Why only money as a gift?"

"Because this is a means to an end the recipient will prefer, whereas a gift other than money is a judgment of what is better for someone else."

"Do you mean they will be given a slip of paper on which is recorded, let us say, $5?"

"That's exactly right, Jim, and this money will be deducted from the record book."

"But wouldn't these young children take advantage of the knowledge that a slip of paper is sufficient to buy certain things?"

"Of course not, Jim, because they will be controlled from hurting anybody, just like an adult, and the principles will be easily understood. Furthermore, they will have already learned to add and subtract, so if they only spend $4, they will know that a dollar is still theirs to spend."

"It does seem very easy."

"It is, Jim."

"What would you say is the primary cause of all arguments between parents and children?"

"Blaming our angels in advance for what they want to do. But it must be remembered that the primary reason parents were compelled to do this was because they were blamed in advance by the priests, the doctors, the government, the school, their friends and relatives, and everybody else. When all these forms of blame are removed, then mom and dad won't have to tell their children what to do. As for asking favors, this arises from a desperate need for assistance and from a desire to have slaves do your work. This latter desire arises from a feeling of superiority towards the person asked, and it assumes many subtle forms. When the transition gets officially launched."

"Couldn't it be launched in each home on a smaller scale?"

"Yes it could, but for these principles to be 100% effective, it is necessary to launch our New Earth on an international scale. However, when it does get officially launched, all forms of slavery, the result of a feeling of superiority, will be done away with, and the desperate need for assistance will be volunteered."

"What do you mean?"

"If a father broke his leg and was laid up in bed, his family would know that he is helpless because he cannot ask favors of others. Consequently, they would ask him if there was anything they could do, and he, not wishing to take advantage of their generosity, would sum up the things he needed so only very little effort would be required. But the children will no longer be the slaves of their parents. 'Get me this and get me that,' or, 'will you get me this or that' (same difference) is coming to an end, and with it all the headaches and arguments that parents have been unsuccessfully trying to remove."

"But Larry, aren't parents the slaves of children?"

"Only for a very little while, just until these principles are understood by the children as well as the parents. However, the work mother is compelled to want to do around the house can be reduced to an absolute minimum by the example she sets and by asking this question: 'Is there anything you would like Mommy to teach you, Jimmy?' If the child is interested in learning what he sees his mother do, he will say 'yes,' but most of the things he will learn by himself."

"What about teaching him to eat with a knife and fork, to brush his teeth, wash his face, etc.?"

"It is obvious, Jim, that up until he is able to do things for himself, mother must do these for him, but if she wishes to lighten her load where he is concerned, she must let him see what she is doing, and when she thinks he is capable of learning, she will simply say, 'Would you like Mommy to show you how to tie your shoestrings, brush your teeth, eat with a knife and fork, dress yourself, make your own bed, comb your hair,' etc.? But under no conditions can she blame him if he doesn't want to learn, if he is slow in learning, if he stops while learning, or if he shows no interest in doing chores for her."

"Do you mean she can't say, 'Jimmy, would you like for Mommy to teach you how to carry out the garbage or wash dishes?'"

"That's exactly right, because this is a means to her end, not his. However, when he is older and knows that his mother will never ask him to do any favors, he will desire to help her of his own free will. 'Let me help you with that, Mom.' 'Thanks, Jimmy.' 'You're welcome, Mom.'"

"You didn't express it that way when discussing marriage, Larry. You said that the husband and wife would ask each other every day if there is something they can do."

"What difference does it make, Jim, when our slide rule works in either case? 'Let me help you with that television set, Julie.' 'Thanks, Jim.' 'You're welcome.' or, 'Is there something I can do for you, Julie?' 'Yes, there is, Jim. I tried to move the TV, but it was a little bit too heavy. Could you help me with it?' 'I don't mind at all.' 'Thank you, Jim.' 'You're welcome, Julie.' Well, Jim, is there a difference?"

"None whatsoever, you win again. Well, what is there left to discuss about our little angels?"

"I can't think of anything offhand, can you?"

"It seems to me that even if you did forget something, your slide rule can be applied by any individual. Well, Larry, any final word before I go to do some shopping and get home to Julie?"

"Just this, Jim. When you and Julie finally have children, it is important to remember that from the day of their birth, they can't be blamed for anything, which means that you are compelled to prevent, without any form of advance blame, what you do not want. To arouse their desire for an end you have determined for them, such as one type of music to another, is a definite form of tacit blame, but to allow them to make their own choice after seeing and hearing the various differences that exist is quite another thing. One method does not consider the innate tendencies of children, which is the source of all contention, only because you feel you know what is better, right, and good for them, while the other method does, which reveals respect for them and true parental love. But we had no choice until now because of the criticism and ridicule that influenced our decisions."

"Do I have a choice now, Larry?"

"You certainly do not, but henceforth nobody is ever going to tell you, influence you, or do anything to try and make you do what you don't want to do. For the very first time, believe it or not, man's will will be completely free to move in the direction of what he knows is truly better for himself. Before this, he was pushed by the desires of others to accomplish their ends. However, to ease your fears about abandoning the so-called knowledge that has been controlling our lives, just remember our simple mathematical rule: 'If you are unable to prevent your children from desiring what you feel will be a hurt, or unable to prevent them from not desiring what you think will be for their benefit (both without any form of blame), then it is rather obvious that what you like or dislike for them, and cannot prevent without blame in any form, is not in any way harmful, existing only as a fear of something imaginary, based upon false knowledge; otherwise, you would definitely have the power to prevent this harm without blame in any form. But should a certain amount of hurt still exist on the part of children to their parents and others, because one-half of the equation is still too young to understand, then it is necessary to continue living for a while longer in the world of free will, even after the transition gets under way, which means that mom and dad will still find it necessary to give their children a choice between hurting others and being punished, as we now do with our laws, and as I would have done had my son used a sofa for a trampoline. But remember, Jim, to punish children, which still might be necessary even though both parents understand these principles, it is extremely important that the hurt you receive from your children must be of a concrete nature, not one that exists only in the imagination. Durant was not hurt when his daughter showed him her marks in arithmetic, but he made her think that he was, and then punished her feeling of guilt by letting her know he would never blame or punish her for this. He didn't mean it to be that way, but such an action is unconscious cruelty personified. I tell you this because it is so easy to abuse this knowledge you just learned when you don't understand it thoroughly."

"But if I do understand it thoroughly?"

"Then there is no chance of abuse."

"I do understand it, Larry, and it has already changed my life. In fact, I can't wait to start a family to practice."

"Or do you mean, Jim, 'I can't wait to practice on starting a family?'"

"Both. Listen, I won't be able to see you tomorrow... I mean, I can't see you tomorrow... I mean, I don't want to see you tomorrow, Larry, because I plan to spend the entire day with Julie. We're going to the beach."

"I think you really have learned what it means that man's will is not free, Jim. You might be my fuse yet. Anyway, I'll see you the day after tomorrow."

"So long, Larry."

"See you, Jim."

# CHAPTER 10 —EDUCATION

Although Jim enjoyed every minute with Larry, he couldn't wait to break away. He dashed to the nearest grocery store, bought several things, and rushed to the apartment. He wasn't sure Julie would even be there because he now knew that she was completely free to do anything she wanted to do without having to account to anyone for her actions. But he also knew that she knew if she left him when he wanted her so desperately, this would break his heart, for which she knew she would never be blamed or criticized; consequently, he was positive she had not left him. However, when he first entered the apartment, his heart skipped a beat because she was nowhere to be seen. But he knew there was nothing to worry about, that it was mathematically impossible for her to leave him just as long as she knew that he loved her and showed his love. It felt kind of funny, though, to Jim, because there was no marriage license, no rings, no wedding ceremony, absolutely nothing but their sexual desire for each other, and yet he knew that he was married for life. He didn't care what she might have been before, and he knew that she didn't care what he had been before. They only cared about their strong sexual passion for each other.

Just at that moment, the bathroom door opened and Jim saw Julie standing in the doorway. She had heard him come in, and knowing that he couldn't approach her for a kiss as had been the custom in the world of free will, unless one of them extended an invitation, she had slipped out of her clothes and put on a see-through negligee, one that came down to her thighs, so he would know, the moment he saw her, that she wanted him very much.

Jim's blood was actually boiling. He could hardly contain himself.

"Hi, Julie!"

"Hiya, Jim!"

Since she was extending the invitation, he knew that he needed to go over to her, and, as if drawn by a magnet, he moved closer and closer and closer. Finally, his hands touched her shoulders, and he planted a very warm and passionate kiss on her lips. They stood there just kissing for about five minutes, and then Jim started to kiss her ears, her cheek, her neck, her breasts, her stomach, her legs. In fact, he kissed her all over, and Julie caught on fire.

She then unbuttoned Jim's pants and began to kiss him all over. Within ten minutes after he walked into the apartment, they were so hot they were about to burst. He made her come four times, and he even came twice. When they were finished, they just laid there in each other's arms. But then both of them remembered simultaneously that the other might not desire to stay there, and that to judge what was right for the other was wrong, so they got up and got dressed. Julie then inquired:

"What did you buy at the store, Jim?"

"A big steak, steamed shrimp, potatoes, and a few other odds and ends."

"What time would you like to have dinner?"

"Anytime you want to make it, Julie."

"How about in two hours; is that okay?"

"It's okay with me."

Jim knew that if he walked out of the apartment without saying anything, Julie would not call after him to question where he was going because this would blame him for not telling her. And Julie knew that if he did go out for these two hours, he would never do anything to hurt her because he knew that she would never blame him. After thinking about it for a couple of minutes, since this change wasn't easy to adjust to, Jim simply said, "I'll see you in two hours, Julie." And she replied, "Have a good time."

In two hours, he returned after playing a few games of pool with his buddies and then ate a dinner he enjoyed tremendously. When dinner was over, he volunteered to help her with the dishes. "Thanks, Jim." "You're welcome." When everything was cleaned up, he had a desire to return to the poolroom, but he didn't want to deprive Julie of an opportunity to use the car. He thought for a minute and then said, "Honey, is there anything I can do for you?" "Yes there is, Jim. I would like to visit my mother. Could you drop me off there?" "Better than that. I'll give you the car, you drop me off at the poolroom, and I'll see you later back at the apartment. Is that okay?" "Thanks, Jim." "You're welcome, Honey."

After visiting her mother, Julie called on a couple of her girlfriends, went to a movie, and then came back to the apartment. Jim had not yet come in, but she was very tired and went right to bed.

A little later, Jim came in. He was also very exhausted. Julie looked so tempting sleeping on the next bed, but Jim knew that even if he only kissed her without being invited, this would be a form of advance blame because he would have to assume that this was what she wanted, and he couldn't do that now; so he left her completely alone.

Julie woke up a half hour before Jim. She, too, had a desire to kiss his lips and his body, but she knew that she could never do this anymore without an invitation, for the same reason. She further realized that if she wanted to kiss his body and make passionate love when he awakened, she would have to extend an invitation so he would come to her. Since she was still a little sleepy, she dozed off. When she woke up the second time, she saw that Jim was already up with his indicator turned on, extending a very warm invitation. Julie then approached him, and their passion was so ecstatic that neither of them could find adequate words to describe it. All they knew was that if the other would leave, it would kill them, but they also knew this was a mathematical impossibility... under the new conditions.

They went to the beach for the day, made passionate love again that evening and the following morning, and then Julie desired to give Jim a lift to meet Larry, after Jim desired to give her the car.

"Bye, Honey."

"Bye, Julie. Oh, wait a minute, I want to get a book out of the car. See you later, Hon."

"Jim was never so happy in all his life. "If only this could continue," he thought to himself, "it would be heaven itself." When Larry arrived, on time, but a few minutes later, he could see that Jim was in a dream world.

"Larry... how can I tell you... how can I describe what my life is with Julie since you taught us what it means that man's will is not free?!! I love her, Larry. I love her, I love her, I love her; I love every part of her!"

"Take it easy, Jim, I know the kind of love that's produced; it's no news to me. Every boy and girl who marries under the new conditions will experience the same thing."

"Please, Larry, don't lie to me, whatever you do. Will it last?"

"It not only lasts for an entire lifetime, but it gets better when you know what makes your partner even more passionate. After all, you just got married the other day."

"Larry, if this is a sample of what your discovery will mean for mankind, then let me be the first to light the fuse and detonate this knowledge across the earth. I only feel sad about the older people who will not experience this because their lives are just about over."

"Don't fret, Jim, because there is nothing to be sad over, as you will very soon see."

"Cut it out, Larry, you know that when they die they are dead and gone, right?"

"Right and wrong, Jim, but I'm not going to discuss this subject until tomorrow. Today, I have education on the agenda, have you forgotten?"

"Of course not, but I just couldn't help thinking of those who missed what I am now experiencing."

"Again, I say, don't fret over it. You will see that Larry knows what he's talking about, and these older folks, as well as yourself and all younger people, will be extremely pleased with certain knowledge I am about to reveal. God let me in on a little secret as a bonus. Instead of paying me in cash, though, He rewards me with tremendous satisfaction."

"Well, Larry, what's what with education?"

"Do you have any idea, Jim, of how many books were written on this subject?"

"Quite a few, I am sure."

"Well, supposing I were to tell you that there is no such thing as education, what would you say then?"

"Nothing you can say would surprise me, but how is that possible? When someone goes to high school and college, isn't he acquiring an education?"

"Is it possible to be born with, or acquire beauty?"

"Absolutely impossible, Larry, because there is no such thing as beauty. Wait a minute, are you trying to tell me that education is a word like beauty, or educated is like beautiful?"

"That's exactly true, Jim, there is no difference between them; they are both words that create and then project a nonexisting value. If education were something actually real, then any symbol would suffice to separate it from the other external differences, as the word sun distinguishes this bit of substance from the word and substance moon. No one living would deny the existence of the sun and moon, would they, Jim?"

"If they did, they would have to be some kind of idiot or epistemologist."

"Wouldn't any word suffice to symbolize the sun or moon, when their differences can be circumscribed with a picture?"

"I don't quite understand, Larry."

"Supposing I draw a picture of an object and then call it X. If I point to the pictured object and say X, wouldn't you know I am talking about the object pictured? And if you have already experienced the object, wouldn't X then become related to the pictured object and the real object?"

"Certainly, I understand that."

"Well, if I drew a picture of the sun, and then called it X, wouldn't this symbol suffice?"

"Certainly. What difference does it make what name is used when the difference between the sun and other objects can be seen through the symbol?"

"That's exactly what I'm saying. The moon, sun, stars, sky, clouds, etc., as apples, oranges, peaches, plums, and pears, are words that accurately circumscribe specific differences that exist in the external world; they are actually pictures of these objects, and when we see the words that symbolize them, we then see, in our mind, a picture of these existing objects."

"Well, that's certainly clear enough, Larry, but what are you driving at?"

"What I'm driving at is this: If education were something externally real, like the sun, the moon, an apple, an orange, a peach, etc., then any symbol would suffice to circumscribe this difference called education, but instead, everybody and his brother defines education according to what they think it is. In other words, the word 'education' is assumed to symbolize something externally real, whatever it may be, and then everybody employs syllogistic reasoning to confirm what they think this reality is. Our description of the sun may be inaccurate, but we know this ball of fire exists. However, we assume education exists, and we try to confirm its existence by giving an accurate description."

"But Larry, there isn't a person living today who assumes the existence of education. It is considered an external reality."

"I know this, Jim, but if it were proven that there is no such thing as education, would it be possible to define the word?"

"Of course not. How is it possible to describe something that doesn't exist? But as far as I'm concerned, it does exist. I, for one, don't have a good education, and are you trying to tell me that I can't acquire this education by going back to school or reading more books on my own?"

"I'm not denying that a person goes to school, graduates, and reads many books, but what has this to do with the word 'education'? I grant that he can read various things, that he can pass various tests, and that he can do any number of things, just as I'm sure there are people, like Gibbon and Durant, who read many many more books than the average college professor, and perhaps could pass many many more tests and graduate with honors; but what has this to do with the word 'education'?"

"Are you trying to tell me that this is simply a word to describe the doing of certain things?"

"Just as the word 'beautiful' symbolizes certain other differences that do not exist."

"I'm a little confused here, Larry."

"The reason you are confused is because you don't like having something taken away from you that has been a source of satisfaction through the years. Do you think Elizabeth Taylor would like to hear that she is not beautiful? Would Gibbon and Durant like to hear that they are not educated? If I took an illiterate person and told you that you are no more educated than he is, wouldn't you resent it, Jim?"

"Yes, I think I would."

"And if I took several girls considered extremely homely, put them alongside Lana Turner and then told the actress that she is not one whit more beautiful, wouldn't she resent this and consider it somewhat of an insult?"

"Yes, I know she would, unless she considered you half blind."

"Now, to understand what is actually going on with words, let us draw a picture of a girl, a picture of an apple, a picture of a boy, and a picture of an orange. We now have four pictured objects; is that correct?"

"That's correct, Larry."

"We shall call the first — object number one, the second — object number two, the third — object number three, and the fourth — object number four. Now, if I ask you to identify each of these objects, can you do it?"

"Certainly, a child can do that."

"Are you absolutely certain that you will not make any mistakes. Let me test you. Point to object number 1... Very good. Now number two... OK, Jim, I'm convinced. Now, let us also draw a picture of exactly what you did in your life that makes you consider yourself educated."

"Not me, Larry; I didn't go that far in school. Use Durant as an example."

"Well, let's imagine that he has read 10,000 books. We will write this figure after a picture of him and a book, OK so far?"

"OK, Larry."

"Next, we shall estimate the number of grades he passed, the diplomas and degrees he received. Let us say 100, is that all right, Jim?"

"More than enough. I get the picture, so you don't have to continue in this piecemeal fashion. In other words, let us say a picture is drawn of his entire life, or better yet, let us say a moving picture was taken of his life."

"I like that. And now we shall take a moving picture of the life of this person to whom we referred as illiterate. We shall call the first life — object number five, and the other life — object number six. Now if I asked you to describe object number five, you would say — 'this individual went to school, read 10,000 books, passed to the 100th grade, etc.', and as a description of object number 6, you would say — 'this individual never went to school, never learned to read or write, worked hard on a farm, did this and did that.' Now tell me, Jim, and be very careful before answering, is it humanly possible for any person seeing these pictured differences to get confused as to which numbers they refer?"

"No chance of confusion at all."

"Now, once again, think very carefully. If there is no chance of confusion by symbolizing them in this manner, why are two of these circumscribed differences symbolized in a manner that does confuse?"

"Do you mean the words educated and uneducated confuse?"

"Aren't there differences of opinion as to which people are educated?"

"Not the two pictured. The illiterate individual is obviously uneducated, but Durant is certainly a highly educated person. However, I know there are differences of opinion as to whether a person is educated because of certain things he has done in his life."

"I purposely drew a strong line between the two individuals pictured, Jim, so there would be no disagreement. Now, here we have taken a motion picture of two people's entire lives, given these differences a symbol to identify them, and you admit that it is mathematically impossible to get confused. We don't get confused over the moon and the sun, do we, Jim?"

"Once I did, remember? I told you about Inez."

"Enough of your jokes, Jim, I'm serious."

"You just blamed me, Larry."

"But you struck me first, so obviously you are still living in the world of free will."

"All right, Larry; I admit I can't get confused over the difference between a cat and a rat."

"Now, if it is possible to identify differences in such a manner that no opinions are necessary, wouldn't you say that this method of symbolism is mathematically accurate and preferable?"

"I certainly would say it is mathematically accurate, but preferred by whom? Durant can't like the thought of losing this value called education, and Robert Taylor wouldn't like to lose that value called handsome."

"Well, Jim, we have finally arrived at the heart of our problem, and you can see how difficult it is when you realize how the college students and professors would react to the news that they are not one bit more educated than anybody else. Did not the doctors react similarly to the announcement that man does not have five senses, and didn't religion react the same way to the news that man's will is not free? But now that these various people understand that the truth didn't hurt them at all, only helped remove the evil in the world, they are grateful for what they learned. The same thing here. Only at first does it hurt to think that you are no more educated than another, regardless of what he has done with his life, because it appears that something of value is being taken away, which is not the case at all, as you will see."

"Is there a way you can clarify this even more?"

"Yes, I think so. To be considered an educated person, in the present world (can you see the syllogistic reasoning present as I speak?) means that others will react to this knowledge of your education by giving you greater respect, greater admiration. Consequently, to lose these values called beautiful, educated, and handsome, you must also lose this reaction of others, which gave such tremendous satisfaction."

"But isn't this an insult and a hurt to these people, and isn't this showing them disrespect?"

"Of course not. Perhaps if I draw up an analogy, you might understand this better. If your income allows you to eat steak, is anything being taken away from you if the janitor who works for you suddenly discovers that his purchasing power has increased so that he, too, can now afford steak? If this sudden increase meant a decrease in your purchasing power, then you would be justified in complaining, but if it also increased your purchasing power, then you would even be happier. Today, great satisfaction is attained by having what others cannot get, but when others can acquire it without hurting you, while allowing you to get more of what you like, can you object?"

"Certainly not."

"The reason people take such pride in having values contained in words such as educated, beautiful, handsome, etc., is because there is so much disrespect shown to those who do not have them. When respect levels off, in other words, when there will be no more criticism and ridicule, these differences will not be missed one iota, nor will they be envied.

For further clarification of this subject, let me quote a passage by Durant and then analyze it as we proceed. Perhaps you will be able to understand more clearly what I'm talking about. Where's that book? Oh, here it is. He writes: 'I believe that it is through reading, rather than through high school and college, that we at last acquire a 'liberal education.'"

"I disagree with him already, Larry. Supposing a person only read comic books, would this give him a 'liberal education?'"

"But supposing there was no such word as 'education,' Jim, then what would you say? You are not disagreeing with Durant about whether a certain type of reading is better for one person than another — as one type of food might be better for one person than another — you are disagreeing only because he didn't qualify the type of reading necessary to acquire a liberal education. If two individuals are standing side by side, and you had never met either, but one was completely illiterate while the other had read everything written, you would desire, under the banner of free will, to give much greater respect to the latter. However, in the new world, it is mathematically impossible to give greater respect to these differences, not only because man's will is not free, which prevents the former from being blamed, but also because it is impossible to credit the other with a great education when the word education becomes obsolete. The slightest shade of disrespect is a hurt which will never be blamed; consequently, all words that show this disrespect, such as beautiful, handsome, educated — plus all their synonyms and antonyms — must be removed out of absolute necessity. Durant, however, not understanding the difference between words and reality, continues to give external value to what has absolutely no existence, for he then goes on to say that Mr. Everett Dean Martin has admirably described the meaning of a liberal education, and I warmly recommend his book to those who wish to know what it is to be mature. The word 'mature' is a synonym for 'liberal 'education' in this context."

"But why does he use the word 'liberal' at all? Why doesn't he just say 'education'?"

"It is Durant's subtle way of avoiding too much criticism by the school system, for teachers and professors, educators in general, like to believe that 'education' belongs to them exclusively. Are you beginning to recognize how an assumption for a major premise, and syllogistic reasoning to give it form, can make something appear realistic? No one is discussing whether education is or is not a reality, but whether the school should have a monopoly on it. No one is discussing whether man's will is free anymore, because this is assumed as a reality. The arguments are strictly over definition, as if definition confirms reality."

"I do understand that, Larry. But isn't it true that certain behavior patterns of man can more accurately be described with words that are almost identical to the meaning of other words, but not quite?"

"Certainly, but the shade of difference in the behavior pattern is a reality, and therefore two different words are required to symbolize this difference. But all the words in the world, 'mature' or otherwise, are not going to better describe what is not a part of the real world. It is this difference that either confused epistemology or those who tried to understand what was not clear to the epistemologists themselves. Anyway, Durant says: 'Today we think a man is educated if he can read the newspapers morning, noon and night; but though our colleges turn out graduates like so many standardized Fords every year, there is a visible dearth of real culture in our life; we are a nation with a hundred thousand schools, and hardly a dozen educated men.'

"Do you see what he's done?"

"I see that he's beginning to separate an 'educated man' from a college graduate, and I can see why the colleges would resent it."

"But why would they resent it, Jim?"

"Because college graduates like to consider themselves educated."

"In other words, they resent his criticizing their method of acquiring what everybody agrees has actual existence."

"That's right."

"But take note how he further separates the school system from this value by saying that regardless of how many schools we have, 'there is a visible dearth of real culture in our life.' The word culture has now become for him a synonym, like the word mature, for this liberal education. But because there are people in the world who have a certain amount of fallacious culture (again, this syllogistic reasoning), he makes sure that you understand he is referring to 'real culture.'"

"I don't think Durant is going to like you."

"Nonsense, Jim. I'm actually not criticizing him at all, but showing how certain words can even confuse the mind of an individual who is supposed to be a clearheaded thinker."

"You just said that 'there are people in the world who have a certain amount of fallacious culture.'"

"This is my way of showing you how easy it is for words to make something appear undeniably real. Once it is understood that the word education is not a symbol for anything externally real, but is a projection of what someone prefers for himself onto a screen of specific differences which he then says are better for everybody because he can define why these are better since they partake of this value called education, then all words like culture, mature, etc., become, along with their synonyms, completely displaced. Or to put it another way, you just said you resented Durant's criticism of what you did with your life. Now, if he understands that you will never blame this criticism, no matter how much it hurts you to be criticized, then he will not be able to say you are not educated because this is a criticism, so the word must, out of necessity, get displaced."

"But wouldn't it hurt him, Larry, to be denied what gave him such satisfaction over the years — this criticism of others?"

"That's the great humor. How is it humanly possible for him to object to being denied the right to criticize, when his very criticism, as well as the criticism of all others, is partly responsible for the very things he is criticizing? It's really no different than a preacher not objecting to doing away with his preaching against sin, when he becomes aware that his preaching against sin is partly responsible for the sin."

"I think we went over this once, didn't we, Larry?"

"Yes, we did, but I want to deconfuse your mind as much as it is humanly possible, so repetition — when I'm trying to start a chain reaction of thought across the globe and ignite the fuse through you — cannot be a waste of time. You asked me for clarification, so I'm trying to give it to you. Remember, this subject we're presently discussing actually ties together just about all the loose ends of our equation, except for death, which I will clear up next. You see, Jim, God felt awfully guilty through the years he made us develop ourselves, because our development necessitated that we fight and kill each other, discriminate and hate each other. When Job cried out to Him for understanding, God actually wept because there was no way He could communicate this knowledge. So, he turned to the ministers of religion and said: 'My dear cohorts, my wonderful assistants through the years, would you please be kind enough to tell all the people of the world to have faith, to believe in me, because I definitely am a reality, and one day, in the very near future, I shall reveal myself through a mathematical revelation."

"Larry, sometimes you send chills up and down my spine, and make me feel that you were specifically sent here by God."

"I was, Jim, but so was Christ, and so were you, and so was everybody else. We're all here at His bidding. Because you do one thing for satisfaction and I do something else, doesn't make me more His son and you less. My talking to you about these things is not done of my own free will because man's will is not free, nor is your listening done of your own free will. Remember, Jim, if you want to thank somebody for getting rid of all the evil, don't thank me because I had nothing to do with it. Thank God; He's my boss."

'You're just being modest, Larry."

"Truthful is the better word, Jim. However, let me get on with the problem at hand. Durant then says, 'No wonder that Mr. Wells and others have questioned the use of a college education. This is pessimism exaggerated to make a point. He apologizes to the schools by blaming Mr. Wells; 'but it is well that someone should check us up in our notion that the multiplication of schools and graduates can make us into an intelligent people.' The word 'intelligent' is now a substitute for liberal education, mature, and real culture. 'Our schools and graduates have suffered severely from Spencer's conception of education as the adjustment of the individual to his environment; it was a dead, mechanical definition, drawn from a mechanistic philosophy, and distasteful to every creative spirit.'"

"What about Spencer's definition, Larry?"

"Is it possible to define what doesn't exist?"

"That's right, it is impossible."

"However, Jim, if you analyze Spencer's definition, you will see that he has done away with further need for the word, just as I am doing. How is it possible to have a word to describe a difference among mankind, when there isn't any? Isn't it obvious that everybody is compelled, by his very nature, to adjust to his environment? It is true that the environment is different for different people, but he has defined education as 'the adjustment of the individual to his environment.' In other words, what he has said is mathematically undeniable; therefore, what is the need of having a symbol when every individual is included in the symbol?"

"Larry, I have to hand it to you, and I see what you mean. But what did Durant mean by 'distasteful to every creative spirit?'"

"Durant, like all other normal people under the banner of free will, resented Spencer only because he didn't understand him, and consequently derived a certain amount of pleasure in criticizing him, for this is one way of feeling superior. Since Spencer had proclaimed that man's will is not free, Durant employed words to twist the meaning of Spencer into something of a mechanical nature, which then made it possible for man, according to Durant, to be creative. He felt that if man's will is not free, then he couldn't take credit for the books he was writing, and he couldn't consider himself a genius."

"A genius, what's that?"

"This is a word like beautiful, educated, etc., which is designed to stratify certain differences by raising someone up, consequently, lowering others. To feel that one is a genius, it was necessary to feel 'creative,' and how was it possible for him to feel this way unless he could prove that man's will is free. Since he knew that it was impossible to prove this theory, he resorted to the next best thing, criticizing those who thought otherwise, not realizing that it is mathematically impossible to prove something false when its opposite can never be proven true. This is another reason why certain individuals resent the thought that man's will is not free, for how is it humanly possible to be proud of anything they have done unless they believe, consciously or unconsciously, in freedom of the will? Durant's chest swelled with pride over his masterpiece, The Story of Civilization, and it annoyed him no end to have someone like Spencer tell him that he didn't create what he spent years creating. But in actual reality, no one is taking this achievement away from Durant, for this is certainly a worthwhile accomplishment. The only thing we are taking away is his pride that he did it of his own free will. For the first time, he is made to realize that God pushed him in this direction, that's all. Of course, words like 'achievement and masterpiece' will no longer be used to describe anything that man does, simply because these words imply that one person's efforts in a particular direction are better than another person's efforts in a different direction."

"I'm beginning to lose you again, Larry."

"There's nothing difficult to understand, Jim. My efforts to write the book "A New Earth" are of no greater importance for the entire world than your efforts to play pool or do something else."

"You have to be kidding. My pool playing isn't going to help get rid of any evil that exists in the world, but your knowledge will definitely do the job."

"But I can't take credit for removing the evil when my will is not free, only for writing the book; there's a big difference, you know."

"What do you mean?"

"Durant's Story of Civilization, his Mansions of Philosophy, and all the other books he wrote, played just as important a role in my discovering what it meant that man's will is not free, as did everybody who ever lived. All knowledge is a gigantic accumulation of what everybody does in their motion towards greater satisfaction. Just because I happen to be at the end of the line when everybody pushes me or sets the stage that induces me to move in this direction for greater satisfaction, does not allow me to take the credit, nor is an individual to blame when everybody pushes him towards murder and war. It is only when all the facts are in that we get a glimpse of reality for what it really is."

"I'm beginning to understand at last. By the way, you still didn't discuss pornography as you said you would."

"I'll get to it soon."

Okay, you can continue now. I'm not lost anymore."

"Durant says next that Spencer's conception of education resulted in 'the conquest of our schools by mechanical and theoretical science, to the comparative exclusion of such "useless" subjects as literature, history, philosophy, and art. So we make good office-boys, good clerks, and good technicians, who, when their workday is over, devour the pictorial press and crowd into theatres that show them forever the same love-scenes on the screen and the same anatomy on the stage.' He constantly criticizes what others prefer, which was natural under the banner of free will. At this point, he qualifies the subjects necessary to acquire this 'liberal education, this real culture, this maturity,' ridicules what the graduates of our colleges do with their learning, and criticizes them still further for considering 'useless' what he has found to be otherwise. He then says: 'This mechanical and "practical" education produces partial, not total men; it subordinates civilization to industry, biology to physics, taste and manners to wealth. But education should make a man complete; it should develop every creative power in him, and open his mind to all the enjoyable and instructive aspects of the world. A man who is heavy with millions, but to whom Beethoven or Corot or Hardy, or the glow of the autumn woods in the setting sun, is only sound and color signifying nothing, is merely the raw material of a man; half the world is closed to the blurred windows of his spirit. An education that is purely scientific makes a mere tool of its product; it leaves him a stranger to beauty, and gives him powers that are divorced from wisdom. It would have been better for the world if Spencer had never written on education.'"

"I remember the passage very well, Larry."

"In this passage, he begins to multiply his synonyms of 'liberal education, mature, real culture, intelligence,' by including 'total, complete men.' Then he qualifies a little more what is required for these values: "Beethoven or Corot or Hardy, or the glow of the autumn woods in the setting sun.' Furthermore, these mechanical, practical, scientific people will have different tastes. They will prefer 'physics to biology, money to taste and manners, and consequently will be uncivilized individuals without knowing anything about beauty and wisdom.' Are you beginning to understand what I mean, Jim, about syllogistic reasoning?"

"I certainly am. In other words, his reasoning is logical, that is, it gives the appearance of being true, simply because he thinks he sees, with 'direct perception,' these external values which he has unconsciously projected, through his eyes, upon differences that in themselves are undeniable — all because of words or slides that stratify personal values into what appear externally real. When these words or slides are removed, or when man stops using them, it becomes mathematically impossible to judge what is right for someone else."

"You're hired, Jim; you start work the day after tomorrow."

"What's my salary?"

"You get paid like I get paid, with satisfaction."

"But I'm not satisfied to get paid only with satisfaction, can't you throw a little money in my direction?"

"I'll tell you what I'm gonna do. If you can get some thinker to take the necessary time to plow through the first five chapters of my manuscript, without skipping anything, I'll give you a hundred dollars cash on the line, and if you can get him to understand its significance — enough so he'll desire to get others to read it — you get a thousand dollar bonus when the money starts coming in. Does this give you greater satisfaction?"

"It certainly does."

"Anyway, Jimmy, my fuse, my detonator, Durant then says: 'It is well that Latin and Greek are passing from our colleges, for they consumed a hundred times more effort than they were worth. As Heine said: 'The Romans could not have had much time left to conquer the world if they had first had to learn Latin.' But though the languages of Greece and Rome are necessary only to philologists, the literature of these nations is almost indispensable to education. A man can conceivably ignore Virgil and Horace, Lucretius and Cicero, Tacitus and Marcus Aurelius, and still become mature; but of all possible instruments of education that I know, none is so fine and sure as a study of Greek life in all the varied scope of its democracy and imperialism, its oratory and drama, its poetry and history, its architecture and sculpture, its science and philosophy. Let a student absorb the life and letters of the Periclean age, the Renaissance, and the Enlightenment, and he will have a better education than any college can give him.' Again, he separates the values he has found preferable, and projects them through his eyes, upon differences that, though they are externally undeniable, are also differences without any external value. He then arrives at the very heart of his definition: 'Education does not mean that we have become certified experts in business, or mining, or botany, or journalism, or epistemology; it means that through the absorption of the moral, intellectual and esthetic inheritances of our race we have come to understand and control ourselves as well as the external world; that we have chosen the best as our associates both in spirit and in the flesh; that we have learned to add courtesy to culture, wisdom to knowledge, and forgiveness to understanding. When will our colleges produce such men?' Well, Jim, are you still confused, or would you like to sum this passage up to show me that you can qualify to earn the thousand dollars?"

"Larry... have you forgotten? In the new world, each person will judge his own qualifications for a job."

"But there is a difference. A person applying for a particular job already knows whether he is or is not qualified by testing himself in various ways, but to know if you qualify here, it is necessary to test your knowledge by a comparison, either by writing down what you understand so this can be compared with what I have written, or else by letting me hear what you think, so I can compare it."

"I think I understand, but you tell me if I qualify."

"I'll be the judge."

"Well... first... it is extremely important to understand that when a word like education is used to describe certain differences, as when beautiful is applied to definite physical characteristics, these differences are real and a part of the external world, but the word contains a judgment of value and consequently can have no corresponding accuracy. There is a world of difference between saying 'I like Julie because her nose is straight, her teeth together, her breasts pointed and firm, her skin smooth and soft."

"You'd better take it easy, Jim, or you'll be rushing home to her in the next few minutes."

"I say, Larry, there is a big difference between saying I like her because of these various things and saying I like her because she is beautiful. Even to qualify it by saying she is beautiful to me does not rectify the inaccuracy of the description because it is mathematically impossible for the word to delineate anything externally real. The sun is not beautiful, although on certain days I like it better than on others; it is simply a ball of fire. Many people, resenting this word 'beautiful' being applied mostly to physical characteristics they did not possess, and yet wanting a share of this value, would parry with, 'Beauty is of the soul, not of the body.' By defining it differently, they derived a compensating satisfaction, as if definition determines what exists."

"You just earned a down payment, but we're discussing education, not beauty."

"What difference does it make, Larry? The same holds true for the word education."

"Considering this an external reality of great value, and resenting the fact that millions of people imagine themselves educated because they completed high school and college, Durant resorts to a definition for the purpose of showing that the prevailing conception of education does not determine an educated man, and he points out why by relating other values, which he judges are external, to his own conception of education, and he is able to do this in a logical manner through the use of synonyms that also do not have any external value, such as 'mature, real culture, total men,' etc. In other words, a person acquires a liberal education when he becomes mature, really cultured, intelligent, etc. Since these college graduates do not develop into this, they cannot be educated. Durant doesn't realize that the 'enjoyable and instructive aspects of the world' are different for different people, that 'the glow of the autumn woods in the setting sun' has no value except to those who enjoy it. He blames those who do not consider 'Beethoven or Corot or Hardy' of greater value than the newspaper, the love-scenes on the screen, the same anatomy on the stage, by calling them 'merely the raw material of a man;' and then because he does not have the ability to perceive mathematical relations, for which he cannot be blamed, he blames Spencer for a definition of education that is so accurate it completely does away with further need for the word, since everybody, regardless of his motion from here to there, acquires an education from the day of his birth as he learns to adjust to his particular environment which included, in the world of free will, the criticism, judgment, blame and punishment of others."

"Are you finished, Jim?"

"Not yet. I'm beginning to understand these relations much better as I explain them. Anyway... since Durant's conception of education 'does not mean that we have become certified experts in business, or mining, or botany, or journalism, or epistemology,' but describes other aspects, all that is necessary to solve his equation is to show him that there is no greater value between one thing a person prefers to do and another, that is, under the new conditions. Larry, I think I see something very humorous; correct me if I'm wrong. It seems to me that without doing any reading at all, those born in the new world will surpass, in every way, what he describes as a 'mature, liberally educated, really cultured, civilized, well-mannered individual.' We are able to control and understand ourselves not because we read the books he recommends as necessary for development, but only because we know at last what it means that man's will is not free. Our knowledge that we will never be criticized or judged by another allows us, for the very first time, to select what is truly best for ourselves, even though we may prefer Zane Grey to Shakespeare, Elvis Presley to Caruso, a pool player as a friend to an author, philosopher, historian. Furthermore, all the reading in the world can never make an individual courteous when he is constantly ridiculed, criticized, and judged by fallacious standards of value, such as culture; nor can it give him wisdom without the knowledge of his own nature, which no one ever understood completely until now. As for 'forgiveness,' how is it mathematically possible for me to forgive you, Larry, for doing what I know you were compelled to do, which reveals that it exists only because man was lacking in understanding."

"I liked that very much, Jim, except for one thing. The word wisdom is no different than education or other words that describe nonexisting external values. Just as Spencer's definition of education is so accurate that it does away with further need for the word, simply because everybody is educated, so does the knowledge of what it means that man's will is not free do away with further need for the word 'wisdom,' simply because everybody then becomes wise. Being no different than any other thinker in the world of free will, he arranges everything in stratified layers of external value and judges what is better for mankind by how close each person comes to these upper levels of stratification."

"In other words, Larry, all words that criticize another for being in a lower level of this stratification must become obsolete; is that right?"

"That's exactly right; everybody henceforth is exactly equal in value, and any words that criticize them for being not equal are a hurt, for which there will be no blame; consequently, these words must become obsolete.

Furthermore, as was already explained, if I should say that a person is educated, cultured, mature, wise, intelligent — or should I ask favors of others — I would only reveal my ignorance of what it means that man's will is not free. Since no one can derive any satisfaction from being considered an ignorant individual, it is obvious that he will be forced to relinquish the use of these words, which will necessitate a complete revision of this aspect of our dictionaries."

"But Larry, it is a known fact that certain things have greater value for certain people, and therefore man will always be drawn towards values that he sees are better for himself. If an accountant makes more money than a bookkeeper, and I desire more money, then this is a value that will attract me. If I see that a particular group of people prefer to associate with those who like to read particular books, like Shakespeare, or listen to a certain kind of music, like Beethoven, then as long as I wish to belong to this group, this type of reading and music will have a personal value."

"That's very true, Jim, but this would not make you superior to someone who desires to associate with a group that likes rock and roll or comic books. There is no such thing as a good book, better music, a classic, a masterpiece; only what you like better. These words try to give external reality to personal taste and values. I might like a painting by Rembrandt better than one by my daughter, but this doesn't make it a masterpiece, nor does it become one because it is liked by the majority of mankind."

"Do you mean that I can't praise Edward Gibbon, Rembrandt, or applaud someone for what he has done? Supposing I went to a nightclub to be entertained, and the singer there sang in a manner that I liked; can't I stand up and applaud, yell Bravo, etc.?"

"You can do anything you want, just so you don't hurt anybody by what you do. If you say to yourself while visiting an art gallery, 'I think this painting by Rembrandt is a masterpiece,' then nobody can be hurt, but if you say this to the person next to you, then you will automatically put him in a lower level of stratification the moment he disagrees with your opinion, because the word masterpiece, or any opinion, is stratified."

"But supposing I don't remark that this is a masterpiece, only that I like it. In other words, suppose somebody is standing next to me, and I say, 'I like that painting, don't you?' Is there anything wrong with that?"

"Certainly there is. You are asking him to agree with what you like, which means you are blaming him in advance for not agreeing. If he should say 'I don't like it,' then you will want to know why; otherwise, you would never have asked. If he agrees with you, then the most you can do is talk about what both of you like."

"Well, what's wrong with that, with finding people who like the same things?"

"Nothing, but what is there to talk about? All you can say is, 'I like Rembrandt,' then he says, 'I like him too.' The purpose of a discussion is to find issues upon which to disagree, and how is it possible to get involved in this kind of a discussion when the very moment you disagree, you blame someone for being different?"

"You know, Larry, while you were talking, I think I found a flaw that will put a kink in your whole system."

"It sounds frightening, Jim, but don't bet your life on it, or your $2000. Remember, this discovery is a mathematical, invariable, inexorable law that brooks no opposition."

"Of course, I admit that I could be wrong, but I was quite surprised when I thought of it. Now tell me, Larry, isn't it true that asking favors is a form of advance blame?"

"Certainly, you know that."

"Well, if asking favors is a form of blame, then asking questions must also be a form of blame because every time you ask a question, you are asking the person to do you a favor by answering the question. In other words, all conversations in the future, if what you say is true, will be statements only. Well, my fine feathered friend, what do you say about that?"

"I was wondering how long it would take you to discover this because it is so obvious. I've been reserving this problem until now because it brings about such a drastic change in our relationship with each other. In fact, I was just about ready to mention it. Anyway, you are right about the first part of what you just said and wrong about the second."

"What do you mean?"

"I mean that asking questions is a definite form of advance blame, because it is asking a person to do you a favor by answering your question.

However, conversation in the new world will not be with statements only, because questions will still be asked."

"But Larry, you distinctly said that all forms of advance blame will be removed, and you just now said that asking questions is a form of advance blame because it is asking someone to do you a favor; now, how do you get out of this impasse?"

"It is apparent that this problem requires a certain amount of clarification, right?"

"Most definitely."

"The answer, however, is rather simple. When you go home to Julie this evening and teach her what I'm going to teach you, you will simply say, 'Julie, I would like to answer any questions you have, ' and then she would proceed to ask whatever is on her mind. But since Julie knows that you will always desire to answer her questions, it won't be necessary for you to tell her each time that you would like to answer any questions. This is equivalent to an individual who has something to sell. A bank wants to sell the use of its money for a price, and therefore, since it knows you will never borrow if you can't pay it back, there is no fear of being hurt. Consequently, when you know that Julie will never desire to hurt you by the questions she asks, and she knows that you will never blame her for asking because you told her to ask, then there is no form of advance blame under these conditions. But this reveals something very humorous . . ."

"But wait a minute, Larry. If that's the case, then why must I ask Julie if there is something I can do for her? Why can't she know that it is a permanent question, and then when she has the television to move or something else she can't do without my assistance, all she has to say is, 'Jim, help me move the television, will you please?' Under the conditions you just described, Larry, this is not a form of advance blame."

"And you are perfectly right, simply because there is no way advantage can be taken."

"Well, why didn't you tell me this before, so I could have saved myself the trouble of saying to Julie, 'Honey, is there something I can do for you,' and saved myself the effort of teaching this to her?"

"Did I know you were going to get married so quickly and test this knowledge? Besides, this is my way of testing your alertness. It was discussed once already, I think."

"Okay, Larry. Well... what is this something that is so humorous?"

"It is also very serious. It has to do with asking questions. You see, Jim, when someone spends a great part of his life accumulating knowledge other than for the purpose of earning a living, it is equivalent to a man spending equal time in developing huge muscles. The latter could never desire to expend this great effort lifting heavy weights if he knew positively that the very moment his body was developed sufficiently to attract the admiration of others, he would be placed on a deserted island where nobody would ever be able to see the fantastic results of his efforts; nor could a person desire to memorize the encyclopedia if he was not granted an opportunity to display this mnemonic feat. However, to walk on a beach in swimming trunks so that everyone can see the differences that exist between one body and another does not impose on anyone, but to show the world the differences that exist inside of one's head does impose."

"Exactly how does it impose?"

"After spending so many years accumulating knowledge that has no value for his employment, man has to convince himself that the effort was worth it and consequently will search for ways and means of demonstrating this information to others so he can reveal his superiority. You see, Jim, in the world of free will, we were constantly faced with this stratification of values, and it was a source of satisfaction to move in the direction of these upper levels. As a result, we developed the habit of asking questions, the answers of which were already known to us. Do you know when Columbus discovered America?"

"I used to know, but not anymore."

"It was back in 1492. This proves, in a mathematical manner, that had a person who asks this kind of question known positively that the one asked would know the answer, he could have gotten no satisfaction out of asking, simply because he would not have been granted an opportunity to reveal this difference in knowledge which he considered important for the other to know."

"I know what you mean, Larry, because I see this happen all the time. In fact, just the other day I was in my car with a friend when a particular aria was played over the radio, and he said, 'Say Jim, do you know the name of that tune?' And when I said 'no,' he proceeded to tell me."

"This kind of question is designed for two reasons: either to make yourself appear superior, and the person asked inferior, or to teach the other person what is thought he should know, which blames him in advance for not knowing. In most cases, the question partakes of both reasons."

"I have an aunt like that. Whenever she would visit, she never failed to ask me: 'Jimmy, how do you spell Constantinople?' "I don't know how, Aunt Lil.' 'Jimmy... shame on you... you should know that; aren't you in the 12th grade? Now come on and try.' "I'll try, but I'm sure I can't spell it; spelling is my worst subject — C O N S T A N D ..." 'Hold it, Jimmy; not D but T I N O P L E, now that wasn't so hard, was it?'"

"Now it is extremely important to understand that any question designed to make the person asked feel inferior is a definite attempt to hurt the other person. However, when a teacher asks this question for the purpose of instructing children, it is not stopped because he wishes to show that he knows more, but only because it blames them in advance for what he thinks they should know."

"Are you trying to tell me that all questions for the purpose of teaching have come to an end, in school and out?"

"Since there is no way this kind of question can be asked without blaming the children for not knowing the answer, we are given no choice, Jim."

"But how will the kids learn if they are not taught?"

"Who said they wouldn't be taught? The teachers will still teach them what they want to learn, and what the kids don't understand, they will ask the teachers."

"Ask without blame?"

"Certainly, without blame. A child is equivalent to a potential buyer in a store, and a teacher is equivalent to an assistant in the store. The buyer knows that the assistant is there to help if he needs help, but the assistant doesn't know if the buyer wants help until the buyer comes to him. The same with teachers and students. A pupil knows that the teachers are there to answer his questions, but they don't know if he wants help until he comes to them. Now tell me, Jim, regarding the other reason for this type of question — the answer of which is already known to the questioner — how is it humanly possible to exert effort in learning various things, except for employment and personal gratification, when there is absolutely no value to this learning? Take your time because this is a very crucial point."

"If there is absolutely no value, obviously, there couldn't be any desire, as this would be equivalent to developing huge muscles on a deserted island, as you mentioned. But my question is this: Are you implying that the very subjects Durant mentioned as having value for a 'liberal education' are now of no value whatsoever?"

"Of course not. They have value for any person who wants to read them. But how is it humanly possible to desire reading things that are not a pleasure in themselves when there is no way this information can benefit the reader as much as one iota where others are concerned? It should be obvious that the books on philosophy have no further value because the knowledge revealed (by knowing what it means that man's will is not free) makes all such books a waste of time since they pertain to someone's opinions regarding a world of human relations that has now become obsolete... unless a certain amount of pleasure is derived from this reading. As for history, unless you are planning to write a book, or you are deriving a certain amount of pleasure, of what value is remembering dates, names, and events when you can't use this information? In other words, if you memorized the entire encyclopedia, it would be a complete waste of time and effort because there would be no conceivable way this knowledge could ever be aired."

"I'm really not clear on this, Larry. You say there is absolutely no value in memorizing anything that will not be used to earn a living? As an example, couldn't someone ask this person who memorized the encyclopedia, when Columbus discovered America, if he really didn't know the answer?"

"Didn't we just get through saying that asking questions is asking someone to do us a favor by answering? If I asked you such a question, when the answer is already in various encyclopedias at the library or in your home, it is obvious to save myself a trip, a phone call, or just the effort required to look it up. Since I can't blame you in advance anymore by asking you to do for me the things I can do for myself, all questions, the answers of which can be gotten without disturbing another person whose job is not for the purpose of answering questions, as is the duty of a teacher or librarian, will be kept to oneself. Now think very carefully, Jim, about what a crucial turning point this is."

"Believe me, Larry, I'm thinking while listening."

"If, for example, you are reading Shakespeare, and you come to a passage you don't understand, you will be compelled to refer to another book for an explanation, because it is impossible to ask favors even of a teacher when you are able to do things for yourself. This also applies to the assistants in stores. Anything you can get for yourself you will get because otherwise you would be asking someone to do you a favor. Furthermore, unless a teacher knows a mathematical answer to a question, an answer that is absolutely undeniable, he would be compelled to be honest with his students. In other words, if you could not find a satisfactory answer to a passage of Shakespeare, unless the teacher knows there is only one possible interpretation, he could not be of any assistance whatsoever, because he is prevented from expressing his opinion, since this blames others for thinking differently. Consequently, he would say, 'I don't know what he means.' Now again, pay close attention, Jim. The only reason a person could ask a question the answer of which he could find without disturbing this individual, and the only reason he could ask a question, the answer of which is already known to himself, is either because he already feels superior to the person asked, or would like to be considered superior, but in both cases there is a subtle attempt to hurt the person asked. Therefore, when it is mathematically revealed that the person who asks is tacitly blaming, judging that the other would desire to answer — which strikes the first blow — this other has a justifiable right, in the world of free will, not to turn his other cheek, which is what he would be doing by answering any question designed in some subtle way to hurt him either by not answering or by retaliating with, 'If you already knew the answer what was your purpose in asking the question? or with, 'Why don't you go to the library for your information?' — making the questioner feel foolish. However, when the person asked fully realizes what it means that man's will is not free (that the one asking cannot help himself), he will lose the desire to strike back by making this other feel foolish, which knowledge that this would be his reaction compels the questioner, who now knows that this person will not desire to hurt him in return regardless of what, to lose his desire to make this other feel inferior and to think very carefully before asking any more questions. Consequently, it is mathematically impossible, once this knowledge is thoroughly understood, for man in the new world to ever accumulate information which only has value in this direction of asking these kinds of questions, for it cannot satisfy him to exert great effort when this will only shipwreck him on an island where it is impossible for others to admire a difference that can only be brought to light by making them feel inferior and himself ignorant, for which no one will ever blame him."

"Larry, you have no idea how much I really enjoyed that, but I would like to know what compels this desire to make others feel inferior, and also — this was never explained to my satisfaction — am I allowed to applaud an entertainer?"

"As you know, Jim, you are permitted to do anything you want to do, but since your applause would blame those who do not applaud..."

"How is that blame?"

"Aren't you expressing an opinion of the entertainer that disagrees with those who don't applaud...?"

"Sort of, I suppose."

"Sort of nothing, Jim. When you applaud, you are saying, 'I like what you just did.'"

"But that's not an opinion, Larry, that's a mathematical fact. I did like it."

"That's true, Jim, but the moment the person next to you doesn't applaud, you are saying in effect: 'I think this entertainer is worthy of applause, why don't you?' The same thing would happen if you started clapping in front of a painting by Rembrandt with someone standing there. You certainly are not applauding for Rembrandt's benefit, and if you were by yourself, you certainly wouldn't be applauding for your own benefit. So obviously you are clapping to get an agreement or disagreement from the person standing there. The effect would be the same if you said to him, 'I like Rembrandt; do you?'"

"But Larry, a painting is one thing, and a live entertainer is something else. The entertainer likes to hear the applause."

"Do you mean, then, that you are applauding because the entertainer expects it?"

"Not exactly, but in a great many cases, yes."

"In other words, he is blaming you in advance for not applauding, which is a judgment of what is right for you. Since no one will judge any person henceforth, for this strikes the first blow, the only reason, in the new world, for applauding is not because the entertainer expects it, but because you like what he did enough to make you want to applaud. However, just as long as more than one person is being entertained, it is impossible to desire applauding without disagreeing with those who desire not to applaud. He knows he is a superior entertainer, not because of what others tell him but by what he tells himself. Therefore, all applause comes to an end because you are expressing your opinion that you think he is worthy of it."

"Won't that be a disappointment to entertainers?"

"Absolutely not. An entertainer will know whether he is entertaining not by the applause, but by comparing himself with others in the field and by the number of people who come to see his entertainment or watch it on television. He knows he is a superior entertainer not because of what others tell him, but by what he tells himself."

"Are you also trying to tell me that after a Broadway show, the people in the audience will not discuss it?"

"What is there to discuss? Either a person liked it or he did not like it, and the cast will never know this except from their opinion of themselves."

"But Larry, I do remember you saying that a child could not be applauded until after he had been taught what it means that his will is not free, and doesn't this imply that he could be applauded later?"

"I didn't say you couldn't applaud; I said you couldn't applaud if more than one is being entertained. If my son walks around the room on his hands to entertain me, that is his business; if I like it, that is my business. However, if no one else is present and I wish to tell him I like it by a clap of the hands, this is also my business. But remember, Jim, my applause could influence him to believe that he is an excellent entertainer, and this is a judgment he must make for himself, which he can only do by comparing himself with others in the entertainment field. Consequently, if he should walk around the room on his hands, he will know that he is entertaining not by any applause, but by the knowledge that he is a superior performer (there are certain mathematical standards that he can use for judging himself). Have you any idea how many children got the impression that they were good at doing something only because others told them they were, or because they didn't compare themselves properly?"

"A high school graduate recently told me that his best subject was algebra, and that he was terrific at it, because his teacher told him so. After finding that he was incapable of solving two problems I gave him, he excused himself by saying, 'I think that's college algebra.' Well then, how am I able to work these out if I never got out of elementary school?"

"That's exactly what I mean, Jim. Everybody has been using fallacious standards to judge themselves because they were compelled to reach out in every conceivable direction for anything that could place them in the upper level of stratification. But all this is changed when each person is compelled to keep his opinions to himself."

"Won't there be critics, reviewers, and write-ups after each show?"

"Absolutely not. All these people get displaced."

"Well, how will an entertainer know if he is really entertaining?"

"I just got through telling you this. He will know simply by the perception and extension of mathematical relations."

"What is that supposed to mean?"

"If you were able to balance your entire body on one finger, wouldn't you consider this a form of entertainment?"

"I certainly would."

"Well, how do you know?"

"Because I can see how the public would react to something like that."

"Well, that's how you know, when you yourself can see, in advance, how people will react to your entertainment, which means that only people with enormous ability will ever tackle the entertainment field in the new world."

"Why can't people with lesser ability entertain?"

"Because the real reward of an entertainer, other than cash and fame, is in the knowledge that he is definitely entertaining, and since he will never know by applause and comments what people think of his entertainment, the only way he will ever know is by what he thinks of himself. Therefore, only the extremely talented will ever perform."

"Do you mean there will be no more talent shows, beauty contests, applause meters, etc.?"

"That's right, Jim; they all get displaced."

"Won't anybody ever tell another whether he has talent or not, whether he is good at doing certain things?"

"Never, Jim, because this is a judgment of what is better for someone else and blames him in advance for not developing in this direction. Furthermore, if he relies on the judgment of others, he could easily be responsible for hurting someone, as a doctor can hurt people by relying on the schools telling him that he is a qualified healer."

"But how could an entertainer hurt someone?"

"He could hurt his sponsor by taking a job for which he is not qualified, and the only reason he thought he was qualified was because others told him he was; he didn't tell himself."

"Your reasoning is a complete mathematical circle, Larry, that proves its truth every step of the way. It is like saying 4 plus 2 is 6 because 4 from 6 is 2 or 2 from 6 is 4."

"Does this mean you agree with me?"

"What else, when it is mathematically impossible to disagree.

"Well, you still haven't answered my other question: What impels this desire to make someone feel inferior?"

"The lack of respect for him. We were born into a world that stratified people according to what they did to earn a living, the amount of their wealth, their social position, their formal and informal education (remember this word will soon be displaced), etc. Doctors, rabbis, priests, and professors were entitled to a specific designation to reveal a difference that exacted greater respect to them than to others who were not entitled to these additional names. The age of a person made him feel that much younger people, like children, should call him 'sir' or 'mister,' and the protocol of government was designed to show deference to someone's position, as in the Armed Services. 'Your Honor, Your Grace,' etc., like all titles, were designed to separate the difference between one person or group of people and others. When two men would meet for the first time in the army, for example, the person who had the kind of position in civilian life that put him in a higher bracket of respect would generally desire to reveal this difference so he could get his share of respect even here.

'Say Harry, what did you do in civilian life?' 'I was a butcher.' Already, the classification has placed him in a category to be treated in a certain manner. 'What school or university did you go to, Harry?' Again, the effort to find out the differences that could separate them. 'I never went to either high school or college.' 'Do you like to work out mathematical problems? If you do, I have a couple of good ones. And how about chess and checkers, do you play these games?' Every step of the way, these types of questions are designed to probe for the differences that can make him feel superior, and they are avoided when he knows that his position is so low on this scale that any difference can only make him feel inferior. Do you like Shakespeare? Have you ever read the Critique of Pure Reason by Kant?' A steelworker is not anxious to ask: 'Where did you work in civilian life?' because he knows he will be asked the same question, and his answer is not a source of satisfaction to himself. Should the answer to his question be: 'I'm the Vice-President of a bank,' then he is sorry he asked."

"I get the point, Larry, but how is this remedied?"

"In a very easy manner, Jim. First, by the very fact that all questions like this cannot be asked, and second by this: In our New Earth, that is, when the transition gets under way, just as we displaced all the material forms of money because this was advance blame, so likewise do we displace all names and titles except those to distinguish one person from another. If parents wish to use one, two, three, four or more names for a child, this is their business, just so the names are not designed to exact greater respect for one person over another."

"But what about in school, will a student yell up to his teacher, 'Hey Larry,' and then ask his question? Won't children say 'sir' and 'ma'am' to their elders? Won't this make matters even worse? I like when this respect is shown to me."

"I know you do, Jim, but do you show this respect to the Blacks, the janitors, the garbage collectors, the street cleaners? Besides, the very moment you show respect to one and no respect to another, you place yourself in a position of inferiority. If I call another person handsome, isn't this an admission that he has something I don't have?"

"I don't quite understand."

"If I say, 'he is quite an educated man,' isn't this an admission that I am not quite what he is? To put it another way — to show you that this is completely mathematical — if you are the champion pool player of the world, is it possible for you to say, 'he is the best pool player in the world' when talking about another player?"

"Of course not, not if I am the champ."

"Well, supposing you consider yourself a champion in the field of being educated, like Durant, is it possible for you to say, 'he has quite an education,' which means, in your eyes, that he is now the champ, when you still consider yourself the champ? In other words, Jim, whenever you use words that give to one person greater respect than to another, you automatically place yourself in a relation of lesser respect. I'm repeating this because of its importance. This is why Durant found it necessary to criticize college graduates and professors for thinking they were educated. Consequently, since it is impossible — once man understands what it means that his will is not free — to judge what is right for others or exact this respect; and since each person knows that to pay others compliments only lowers himself, he is given no choice but to relinquish every word, habit, custom, convention and motion from here to there that pushes another up, which, out of mathematical necessity, must push himself down."

"But Larry, what about all the people who try to push others down to elevate themselves?"

"How is it possible to do that, Jim, when this would be a hurt for which there would be no blame or punishment? In other words, you won't have to continue calling a person doctor, once the transition begins (this must be qualified); he won't expect it; and you, because this would be a hurt to him for which he would never blame you, cannot ridicule him by saying... Hi Doc ole buddy!'"

"Are you referring to the expression, 'familiarity breeds contempt?'"

"To become familiar, in this sense, with another person, is a definite form of hurt; it is a sign of disrespect which cannot be done under the conditions because no one will want to do it."

"In other words, Larry, if I try to elevate you, I am showing disrespect to myself, and if I try to lower you, which I cannot do, of course, I would be showing you disrespect. Therefore, when these conditions are removed, we will have a perfectly balanced equation of mutual respect."

"Excellent, marvelous, wonderful, Jim!"

"Now wait a minute, Larry. You distinctly told me... "

"I know what I told you, but am I lowering myself by paying you this compliment? All I actually said was that I liked the way you expressed yourself, and since no one else is present to disagree, no one is being criticized."

"But you said all words that project external values are being displaced. You also said that even to say 'I like that very much' will have no further value. Do you mean, then, that if I wanted to go home and tell Julie that she is the most beautiful girl in the whole world, the most wonderful, the most precious, the most adorable, the most educated, the finest, the best, the greatest, the loveliest — I can do it if I want to?"

"Certainly not, Jim. I was only testing your alertness. These words will definitely become obsolete. However, it won't be necessary for you to say these things to Julie because just as long as you desire to make passionate love to her, which she can control, you will desire to display the meaning of these words with actions that speak much louder. After all, when you find yourself desiring to kiss her body, what is this but another way of saying, 'Julie, Honey, Baby, you mean so much to me, and I love you very much.'"

"Am I to understand that the dictionaries will definitely be revised?"

"Of course they will be."

"Supposing she prepares something for dinner that I like very much, can I compliment her?"

"Certainly not, for this blames the meals you don't compliment."

"Well, supposing she makes something I don't like, can I tell her it was bad?"

"Wouldn't this be a hurt to her, Jim?"

"Yes, but she is striking the first blow by hurting me with a tasteless meal."

"She is well aware of this possibility, and she knows that you would eat what she makes, no matter how much it is distasteful, because you know she can't help preparing it this way. But she knows she doesn't have to prepare what you don't like unless she wants to, for over this she has mathematical control... "

"It never fails to work, does it, Larry?"

"Never, Jim."

"But how about lovemaking? Does this mean that I would desire to make love to her regardless of how I feel at the moment, just because she extends an invitation? You just said that I would desire to eat whatever she prepares because if I didn't, this would be a hurt to her. You also said that she, knowing that if I ate what I didn't like, would be hurting me, which prevents her from preparing dishes that are not tasty for me. But supposing I'm not hungry even for what is prepared in an appetizing manner; must I eat anyway; must I make love anyway? Remember, Larry, Julie can eat by herself, but she can't make love by herself. If she extends an invitation because she is in the mood, and I'm not in the mood to accept, wouldn't this be a hurt to her?"

"If Julie wants you to partake of her body, then she must arouse your desire to do so, and if she can't, then she must bide her time until you are in the mood. But remember, she can say and do anything she wants to excite you, just so she does not touch you in any way."

"To change the subject, will the signing of autographs also come to an end?"

"Certainly. How is it possible for you to ask me for my autograph when this is asking me to do you a favor?"

"Well, couldn't someone say to an audience, 'I will answer any questions you may have, and couldn't a person then ask, 'May I please have your autograph?'"

"You're a rascal, Jim, but one hundred percent right."

"Are you sure that I can't ask for an opinion on something?"

"Of course you can't, for this blames my not agreeing with your opinion."

"But supposing it isn't an opinion I am asking about?"

"Then why did you ask the question? If you know that two plus two equals four, you are not going to ask me how much this is, right?"

"Right."

"And if you don't know the answer to something, the library is available, right?"

"Possibly. But supposing what I want to know isn't in the library? Supposing I wish to ask you a question regarding the knowledge you just revealed, what then?"

"Then you are not interested in my opinion of something, but in my explaining a mathematical equation you still have not understood."

"Won't this affect the kind and quality of the conversations in the future, in the new world, that is?"

"Tremendously. No one will ever ask others where they work, for this is not their business. In fact, very few questions will ever be asked, and these will be of great importance. Besides, when all disrespect is removed, no one will want to know."

"What about all the conversations regarding various books?"

"What is there to talk about? Didn't we go over this? Either you like something or you don't. Don't you like making love to Julie?"

"I love it."

"Well, is there something to talk about?"

"No, there isn't."

"I loved reading Gibbon's Decline and Fall of the Roman Empire solely for the pleasure I experienced and what I learned, but I have no desire to talk about it. I enjoyed watching a Western on television the other night, but I didn't feel like talking about it. The people who desire to strike up a discussion are unconsciously interested in showing off something, and they either want to put you down or elevate themselves. Since this is an impossibility in the new world, they will lose their desire to strike up a discussion."

"But sometimes it is awkward just standing around when nobody says anything."

"That's only because you were expected to say something. But in the future, no one will ever expect you to do anything, for this is a judgment of what is right for you; consequently, the awkward feeling disappears."

"You seem to have all the answers."

"I do, Jim, because this discovery is completely mathematical in every way and is a law that defies anyone to move in the direction of dissatisfaction."

"But Larry, I still think you are wrong about applause. You yourself said that it is perfectly all right to do anything that does not hurt another individual, which hurt is prevented by the knowledge that there will be no blame, and that it is perfectly all right to do anything that doesn't partake of advance blame. Now, if I want to applaud, this is my business, I'm not hurting anybody, and I'm not blaming anybody for not applauding. Besides, it gives me a certain satisfaction to know that the entertainer enjoys my applause. I can understand that it would be advance blame if I asked the person next to me, or someone else, for his opinion about the performer, and I can also understand that the question itself, being the kind it is, would be considered a form of advance blame, but for the life of me, I can't see where my applause is a form of advance blame."

"I can't seem to confuse you, can I, Jim? Now, doesn't this prove that you don't need me or anyone when you have this slide rule to prove the validity of my statement?"

"Oh, so you agree that I'm right! Well, what do you know, the great Larry conceded!"

"How can I argue against mathematics?"

"You can't. By the way, did you ever read the book: How to Win Friends and Influence People?"

"No, I never did. But what difference does it make now when there is no possibility of making enemies? So many books will be displaced, you have no idea."

"Isn't it important to develop a large vocabulary and speak in a manner that attracts attention, so that a person can draw to himself the kind of friends he likes?"

"What difference does it make how you speak and write when no one will ever disrespect you for it?"

"But supposing an individual speaks in a way that grates on your ears, and it actually annoys you as certain types of music can do; what do you do then?"

"You find the kind of music you like."

"But supposing this person likes to talk to you?"

"About what?"

"About any number of things."

"You've just set up a very unmathematical equation, because there is absolutely nothing for him to talk about with me, so how can his voice grate on my ears? A person either has something important to say or he has nothing of importance to say. He can't ask me questions that refer to opinions, and he can't ask me questions that refer to facts, so what is he going to talk about?"

"The women won't like this very much."

"Not upon a first glance, but they won't be given any choice. From now on, Jim, actions will speak much louder than words, and the actions can only go in one direction."

"Well, what about the school system, Larry? Have you got this all figured out?"

"Yes, I do, and it is marvelous to behold; fantastic, in fact."

"Well, tell me about it already. By the way, Larry, if I go back to high school and then on to college, could I become an educated man?"

"That question makes absolutely no sense anymore, Jim. Children go to school to learn specific things that interest them for various reasons; they don't go to acquire an education, for there is no such thing."

"At what age do they start school?"

"There is no specific age because this is a judgment that the child is ready, which blames him in advance for not wanting to go when the parents and school think he should."

"Well, when do you think a child would think he is ready to go?"

"When he is taught the basic principles in this book, which will not be difficult to do. Each home will have commandments placed on the wall, as we have the Ten Commandments today, and these will say... Thou Shall Not Ask Favors... Thou Shall Not Tell Others What To Do... Thou Shall Not Judge What Is Right For Someone Else, and so on. The parents will explain what this is to their children. Once they are taught the many ways other children and teachers could be hurt, for which they know they would never be blamed, then they will be ready."

"But supposing they should desire to start before they learn these principles, wouldn't this blame their desire?"

"Remember, Jim, until they do learn, they will be living in the world of free will, and the teachers and children must be prevented from being hurt; consequently, if a child should ask why he can't start, you would simply tell him the truth, that he will be allowed to go to school just as soon as he learns what it means that his will is not free."

"Will it be hard to teach children this?"

"Under our present conditions, yes, but by the time our New Earth gets launched, it will be relatively simple."

"Assuming that a child has been taught the necessary fundamentals, what's the next step?"

"The parents will show him the school, show him the fun children are having, and then ask if he would like to go — after explaining that the purpose of the school is to teach him anything he wants to learn of which there is knowledge."

"Supposing he still doesn't want to go?"

"There is nothing you can do but try to arouse his desire."

"But you said that it was wrong when Durant tried to arouse his daughter's desire to play the piano."

"It was wrong because he judged what the end should be. School is not an end in itself but a means to the child's end. Durant decided what he wanted his daughter to be, and this blamed her desire to be different."

"Do you mean, then, that anything is permissible to arouse the desire of a child to go to school?"

"Anything at all, once he has been taught what it means that man's will is not free. However, he will desire to go because there will be no force or persuasion."

"Will the school have specific hours?"

"Not the school, the teachers. Each one will judge what is better for himself because this is his business — teaching — and he will tell the children what time class begins and what time it will be over."

"Doesn't this blame them for not being there on time?"

"No more than a traffic light blames an individual for going through when it is red. The children know that they would hurt the teacher by being late with their interruptions, as well as disrupt the class, and they also know that they would never be blamed for hurting or annoying others this way. Consequently, they will desire to be there exactly on time, and if something did occur to make them late, the teacher and everybody else would know that it was unavoidable, and no questions would be asked."

"But supposing it was avoidable?"

"How is that possible when man's will is not free, and how is it humanly possible for them to be late either carelessly or deliberately when they know others will be compelled to excuse what they can never justify? No, Jim, they will desire to be on time and will set their own alarm clocks, which the parents will have already taught them to use."

"Can you describe a child's first day at school?"

"Very easily. When he arrives, he will be greeted by someone who will ask him if he would like to be shown around. If he doesn't want to be, this is his business, and he is not to be persuaded. However, these children will desire to be shown around the school. When this has been done, they will be asked if there is anything special they would like to learn. Then the teacher will ask them if they would like to learn how to read and write, add and subtract, etc. They will then be placed with the proper teacher who will address them by their first and last name. The teachers will also be addressed by their first and last names. No Miss or Mrs. or Master or Mister or Professor will be used. If the teacher prefers calling a child by his first name or last, this is his business, but by the same reasoning, this privilege is also extended to the children. Under the new conditions, however, there can be no disrespect whatsoever."

"If the children could be of different ages when they start, depending on how long it would take them to learn what it means that man's will is not free, then it is very possible that a four-year-old child could be in the first grade with a seven-year-old, isn't that true?"

"That's very true."

"Well, wouldn't that make it very difficult for the teacher?"

"On the contrary, it would be very easy since this would make them all equal when they start. However, there will be no more grades, no report cards, and no graduation."

"What about homework?"

"How is it possible for a teacher to give children something to do at home, when this blames them for not doing it?"

"Isn't this the same as a teacher telling a child what time to be in school?"

"Of course not. The time is the teacher's business, but what children do at home is their business. However, many may desire to do some studying when they get home, but again, this is strictly their business."

"Did I hear you say, 'no more grades, report cards, or graduation?'"

"You did."

"But how is that possible when these things allow the teachers to know what's going on?"

"It is not the business of teachers to know anything about a child except his name, address, and phone number."

"Why his address and phone number?"

"Just in case of an emergency."

"Do you mean there will be no records or tests of what a child has learned?"

"Absolutely none, although he will constantly test himself. There will be no passing and no failing. The only other thing teachers have to know about a child is what he wants to learn. Since they cannot blame him in any way, shape, or form, just as I can't blame you, Jim, for not understanding these principles (should you not understand them), they will have to make everything so clear there can be no misunderstanding."

"But just suppose that a child doesn't understand in spite of everything, then what?"

"Then when the teacher asks, 'Is there anything that is not understood?', Mary Jane will stand up and say, 'I didn't understand so and so.'"

"Why does she have to stand?"

"She doesn't; this is her business."

"How often will the teacher ask that question?"

"Until she gets no answer to it. If she doesn't like repeating the same lesson over and over again, she had better start thinking of ways and means to teach these children so they won't have any reason to take longer to learn. Teachers will have nothing to say to a child other than what they are teaching and only two questions to ask. Children will be permitted to ask any questions they wish once they have been taught the types that cannot be asked because they are the buyers, and the teachers are the sellers. The children will also be asked if they would like to learn how to swim and do other physical things."

"Will all the new schools be equipped with a pool?"

"The definition of a school is a place to teach children what they want to learn."

"But supposing, when the transition begins, some schools do not have pools, what then?"

"Then the teacher wouldn't ask."

"But supposing the child asks?"

"Jim, are you trying to be funny?"

"After telling me about all the changes, Larry, I truthfully don't know what to expect next."

"And you're going to be my fuse. Anyway, if the child asks, the teacher would simply tell him the school doesn't have a pool."

"What will be the subjects of the elementary schools?"

"Reading, writing, spelling the words used in everyday conversation, and also arithmetic."

"Will there be a recess period?"

"Certainly."

"Will there be games played?"

"Only for those children who want to play and who want to be taught."

"When they have learned these elementary subjects, what do they do then?"

"It is important to remember, Jim, that there is no time limit to when a child knows the subject he is interested in. He may take a couple of books home with him, and within a week, understand these symbols. All words that create external values will never be used or taught, but since many books will contain these words at the start of the transition, the children will be given a list of obsolete words and then told why these are obsolete. Once a child has learned to read, he is ready for the next stage of his self-development."

"What about music? Supposing a child has enormous talent in this direction, as observed by one of the teachers who saw him fiddling with the piano or playing with the fiddle, can he be asked if he would like to learn this instrument?"

"Absolutely not."

"But why? Didn't the teacher ask the children if they would like to learn how to read, write, spell, etc.?"

"But there is a big difference, Jim. These elementary subjects are strictly a means to the end the child will select for himself, but a musical instrument is an end in itself. The child may prefer any number of instruments or even an altogether unrelated field. By asking him if he would like to learn the piano, it is possible that he could be slightly influenced, and since this is not a means to his end but the end someone else thinks he should strive for, he must be left alone. If he wants to learn anything at all, including how to swim, he will approach the teacher. However, anything that is a means to an end he will select for himself, can be mentioned to him, as was already explained."

"Well, what happens after they have learned these elementary subjects?"

"They will continue developing in the direction they want to go. Many will prefer to compete in chess, checkers, swimming, boxing, mathematical games, etc., while others will prefer to read, write, dance, sing, act, do tricks, and many other things."

"But I understood you to say there would be no tests or contests."

"As long as a contest has a mathematical standard by which the winner can be determined, there is no harm, and it allows children to test themselves. Applause meters and judges become obsolete because they do not employ a mathematical standard."

"What about boxing?"

"There will be no more judges. The fight will be over when someone gets knocked out to the tune of ten seconds or when he quits."

"But supposing a fighter hits below the belt or does other things not allowed in the fight game?"

"How is it possible for him to desire to do the things not allowed when he knows he will not be blamed by anybody, even though he may rupture or kill his opponent? Aren't there rules in the game of chess?"

"Yes."

"Well, couldn't one player move the king like the queen if he wanted to get himself out of checkmate?"

"If he wanted to, yes."

"But why wouldn't he want to?"

"Simply because it isn't fair; it's just not the way chess is played."

"That isn't the reason, Jim. He wouldn't move the king like the queen simply because his opponent would never blame him, never criticize this move in any way because it is known that he can't help himself, that he must do things like that. Since he knows he doesn't have to do that, and since he can get no satisfaction from being excused for what he cannot justify, is he given a choice? When a boxer decides to hit his opponent below the belt and remembers he will never be blamed or criticized, is he given a choice?"

"None at all, I know that, Larry. Well, what's next with the kids?"

"After several years of getting acquainted with themselves..."

"Wait a minute; what about Geography, History, Algebra, Geometry, Grammar, and all the rest; won't these subjects be taught?"

"Certainly they will... if the children want to study them. Nothing is stopping a child from reading anything he wants to read, because this is his business, but how is it humanly possible to desire reading or studying anything unless it is for the purpose of earning a living, the pleasure derived from the reading itself, or because there is a deeper purpose, other than just for earning a living, such as developing in a particular direction to become famous. But fame will be so different in the new world, especially when all disrespect is removed (which means that no matter how famous you become, you will never get one ounce more of greater respect), that only the extremely talented will move in this direction, their satisfaction coming mostly from the sheer pleasure of personal development. As I started to say, Jim, after several years of getting acquainted with themselves, children will be shown, through films and personal tours, the entire economic world, and what is the potential purchasing power of particular positions. However, by the time the transition gets under way, especially with the development of atomic energy, there will be a greatly diminished difference between the rich and the poor; and when our New Earth gets officially launched the difference will still be smaller because there is a limit to what a person can buy and a limit to what he can invest in, and prices must come down."

"Supposing someone doesn't want to study anything, and is satisfied to take a laboring job when he gets older?"

"That's his business, and he will never be respected less for this preference or more for becoming a scientist."

"Do you mean that school could be over that quickly?"

"There is no time limit to school. You go just as long as you want to, just as long as you, no one else, see some value to it. If a girl wants to learn how to prepare meals, how to make her husband more sexually satisfied, there will be teachers to explain everything, of which there is undeniable knowledge. The boys will also learn about the female, and though both sexes will get somewhat excited in learning these things, no harm can come of it because marriage, in the new world, is the only sexual outlet."

"But Larry, isn't sex a personal thing? What I mean is, couldn't a boy make a girl passionate without all this learning?"

"Yes, that's true, but the boy doesn't want to take any chances of not satisfying his wife, nor does she want to take the risk of not satisfying him, and since they have had no personal experience, it is obvious that they will want to learn all they can about sexual intercourse. In fact, television and motion pictures will be a school in itself, since everything will be shown without the slightest fear that anything could go wrong. Everybody watching these sexy stories will desire to make love if they are already married, and desire to get married if they are not. Same difference."

"Do you mean there will be no censorship of certain films?"

"Of course. Wouldn't this be a judgment of what is right for others?"

"Do you mean that we will actually see people making love right on television?"

"You will see everything, no holds barred. But remember, the lovers on screen and television will by necessity have to be married to each other."

"But what about the younger children seeing these shows, children who are not yet ready for marriage?"

"Who will determine whether or not they are ready? If a boy sixteen wants to take a wife, who is to stop him when there is no possibility of him hurting anybody? Don't you remember, Jim, that since he doesn't want to hurt his or her parents, he will prepare himself by taking a job. In most cases, however, his desire to develop himself in a particular direction before taking a wife will prevent him from getting married at too young an age. But even if they wished to get married at the age of sixteen while still going to school, they could easily do so without imposing on their parents, because they could easily avoid pregnancy. What difference does it make to the parents if their daughter goes the extreme with her first date, even at the tender age just mentioned, just so she will never be hurt and they will never be criticized, and just so this boy will be her husband until death do they part. Unless you fully understand the mathematical relations that do completely away with all forms of hurt in sexual experience, you will not grasp why there can be no harm in young people getting married at a very early age."

"But Larry, what about the much younger children who are not conscious of sex, watching these sexy television shows?"

"And what about the horror stories that could scare children half to death, right?"

"That's right, what about these things, and what about all the pornography (snapshots and comic books) that is in circulation? You never did discuss that subject, although you were going to when you discussed children or the sexes."

"Since you can't tell the motion picture and television producers what to do, nor can you tell your children, the only alternative — if you are that concerned for their welfare and fear they would be hurt — is to move to some island where you can control the environment by getting rid of all people. But remember, this means that you would have to sacrifice the great pleasure of seeing these shows yourself. However, if you remember God's mathematical standard set up regarding children, derived from the knowledge of what it means that man's will is not free, you will know that when it is impossible to prevent your child from doing something without advance blame, the cause of your fear exists only as a fallacious perception of syllogistic reasoning or logic. The reason horror stories are frightening in the world of free will is because they are related to ways of actually getting hurt, but when hurt becomes a mathematical impossibility, these stories will be equivalent to fairytales; and until a child becomes conscious of sex, lovemaking will have no interest for him, and he will prefer cartoons. There is absolutely no way pornography, which loses its derogatory connotation in the new world, can hurt anybody when it will be so easy to have a sexual relation (get married), and so impossible to get a divorce or commit adultery. Don't misunderstand me, Jim. The hurt our moralists tried to prevent in the world of free will regarding sex and censorship was real, but when the possibility of hurt is removed, the need for moralizing censors has been obviated."

"But what if a child should desire to masturbate because he sees passionate lovemaking?"

"Will he see masturbating on the screen, Jim?"

"No, I guess he wouldn't."

"Well, if he doesn't see it, who is going to teach him?"

"He may just stumble on the fact that there is a thrill associated with his penis."

"Well, if he does, is this your business or his?"

"His."

"Is he hurting you?"

"No, but he might hurt himself. In fact, some doctors say it's unhealthy."

"Bear in mind, Jim, that many things a doctor said under the conditions of free will might have had an element of truth; therefore, you must constantly view the knowledge you are learning in the light of what it means (you should know by now what it means) that man's will is not free. But doctors are completely finished with expressing opinions. If they want to study the human body while in school, there will be teachers to give them only mathematical answers — answers that cannot be denied. Remember, there will be no more diplomas, no titles, no graduation ceremonies, no more failures; only some people who stay in school longer than others and who study one thing in preference to another."

"Will this schooling have to be paid for by the taxpayer?"

"Absolutely not. It will be paid for only by those who want to satisfy the desire of their children to go to school."

"Won't there be scholarships?"

"What the rich do with their money is their business, but only the children themselves will judge whether they are deserving of this free tuition."

"How will they be able to judge without some kind of test?"

"There would be a contest between the applicants for the proposed scholarship. Since every applicant is automatically qualified by the fact that he presented himself, the test will simply be the drawing of a name from a hat, nothing else. If two people apply for the same job, it is obvious they are both qualified under the conditions. Therefore, the employer would simply flip a coin. What else do you want to know?"

"Is it possible for a father to waste his money on a child's college education?"

"If you would think for a minute before asking, you would see that it is absolutely impossible, because the child would never take his father's money unless he knew that he had the necessary ability to become what he himself wanted to be; otherwise, he would hurt his father, who would never blame him for this."

"I think I have something that is going to stump you. At the rate population is increasing, and with no more wars, no automobile accidents and sickness to take our lives prematurely, the earth will soon be too small to feed, clothe, and shelter everybody. Where is man going to build his house when there isn't any more room, and how is he going to feed his family when there is a food shortage? And since you said that nobody can tell another what to do, everybody can have just as many children as they want. Now get out of this one."

"If you think for a moment, Jim, you can get out of it yourself."

"I give up; what's the answer?"

"If you are earning, at present, $100 per week, can you actually afford to support 8 children?"

"I should say not."

"Then to have this many, in the new world, with that kind of an income, would definitely hurt the taxpayers because they would have to supply your family with what you are unable to give them. Therefore, since it cannot satisfy you to hurt them when you know they will never blame or criticize whatever you do, you are given no choice but to bring into the world the number of children you know positively you can adequately support. Consequently, since money is related to what you can buy with it, and since there is a limit to what can be produced, the newspapers will periodically announce the value of your dollar in relation to the raising of one, two, three, four children, etc. If, after checking these figures, you can see that all you can afford is one child, unless you hurt others, are you given any choice when you know you will never be blamed or punished?"

"You're right, Larry, I'm given no choice. But wouldn't the total needs of the economic system also determine the amount of population?"

"Certainly it would, but all this is included in the general information given to the public so each person can decide for himself the direction which is better for him. The Catholic religion had no choice in teaching what was and is still being taught, because it was God's will, but it is not His will anymore, and all people everywhere, by understanding this knowledge, will know this to be an undeniable fact because they are given no choice in this matter whatsoever."

"I have to agree with you, Larry. What is so fantastic is the fact that at the very moment all premature deaths are reduced to an absolute minimum, which increases the overall population tremendously, we are compelled, but of our own unfreely free will, to desire to control the birth rate to meet whatever conditions may arise."

"If this discovery didn't come to light, man would, sooner or later, destroy himself. But since man's will is not free, he has absolutely no say in this matter whatsoever, which proves that God is a mathematical reality that can no more be denied. But this is humorous; religion is founded on faith in God, and the moment we discover that God is an undeniable reality by actually delivering us from all evil, faith is no more necessary, just as it is impossible to have any more faith that the world is round because we know, beyond a shadow of doubt, that it is."

"I can see that we have been confused about a lot of things, Larry. By the way, what about incestuous marriages, and are not these harmful to children born from such close inbreeding; and how is it possible to control it if it is harmful?"

"I know of an uncle and niece who had 13 children, eleven of whom died shortly after birth, but I also know of a similar relation in which the children were not only normal, but their ability to think was above average. Do the experts on heredity really know or think they know?"

"Are you trying to tell me that an incestuous marriage is healthy and safe for children, that is, at least fifty percent? Supposing a deformed child was born, what then?"

"The parents would need to decide whether or not they wish to end the baby's life."

"But this is a terrible sin, Larry; they would be taking the life of another human being."

"Well, before you criticize me for it, Jim, why not see what God has to say. Who carried the child for nine months?"

"Obviously, the mother."

"Then isn't it up to her to relieve her baby's suffering, if she wants to? Supposing she wanted to remove one of her fingers, isn't this her business?"

"It certainly is. But supposing she wanted to take the life of a normal, healthy baby, what then?"

"Is it possible for any mother to do what she doesn't want to do? Remember, premarital pregnancies and the inability to support a family (factors that led to these infanticides) will not exist in the new world. Consequently, she could no more desire to take the life of a normal child than she could desire to remove one of her fingers. However, should any baby be born in such a manner that he would have no quality of life — which the parents recognize — they have a perfect right to put this child out of its misery. Besides, Jim, when you learn what death actually is . . ."

"Do you really and truly know what it is, Larry; no guessing or opinions; no theories?"

"I most certainly do, and I'll tell you all about it tomorrow. Anyway, when you learn what death actually is, you will not be so concerned about this deformed child being mercifully put out of his misery by his parents.

What I have been trying to bring about, Jim, is that a boy and girl shouldn't sacrifice their desire to get married, regardless of their relation to each other, when the only people to be hurt are this girl and boy, providing they want normal, healthy children and are denied this by this close inbreeding. However, I am an offspring of first cousins, and so is my wife, so where can the line be drawn, and who will draw it?"

"I suppose God will draw the line."

"That's right, Jim, he does. He tells us to mind our own business. Children will study all the available knowledge on genetics and will know what is a fact and what is an opinion. Then if they want to get married, brother and sister, uncle and niece, cousin and cousin, this is their business, not yours or mine. For the first time in our history, God is making us aware of who is striking the first blow — a blow, however, that had to be struck in the world of free will because otherwise, matters would have been still worse. In other words, a still greater ignorance needed whatever assistance this lesser ignorance was able to supply."

"It just dawned on me, Larry, that if our needs reduced a family to one child, wouldn't this be a hurt to that child because he wouldn't have someone to play or grow up with?"

"And of course, Jim, this was a mathematical observation, right? It wasn't just your opinion?"

"No; many people told me that they were sorry they didn't have more than one child."

"Jim, my ex-fuse, what am I going to do with you? Can't you see that it is mathematically impossible to hurt a child with something that doesn't exist?"

"But when he sees brothers and sisters or brothers and brothers or sisters and sisters playing together and having fun . . ."

"And he wouldn't be having fun, is that right? And how do you know this? And to prevent him from not having fun, it is important to have two or more children, so then he will have somebody to play with; otherwise, he would be unhappy, right, Jim? And this is not an opinion but a mathematical fact because somebody, in the world of free will, whose child was unhappy because he had no brother or sister, told you that this was why her child was unhappy. And man has free ill, five senses, the world is flat, and you are fired. God, send me somebody else for a disciple. Jesus Christ, Jim! Have I been wasting my time with you?"

"You know better than that, Larry. Don't get so excited, can't a guy make a mistake? Boy, you sure don't live up to your own principles. You just blamed the hell out of me."

"I'm sorry, Jim, but my nerves are on edge. This sound barrier of learned ignorance is enough to make a guy go out of his mind. Nobody knows, yet everybody is judging what is right according to this fallacious, syllogistic, logical reasoning you just demonstrated. Besides, when you talk the way you just did, you force me to continue living that much longer in the world of free will, which justifies my outburst. Only you can control my criticism of you, but since this requires..."

"I definitely got you this time, but good, Larry. Since my ignorance compels you to live a little longer in the world of free will, then it is mathematically obvious that by dispelling this learned ignorance, as you call it (although I am not learned), you can accomplish your purpose. Therefore, since this is within your power, providing you explain your knowledge so my ignorance will be dispelled, my fallacious reasoning can give you no justification because it is the result of your inability to explain yourself in such a manner that no confusion is possible."

"You devil you; you just reinstated yourself. Well, Jim, any more questions about the subject of self-development?"

"I just can't get used to the thought of a boy marrying his sister."

"I didn't say he would. But if he decides to, this is his business, not yours or mine. You just can't get used to minding your own business. This boy and girl (remember, they will be taught whatever accurate knowledge exists on the possibilities of close inbreeding) will hurt absolutely no one. No girl likes the thought of carrying a child for nine months only to lose her baby; consequently, she wouldn't desire to marry her brother if she thought this was a possibility. But is science so well-established in this field that our geneticists really know, beyond a reasonable doubt, which marriages will produce deformed children? Look how many come into the world defective in spite of no close inbreeding. Besides, aren't we all brothers and sisters when you come right down to it? Don't worry about it, Jim; just remember our slide rule. What people do from now on is strictly their business when it becomes mathematically impossible for them to hurt others. These so-called experts will keep their opinions to themselves henceforth. But nothing is stopping them from doing continuous research to find the truth. It is there for them to see if they look deeply enough. Just remember that there is no such thing anymore as an education. Each person can go to school for just as long as he wants to and can afford to, but if he remained there all his life, he would still not be one iota more educated than anyone else. In other words, if you meet (and you will, in the new world — you'll be there) someone who has gone to school for twenty years and another who has been there for only three years, you will have no desire to show any less respect to the one or more respect to the other."

"I wouldn't know this difference anyway, would I, Larry?"

"No, you wouldn't. All unimportant questions must come to an end, as do statements. If you like to read Shakespeare, listen to Beethoven, and do the various things Durant judged the preferences of a cultured, mature, liberally educated individual, this is your business, but if someone else likes to read Zane Grey, listen to the Beatles, shoot pool or bet on the horses, this is his business, and there will be no lesser respect given to one over the other. If you want to be a teacher, this is again your business, but there will be no distinguishing titles to exact greater respect. Remember, this is God's will, proven mathematically by what it means when you fully understand that your will is not free. If at first your habits and customs seem to conflict with this new way of life, it is only because you like to tell others how to live, and you derive great satisfaction in being able to talk about other people, to bring them down to a lower level of stratification. However, you are given no choice as to whether you will be able to continue living as before, simply because the knowledge that others (all mankind) will never blame or criticize you no matter how much you annoy them — because it is now known that you cannot help yourself when you know you can help yourself if you want to — forces you to desire making a great change in your conduct because it can give you no satisfaction whatever to be excused for doing what can no more be justified by any living soul, including yourself."

"You know, Larry, what I've learned from you in these last few days is so utterly fantastic that I find it difficult to adjust to, even though I know it is true. I can't believe that all government, all religion, all premarital relations, all adultery, all divorce, and all hurt in human conduct are coming to a complete end. And yet it is so funny because the very people involved in trying to accomplish the things your revelation brings about are actually not too happy over the news. When you get your book published, I'll buy a copy so I can read it at least two or more times, and even then, I doubt if I will understand it completely."

"I'll give you a complimentary copy, Jim."

"Thanks, Larry. Isn't there anything else to be discussed in this field of self-development?"

"There might be, but what difference does it make if I don't undertake all the details when our slide rule is applicable, no matter where it is used?"

"You're right. Well listen, I'm going to take off. I don't think I'll sleep tonight thinking about tomorrow. Are you really going to demonstrate something about death that was never understood?"

"Wait and see."

"Okay Larry, I'll see you tomorrow."

"So long, Jim."

# PART 5

# THE DISCOVERY AND EXTENSION OF A

# MATHEMATICAL STANDARD TO UNDERSTAND

# DEATH

# CHAPTER 11 — IMMORTALITY

That night, after Jim and Julie made passionate love, he was so exhausted that he slept like a baby. The next morning, he was up bright and early, took his accustomed hot and cold shower, was not hungry, so he didn't eat, and left the apartment. Julie was about to say, "Why aren't you eating, Jim?" when she realized it was a very foolish question because he didn't want to eat, that's why. She also thought, "even if I did make a mistake (after all, it isn't easy to remember everything), why couldn't Jim just say, 'Julie, you made a mistake,' and then show me where. It wouldn't be a criticism then." And she was right, because under the new conditions, there is a mathematical standard to demonstrate who is right and wrong, just in case someone slips up. Jim had been thinking the same thing because he saw that she was about to say something when she changed her mind. He wanted to iron this one thing out with Larry.

"Good morning, Larry!"

"Good morning, Jim!"

"I have a question to ask before you get started."

"Shoot."

"Supposing children and adults make mistakes while trying to change over from one world to the other, and say and do what they are not supposed to because it partakes of advance blame, can they be corrected just as we correct someone who thinks that two plus two equals five?"

"Certainly. It is perfectly all right to show them where they made this mistake because this is not a matter of opinion anymore but an undeniable reality. Then, when this is explained, the person who made the mistake will be given no chance to disagree. Can you disagree with something that is mathematically undeniable, Jim?"

"Not very likely."

"By the same reasoning, if Julie should ask, 'Where are you going?'... instead of answering by telling her where, you would point out, 'Julie, by asking this question, you are blaming my desire not to tell you. Since all forms of advance blame are being removed, this question strikes a first blow.' Then, realizing that you don't want to tell her where you are going, not because you are concealing anything that she shouldn't know, but only because you don't think it is important to tell her, which is your business, she will not mind learning the difference between what is right and wrong."

"Can children correct their parents?"

"Certainly, if they do what is wrong. If your mother went about telling people the world is flat, wouldn't you correct her because it couldn't satisfy you to let others see such obvious ignorance in your family?"

"But they wouldn't say anything, nor would they talk behind her back."

"That's true, Jim, but you would know they know she is an ignorant woman, and this in itself cannot be a source of satisfaction. Consequently, you would take pains to show your mom why the world is not flat, and then she would say, 'You're right, son, thanks for telling me.' Now if your mother is unaware that she is blaming others in advance by asking them foolish questions which they will answer because they don't want to hurt her for doing what she is compelled to do — when you know she would not be compelled to do this once she understands what it means that man's will is not free — then it would give you greater satisfaction to correct her."

"You have answered my question, Larry. Now what's the latest word on death? Boy, does that word give me the shivers! I can't stand the thought that one day I'll be gone from this earth, that I won't see the sun, the moon, the stars, won't enjoy eating, sleeping, making love. What a horrible thought! And above all, that I might not even be here when this New Earth gets officially launched if it ever does."

"It'll get launched, don't concern yourself about that. Your thinking, Jim, is typical of the majority of mankind."

"But a lot of religious people don't think that way. They believe that when they die, they are going to heaven or some such happy hunting ground and, consequently, have no fear of death whatsoever."

"Yes, I know that, Jim. There are all kinds of explanations about the hereafter, this spiritual world of souls, but I'm not interested in words, just the flesh. Besides, does it satisfy you to live forever in a spiritual world where you couldn't make love to her?"

"It's better than being dead and having no Julie at all. Besides, maybe by then I'll take up Bridge, or who knows, maybe where they send me there will be pool tables."

"But what about Julie, supposing she isn't sent there?"

"On second thought, if I can't have her body, I'd rather have pool."

"So you would like to have Julie forever in the flesh, is that right, Jim? Supposing I show you that you will always have her, would the thought make you happy?"

"Naturally, it would. But how in the world is it possible to do that?"

"Let me show you."

"Are you going to use your slide rule?"

"Although it has been an infallible guide and miraculous catalyst through the labyrinths of human relations, it cannot assist us here; but it did not help other thinkers to discover atomic energy, nor was it used to reveal itself. However, that of which it is composed, this perception of undeniable relations, will take us by the hand and demonstrate, in a manner no one will be able to deny, that there is absolutely nothing to fear in death because we will be born again and again and again. But this does not mean what you might think it means, because the life you live and are conscious of right now has no relation whatsoever to your consciousness in another life."

"This is confusing, Larry. I'm conscious now, and I know nothing of a consciousness in another life."

"I realize that, Jim, but doesn't it seem strange to you that of all the millions of years the earth has been in existence, you, of all people, should be born at this time to see the wonders of the world and the inception of this New Earth? Why weren't you born back in the time of Socrates, or why shouldn't you be born a little later on when our New Earth will unfold?"

"I was born now because my father met my mother, fell in love, and got married. They gave birth to four children, and I am the third of the four."

"This is all very true, Jim, but it doesn't reveal a deeper truth. Does matter itself reveal atomic energy? Do the individual planets, moon, and sun reveal the solar system, unless you look into this deeply? Do individual people reveal the mankind system? Does all of it together reveal the reality of God, unless certain mathematical relations are perceived? Certainly, your mother and father got married and had four children, and you are one of the four, but this tells us nothing about the laws it is necessary to understand to know why there is nothing to fear in death. At one time, we even feared thunder and lightning, thinking it was the wrath of God, but now we don't fear the thunder and try to protect ourselves as best we can against the lightning. Until man discovered the cause of an eclipse, which required a knowledge of the solar system, or, to phrase it differently, a knowledge of the laws that inhere in particular bodies in motion, he was afraid that something terrible was going to happen. This became an ominous sign that was blamed for what followed."

"But Larry, I see that death is a terrible thing."

"For the living only, Jim. The dead don't know it, right?"

"It's true that they don't know it, but I know that they don't know it, and that's what disturbs me because one day I will also be in their position, and I don't like to know that I won't know from nothin.'"

"I know this is a disturbing thought, Jim, and one that science has not yet been able to solve, that is, how to get rid of this disturbance, but once the laws relating to death are thoroughly understood, just as the laws pertaining to man's motion are understood, then this disturbance will come to an end."

"The problem, then, is to discover and understand the various laws of this universe . . ."

"But it isn't that simple. It took me two years to understand what it meant that man's will is not free, and an additional three years to break through this sound barrier of words."

"Not ignorance anymore, Larry?"

"Just words, Jim, this is the source of the unconsciousness and the ignorance. However, without these words we could never have discovered the laws necessary for an adequate understanding of ourselves and the world in which we live."

"How do words play a role in death? There is certainly a big difference between the theory of free will and the obvious evidence that when you're dead, you're dead."

"But when you use the words 'you, I, him, she, he,' etc., you are making an assumption and not using mathematical language. We discussed this once before. The word 'orange' circumscribes an undeniable bit of substance, but the word I, Jim, what does that circumscribe?"

"Me, Larry; little ole me, from the tip of my toes to the top of my head."

"And you feel that when they lay you out in a coffin . . ."

"Do you have to use that word, Larry? It sends shivers up and down my spine."

"When they lay you out in a box, this body is still you, is that the way you think, Jim?"

"I don't feel this way; I know for a fact that when I looked at my dead uncle, it was my uncle, not anybody else."

"But if I can prove to you, beyond a shadow of doubt, that the word 'I' not only pertains to you as you are now existing, but also to the sperm and ova that are still living in an unborn state, then you will know that when this part of you dies, the other still lives on."

"Is that supposed to satisfy me, Larry? To know that when I die, I am part of a stream of ova and sperm that still continues to float around in a protoplasmic world?"

"Of course not; but it is supposed to reveal that when you say a certain word circumscribes you from the tip of your toes to the top of your head, this is an assumption, because before you were born you were nothing but the union of a spermatozoa with an ovum, and according to you, if that particular spermatozoa had never united with that particular egg, you would never have been born, is that right, Jim?"

"That's perfectly right. And if my father had never married my mother, I would never have been born."

"You mean by 'I', your body, right, Jim?"

"That's exactly right."

"Now, to solve this apparently unsolvable problem, it is first necessary to gather together certain undeniable facts. Therefore, let me begin by asking you if there is such a reality as the past?"

"Of course... yesterday is the past, today is the present, and tomorrow is the future. And this is a mathematical relation."

"Well, when does the present become the past? I actually want you to demonstrate how the present slips into the past."

"That cannot be done, Larry, by God himself. The past is simply the perception of a relation between two points. As I move from <u>here</u> to <u>there</u>, the past is what I leave behind while in motion; it is my ability to remember something that happened. I know that we were talking yesterday, and that I was talking a fraction of a second ago, and that I am still talking."

"In other words, if man wasn't able to remember what he did, there would be no such thing as the past, correct? If I said to you, 'Jim, what did you do yesterday?', and you were unable to understand my words, only the present would exist for you. Is the sun ever shining in the past? Therefore, the word past is strictly another symbol for memory, and nothing else. The recollection of the various things you did in your life, or, to put it another way, the recollection of your past, is just as good as your memory, but to think that anybody ever lived in the past is completely false. Socrates never lived in the past; he lived in the present, even though this was thousands of years ago. In other words, Jim, all we can ever have is the present. If you were sitting up on a high cloud these last ten thousand years, never asleep, as is the sun, you would have watched Socrates in the present, just as you are watching me write this book in the present."

"I know that all we have is actually the present, Larry, so does everybody else, but what does that prove?"

"It is just fact number one; there is no such thing as the past or future because the only thing we can ever have is the present. Are we in agreement so far?"

"I can't disagree, so I guess I must agree."

"Now let's establish fact number two, which is to prove that the only consciousness that can ever exist in the universe... is your consciousness, not hers or his, but only your consciousness."

"Are you trying to tell me that I am the only one conscious?"

"You know that's not what I mean, Jim. Other people are conscious of what is going on in their lives, but their consciousness only exists as a relation to your consciousness. In other words, it is mathematically impossible to see this universe through anybody's consciousness but your own, even though you are aware that others are conscious. Do you agree that it is mathematically impossible to see this universe through anybody's consciousness but your own?"

"Isn't it true that when I read a book, I am looking at the world through the eyes of the author?"

"That may be true, Jim, but no matter what people say, do, or write about, these things are perceived through your consciousness, even though you are aware that others are conscious of these things also. I see the sun, and I also know that you see the sun, but I cannot see it through your consciousness, only through my own; do you understand?"

"Yes, I do, and I agree."

"Then we have established fact number two. Now, fact number three is that you are conscious of your existence at this exact moment of time; is that correct, Jim?"

"How can I deny what is undeniable?"

"Now let's put these three facts together so that we can look at them more closely. One, there is no such thing as the past; therefore, all we have is the present. Two, it is mathematically impossible to see this universe through anybody's consciousness but our own. And three, we are all conscious of our existence at this moment of time."

"What are you driving at, Larry?"

"Just this, Jim. Now observe this mathematical reasoning, which I will later prove in a different manner. Since there is no such thing as the past, only the present moment of time, and since we are conscious, at this moment, of our own existence, and since it is mathematically impossible for us to see this universe through any consciousness but our own, it becomes apparent that our consciousness of existence, not our body, must always be present during every lifetime."

"Are you trying to tell me that because I am conscious of my existence at this moment of time, I will always be conscious of my existence, from now to eternity?"

"Didn't you just admit that it is mathematically impossible to see this universe through any consciousness but your own?"

"I did, and it's an undeniable fact."

"Then your consciousness, not your body, must always be present at each moment of time, simply because it is mathematically impossible to see this universe through any consciousness but your own. Remember, however, the words 'your consciousness' apply to everybody who is presently conscious. In other words, if I lined everybody up and then said to each one, 'Is it mathematically possible to see this universe through any consciousness but your own?', they would all answer simultaneously, 'No, it is not possible.' Confusion arises when we think in terms of his consciousness, but remember, 'his consciousness' can only have existence in relation to our consciousness."

"You fa dddait my cup, Larry. Can't you explain this in an easier way?"

"Yes, I can, Buddy Boy, but it was necessary to establish certain undeniable facts from which to do other reasoning. Are you ready, and do you have on your thinking cap?"

"Let's go, I'm as ready as I'll ever be."

"Now, supposing we let A represent all the sperm in the entire world and B all the ova pertaining to mankind, while the combination of one with the other will be designated C, which is you, your potential consciousness of existence. Let us further suppose that A joins up with B, and during their uterine journey, you, C, whom we shall call Number One, end up as a miscarriage, which means that you, number One, just died. Consequently, you are not conscious of your existence because your body was never born to give you this consciousness, and therefore the relation expressed in these words, 'he died, she died, or it died,' would have no meaning where you are concerned because you just died, not someone else, and your existence is absolutely necessary for the relation. Do you understand it so far, Jim?"

"I can understand that 'he died' must be in relation to someone living, so continue."

"Now this potential mother and father still want child number One, they want you, which word symbolizes human living substance, and so they try again. This time you are born, but one month later you die of a heart attack after taking a good look at your father. But still persistent, and having a lot of fun, this boy and girl who want you very much, number One, try again with viable success, but 18 years later, you end up in a hospital where you die. But mom and dad, much older, of course, but still capable of propagating, are not satisfied to lose you, number One, so they try again to bring you into existence. Now think very carefully, Jim, is there any difference between the death of you in the uterus, the death of you one month after birth, or the death of you 18 years later?"

"You fa dddait my cup."

"Your Yiddish is as bad as mine. Anyway, in actual reality, though hereditary differences exist between the three C's, the word you is a designation only for the viable substance that comes into the world and is identified with a name or number to establish these differences, which mom and dad grow to love. But what is the difference between the you who died during the uterine journey, one month after birth, or 18 years later? Because you are conscious of your existence and individuality during those years in the present, write a book, build a home, make a lot of friends who cry when you die, doesn't take away from the fact that you are a combination of A and B, which continues in existence even while you are alive and regardless of what happens to C. If you had died a hundred thousand times in the uterus of somebody, eventually you — which is a word describing the consciousness of differences about yourself — would have been born because you are also any combination of A and B, which continue in existence from generation to generation with a potential brain that is capable of consciously perceiving the differences of individuality about yourself. Consequently, the consciousness you feel, the knowledge of your own individuality, without understanding that you, this individual person is not only C, which represents the hereditary differences that die, but A and B which never die because they are carried along from generation to generation and when united develop into the potential consciousness of individuality belonging to any C, makes you perceive an improper relation for you have not considered undeniable facts."

"I'm not arguing, I haven't considered anything because you fa dddait my cup. However, it sounds good, and it has a musical quality, so keep on playing the same tune."

"Anyway, Jim, because the entelechy of A and B develops into the consciousness of C, which permits the recognition of individuality, doesn't negate the substance from which C is derived. Even if all the individual characteristics lie potential in the germ plasm, this still has nothing to do with consciousness, which is not an individual characteristic like your face.

The word I or you not only reveals these individual differences between yourself and others, but your consciousness of these differences."

"Larry, I'm getting tired of that song; isn't there a simpler way this can be explained?"

"Let me try this melody. As was just shown, if number One had died during his uterine journey, and mom and dad still wanted you, number One, they would have tried again, but since you survived this last time, you, number One, are now existing and conscious of yourself. However, mom and dad are not satisfied with only one child, so they try for number Two, who is not you, number One, because you are now existing and conscious of yourself, although this new conscious individual is you, number Two. But if you, number Two, should die one month after birth, and mom and dad were still determined to have you, then you would come into existence and receive the name of number two. Both number One and Two grow and develop and become conscious of their existence. In the meantime, mom and dad give birth to number Three, Four, Five, Six, Seven, Eight, Nine, and Ten.

Several years later, number One got married and gave birth not to number One, because he is still in existence and fully conscious of himself and those being born and dying around him, but to numbers Eleven and Twelve. Shortly, thereafter, number Two got married and gave birth to Thirteen, Fourteen, and Fifteen, and number Three gave birth to Sixteen, Seventeen, Eighteen, Nineteen, and Twenty. Before long, there were 200 others, from grandchildren to great-grandchildren. Are you still with me, Jim?"

"As much as I can be."

"Anyway, after reaching a ripe old age, number One dropped dead from a heart attack, which means that you, number One, are not in existence any longer. But the children in your mankind family still want you, number One, since they don't have you any longer, so the next child born is not Two Hundred One but you, number One, who will grow, develop, and become conscious of your individuality and existence. However, had number One not died, this new child could not possibly have been you, number One, but him or her in relation to you, although you, number 201, will grow and develop and become conscious of your existence.

There is absolutely no difference between the dying of number One during the uterine journey, after one month of existence, or many years later. When number One died during the uterine journey, mom and dad still wanted you, number One, which is a designation for any child, and they tried until you came into the world. Remember, Jim, the word you cannot apply to this substance that died, but only to living substance. Also remember that the conditions are exactly the same before your birth as after your death. Since you can never see this world through the consciousness of another, when you die, what consciousness exists belongs to number Two, Three, Four, etc., not to you, number One, because the bubble of your consciousness just burst with your death. However, since you are no longer conscious of your existence when you die, and since it is mathematically impossible to see this world through the consciousness of another — only through your own consciousness — and since everybody who is still alive has their own consciousness, it is obvious that the next person born after your death is not him or her, because this can only be in relation to your consciousness which is not here anymore once you died, but you, not the person who just died, but an individual who grows and develops and becomes conscious of his existence and individuality.

From the time of your birth, Jim ... Jim ... Jim... wake up Jim..."

"I agree, Larry. I think it's terrifically musical like Gibbon, but you lost me again, and it was so nice dozing off."

"As I was saying, Jim, from the time of your birth your body contains the consciousness of your existence, and no matter how many live or die around you everything is seen in relation to your consciousness, which makes it obvious that any child born after your birth cannot possibly be you while you are still living, for there is a mathematical relation between your consciousness and the existence of others. But all the individual consciousnesses that presently exist, represented by everybody alive, do not include those who have not yet been born, consequently, you, number One, who just this second came into the world, will have a relation to all those alive and those yet to be born while you are living; but should you die at any time during your uterine journey, at the age of one month, two years, 18, 67, or 100 years, you immediately lose your relation to the living, therefore, any bit of consciousness that remains in the world cannot possibly be yours at that moment of time. Since it is mathematically impossible to see this universe through any consciousness but your own, and since your consciousness is no longer here, the next person born is not his or her consciousness, for this must be in relation to you, and you are not here because you just died... but your consciousness. It is you who were just born, not number One who just died, but you, whatever name you are given, whatever your sex, for you will now represent the consciousness of existence and your own individuality. But as long as you are living, number One, Two, etc., any person born cannot possibly be you. However, when you die, this you, this consciousness, is gone, which makes it impossible for a newborn child to have any relation to you, only to him or her, or those still living, who refer to this newborn child as him or her. Therefore, since this newborn child cannot have any relation to you and his relation to those alive is to him and her, and since it is mathematically impossible to see this universe through his or her consciousness, only through your consciousness, and since your consciousness just died, it is mathematically obvious that this newborn child contains not his or her consciousness but your consciousness."

"Jesus Christ, Larry! Do you have this in your manuscript?"

"I do."

"I sure hope others understand it better than I do, and I sure want to thank you for clarifying it. What the hell would it have been like had you not made it so clear? Are you finished; can I go now?"

"Not yet, Jim. I'm going to clarify it a little more. You see, all the sperm and ova in the entire world of mankind represent your potential consciousness and existence before your birth. When a child is born, it is you, Jim, you, Julie, you, Mary, you, Inez, you, Jerry, you, Larry. These children will grow, develop, and become conscious of their existence, but everything they see will be in relation to their consciousness. However, there can be no relation if these children were never born, or if, let us say, they were all killed in an automobile accident. At this point, we are right back where we were when all the sperm and ova in the entire world of mankind represent your potential consciousness and existence before your birth. Then, when a child is born, it is you, Jim, you, Julie, you, Mary, you, Inez, you, Jerry, you, Larry. These children will grow, develop, and become conscious of their existence, but everything they see will be in relation to their consciousness. However, there can be no relation if these children were never born, or if, as just happened, they were all killed in an automobile accident."

"I think I'm beginning to understand at last, Larry. Just keep going."

"Consequently, Jim, since there is no such thing as the past, and consciousness can only be your consciousness (never that of another), which can only exist in the present, your consciousness, not your body, will always be here during every moment of time because it is not a personal characteristic like the shape of your nose, but that which applies to the living substance of all mankind, and is given to each person upon his birth enabling the perception of his individuality.

This I or ego that you feel is definitely a reality, for it is you, no one else, that tastes, touches, smells, hears, and sees. But this consciousness is not only an individual thing, like the various differences about yourself which we have considered C, but also A and B, the potential consciousness that exists in the germinal substance. Since this germinal substance is that from which your ego, the feel of yourself as an individual, is composed, and since this I or ego is also the conscious expression of this germinal substance, both are one and the same thing. Consequently, the consciousness of all mankind is the ego or I of the germinal substance, which imparts individuality upon the birth of a child as a tree does to a leaf in the spring of the year. But this all pervasive consciousness which exists always in the present (and here's the mathematical solution), this ability to say to yourself — 'With all the millions of years the earth has been in existence, and with all the millions of years yet to come, I was born not in the time of Socrates, not in the future, but right now to see this wonderful universe' — this all pervasive consciousness, I say, can only be your consciousness, because there is no such thing as the consciousness of another. His consciousness, her consciousness, can only have existence in reference to your consciousness. When your consciousness is no longer here for those existing to have reference to, the new consciousness that comes into existence is not his consciousness or her consciousness, because this can only have reference to your consciousness, and your consciousness is no longer here since you died. Consequently, it makes no difference how many years the Earth has been in existence. Since all we have is the present, the eternal present, any child born after your death is not you as you now know yourself, but an individual who grows and develops and becomes conscious of his individuality."

"Little by little, Larry, I'm beginning to understand, but this is not easy. Can you tie it together in some way that my weak brain can more easily grasp?"

"Let me try. This all-pervasive consciousness can only be your consciousness because you are an individual expression of the consciousness which pervades the universe and continues to exist in the potential of a protoplasmic state. Consequently, each child born comes into the world with this I or ego which, since it is just an individual expression of the germinal or protoplasmic ego, continues to exist after the body dies; and the very moment after death his ego, the feel of himself as an individual existing which has never died because it exists as the potential of germinal substance from which all self-consciousness, this feel of himself, is derived, is born into the viable substance of any A and B combination. Since it is mathematically impossible for man to have any but his own consciousness, and since he cannot see this universe through any consciousness but his own, he, C, which is every conscious individual, must die before he, the new combination of A and B, the individual consciousness which is also the potential self-consciousness existing in the germinal substance, can be born again. But actually, he, C, representing differences, is not born again in any sense of the word, because there is no relation whatsoever between himself now and someone in the future. You, Jim, the conscious perception of your individuality, are you, the present moment in which you perceive these differences about yourself is the present moment, and there is no such thing as the past or future, only the present. Since it is mathematically impossible for you to see this universe through any consciousness but your own, you, not your individual characteristics but your consciousness of these; you who are conscious right now of this universe, who are conscious of yourself, have always been conscious simply because you, an attribute of self-consciousness which continues from generation to generation in the potential of the protoplasmic substance, never die as you are the consciousness of existence. Consequently, any child born, once your body dies (I realize I've been repeating, Jim), will contain your consciousness through which this new person sees the world and the differences about himself, since it is impossible to see this universe through any consciousness but your own. If you are still living when a baby is born, it is obvious that the consciousness through which he looks out upon the world is not your consciousness, Jim, because you are still alive and conscious of your own existence — but his own consciousness. However, since it is mathematically impossible to see this universe through any consciousness but <u>your own</u> (this is the point of confusion, Jim, so observe very carefully), the words '<u>your own</u>' only means your body seeing itself, and since your body, you, your consciousness, just died, which means that you cannot see this universe or your body any longer through your consciousness, but yet it is mathematically impossible to see this universe through any consciousness but your own, then it becomes mathematically clear that the next child born, whether it be Jim, Julie, Mary, Inez, Larry, Jerry, is your own body, you, looking at the universe through your own consciousness. To put it another way, just imagine that God fashioned your body out of clay and then gave you a name, then life, then consciousness of yourself. You look around, see the universe, which includes people dying, and wonder when it will be your time to go. Then God, who gave you your body, your life, and your consciousness, decides to remove this bit of clay that he has fashioned. Now you are not there. However, God picks up some more clay and fashions your body a little differently; this time, he makes you a girl instead of a boy. He then gives you life, a name, then consciousness of yourself. You look around, see the universe, which includes people dying, and wonder when it will be your time to go. The secret or mystery of death, Jim, lies in the fact that there is no such thing as the past, only the present; that we are conscious, at this moment, of our existence; and that it is mathematically impossible to see this universe through any consciousness but our own. If it is mathematically impossible to see this universe through any consciousness but your own, whose consciousness and body are you looking at the world through when you are no longer here because of your death?"

"Some other guy, Larry, not me. I see babies born every day, and not one of them is me. This is me, Larry, and nobody else is me."

"Well who are you when you die, Jim?"

"It's still me, but just dead and gone. I've seen a lot of them get laid out, but I've never yet seen one return."

"Have you ever seen yourself get laid out?"

"Of course not; it's impossible for me to see myself get laid out."

"Well, if it's impossible to see yourself dead, how do you know if it's impossible to see yourself return? Isn't this an assumption, Jim?"

"Yes, it is, but it certainly is a pretty substantial theory."

"However, just as long as you admit it is possible to return, and you admit that all we ever have is the present, and you admit that you are conscious right now of yourself, and you admit that it is mathematically impossible to see this universe or yourself through any consciousness but your own, then when you die and are no longer here to see your body and this world, whose body and consciousness will be the next newborn child?"

"His or her consciousness, Larry, not mine."

"But how is it possible to say his or her consciousness when you are no longer here to say it?"

"Well, if it is impossible for me to say it is 'his or her consciousness,' whose consciousness is it? Is it their consciousness?"

"But that's saying the same thing, Jim. If you say it is not your consciousness, and you just admitted it isn't his or her or their consciousness — because this must have reference to your consciousness, and your consciousness is no longer here since you just died — whose consciousness are we talking about, Jim?"

"If I'm no longer here, I wouldn't know."

"But you do know, Jim, if you stop to weigh all the facts. Since it is mathematically impossible for this newborn child to have anybody but his own... and since it is mathematically impossible for him to see this world through any consciousness but his own... and since it is mathematically impossible for you to see this world through any consciousness but your own... and since you and your consciousness are no longer here once you die, which means that his consciousness no longer exists since this can only have reference to your consciousness or my consciousness."

"Wait a minute, Larry, just because I suddenly die doesn't mean that his consciousness stops existing."

"I know that, Jim, let me try explaining it this way. Here are five people... Jerry, Julie, Inez, Jim, and Larry."

"And they all have their own consciousness, right, Larry?"

"Let us say you have your consciousness, Jim; Larry, you have your consciousness; Jerry, you have your consciousness; Julie, you have your consciousness; and Inez, you have your consciousness. Now, if you just died, Jim, I can't say 'you have your consciousness,' right?"

"That's exactly right."

"Now, instead of calling everybody by name, we shall use numbers. You are number One, Jim, and you have your consciousness, number One, right?"

"Right, number Two."

"Now you just died, number One, which means your body and consciousness are no longer here. However, as you look out upon the world before you die, number One, it dawns on you that everything can only be seen through your consciousness. You are aware of my consciousness, the consciousness of numbers Three, Four, and Five, but only through your own consciousness. Since you just died, number One, which means that you are no longer conscious of anything, because you are dead, this ends your consciousness of existence. But I haven't died, and I look out upon the world before I die and realize that everything, even your death, can only be seen through my consciousness. Now when a new child comes into the world, and since nothing exists for him except what he sees through his own consciousness, which is numbered according to the number of individual consciousnesses that exist, and since you, number One, are no longer in existence, then this child replaces your number, and you, number One, become conscious of yourself and the world in which you live. Picture an assembly line turning out newborn babies, and let's assume that there are no more than 100 people in the world at any one time, ten of which are the workers on the assembly line of forty births a day; ten more are workers on the assembly line of forty deaths a day. Also, remember that each person can only have his own consciousness. As death number 21 gets laid out, who is now nonexistent and can't say anymore that everything is perceived through 'my consciousness,' baby number 21 is born, who soon knows that it is mathematically impossible to see this universe through any consciousness but his own, and who then says, 'everything is perceived through my consciousness.' The numbers are only significant to show you that just as long as birth number 21 remains alive and conscious of his existence, there can never be another consciousness through which he will see the universe. However, when number 21 drops dead, and numbers 22 to 100 are still in existence and conscious of themselves, it is obvious that the next birth is not 101, because this number must have reference to number 100 and there are only 99 in existence when number 21 dies; consequently, every person who dies loses his bubble of consciousness, which is immediately picked up by the next birth. Therefore, no matter how many times you died during your uterine journey in the form of individual characteristics, your consciousness of yourself would have been born from any combination of A and B into viable substance; and whether you die at birth, the age of twenty, thirty, fifty or one hundred years later, does not alter the fact that immediately after your death any combination of A and B into viable substance is your potential consciousness of your individual characteristics and existence. Because a mother and father become attached to the individual characteristics which are you, it naturally hurts them to lose what they have grown to love but this has nothing to do with you who, upon your death, not only have lost your consciousness of existence, but who are born immediately by a new combination which allows you to once again become conscious of yourself. Mathematical proof is the very fact that it is impossible to see this universe through any consciousness but your own, not his, hers, or theirs. Consequently, when you die, and it is mathematically impossible to see this universe through any consciousness <u>but your own</u>, it is your consciousness that is born again into viable substance."

"Would you believe it, Larry? For the first time, I can actually say I understand, but it certainly took a lot of repeating and hard work, didn't it? Do you think everybody is as dense as me?"

"Nobody is dense, Jim. This is just a word that has no significance. However, it is true that some people can think more clearly than others. But even if they didn't understand it as you did, if they stop to weigh the obvious fact that there is no such thing as the past (only now, the present), and this moment of time can only be perceived through their individual consciousness, not that of another, and that they are not only individual beings but are also part of the protoplasmic substance of this universe or God as an attribute of his self-consciousness, which is carried along in the germinal substance of A and B, the relation will soon dawn on them that consciousness (which is not only a personal characteristic) is the eternal window of God through which we, all mankind, or you, the individual attribute of ego of this all pervasive consciousness which belongs to every living soul, look out upon this magnificent universe in all its glory and mathematical harmony — once it is understood that man's will is not free and what this means. It should be further obvious to them and you, Jim, that God can have absolutely no recognition for his existence and achievements unless through the consciousness of man, who is an eternal attribute of God himself. And once man fully realizes that he is the conscious expression of God who exists eternally because there is no such thing as the past or future, only the present, which is eternal, he will become conscious of his own eternal life; otherwise, he will be eternal unconsciously."

"I liked that very much, Larry, and I'm beginning to understand it even more clearly."

"The perception of these relations, Jim, make it obvious that the same general experiences we have gone through of being little boys and girls with a mother and father, growing up, getting married, raising a family and remarking about the time way back in the olden days when man used to believe the earth was flat and his will free, will continue throughout eternity, because there is no such thing as a beginning and end since time, space, and consciousness are infinite and eternal attributes of the present.

When someone dies, it is true that he is gone and will never return in our lifetime because these relations are also undeniable to our common sense. But I also know that my father and his father before him were derived from this protoplasmic substance that never dies and is handed along from generation to generation. It is very true that we have grown to love our fathers and mothers, sisters and brothers, husbands, wives, and children, but their time of death and our relationship to them do not change reality. 'If my father had died during his uterine journey, does this mean that I would never have been born?' Of course not, Jim, because the word 'I' is a symbol of any individual that is derived from this germinal world of potential consciousness. This 'I' is given to us upon being born and taken away upon our death. Our perception that we are derived from two specific people doesn't alter the fact that our consciousness of these relations is not derived from them but from the inherent ability of man's brain to perceive these differences in relation, which ability is carried along in the germinal world of potential consciousness that imparts individuality upon being born. If I should die this instant, it only means that I, not Larry, but someone born of two new parents, would start my life over again because this consciousness of individuality is given to each person at birth and has nothing to do with individual characteristics themselves. But it is impossible for me to have my consciousness and that of another; therefore, the differences that are now me must die before the new differences, containing the same consciousness of existence and individuality, can be born again. Consequently, death is a mirage to the dead and a reality only to the living, and it is our ability to recognize these deeper relations that gives us our knowledge of immortality, for then we know that even though God sweeps away our aging flesh, we will be born again and again and again. This is an actual reality, not a figment of the imagination, and it can very easily be verified when you realize that with all the millions of years, you, of all people, are born right now to see the universe. But you will also be born a million years hence because all we have is the present, and this universe can only be seen through your consciousness, not the consciousness of someone else. However, no one likes to lose a loved companion, but God's infinite wisdom, by revealing that man's will is not free and what this means, prevents in 90 percent of the cases any premature deaths by eliminating all war, crime, and all the other forms of hurt that gave rise to a justifiable retaliation, while giving man the intelligence to wipe away even the other 10 percent. In our New Earth, Jim, the inception of which will take place very shortly — just as soon as enough people understand the principles involved — we will fall mutually in love, raise a family in complete health, security, wealth and happiness, live to a ripe old age, and die only to be born for the same happiness again and again and again. Well, Jim, you tell me; is God a reality and is He good?"

"You make tears come to my eyes, Larry. God is simply wonderful, beautiful, magnificent! I mean, I like Him very very much. He is everything there is, and I know, at last, that we are in capable hands."

"The full realization of what death actually is will destroy the desire to preserve bodies in cemeteries, mausoleums, etc., for this is only a waste of land and the bodies of the deceased. No one will deny that it is sad to lose a loved companion, but satisfaction in preserving this unliving bit of matter can only be gotten when ignorance of the truth engenders the desire."

"This news, Larry, is so unbelievably wonderful (I keep forgetting... I like everything you taught me so very much) that I can't praise God enough or thank Him enough for my existence. At the very time that I have learned of this new world soon to unfold, which would make me sad to think that I might not be here to enjoy it, I have also learned that death is a realistic mirage, and that this New Earth will not only belong to our posterity, but also to ourselves. I only wish all the people who suffered and died would have had an opportunity to know this before they died."

"What difference does it make now, Jim, and are you forgetting so soon? Just before your birth, you were among those individuals who were about to die. It might not have been you that got killed on the battlefield of World War 1, but you were living during that period and died during that period."

"Do you mean that I lived through every period of history?"

"Yes, you did, only, of course, you don't know who you were, or whether you were a male or female."

"This is just too fantastic. In other words, Larry, once it is understood that man's will is not free and what this means, our people, the Jews, cannot blame Hitler for slaughtering 6 million of us, nor can we feel sorry for the dead because we are not dead."

"But you must remember, Jim, that anybody living who lost someone loved in this carnage will never get over it. However, when he fully realizes that all evil came into existence because God needed it to develop mankind, and now that we are developed, it will be forthwith removed, he won't ever again be able to blame another because there won't be anything left to blame."

"It is just too unbelievable, Larry, and I just feel like crying for sheer happiness."

"So will all mankind, once everything sinks in."

"It is like the unfolding of a drama."

"Only the players were unconscious of the role they played."

"Gosh, Larry, I certainly wish there was something I could do to get this New Earth started in a hurry."

"There is, Jim; just tell others about this knowledge in a manner that lets them understand it, and before long it will spread like wildfire right around the entire globe."

"I'm going to get started right away, that is, I want to finish explaining certain things to Julie. Then I shall pick my customers. After all, if this isn't explained carefully, you know they'll call me a crackpot, right?"

"They will, so be careful. But remember, they will not call you anything once the principles are understood. Until this knowledge is understood, however, those are the risks I (you too, Jim) have to take. My only hope is that no one will jump to conclusions until they read thoroughly what I have written; then I don't care how much they jump because they will be prevented from jumping, providing — it must constantly be qualified — they understand mathematical relations."

"Larry, you'll never know how much I appreciate what you've done."

"But always remember, Jim, don't thank me... thank God."

# CONCLUSION

**B**ecause the knowledge herein is completely scientific and mathematical (undeniable), as with the simple equation given in the Preface, it should be obvious that if you find yourself in disagreement, then there must be something you do not understand. It is for this reason that my work must be studied thoroughly, chapter by chapter, and also why it must be read more than once.

When you have read it at least twice and realize that the solution to all problems in human relations has been unquestionably solved, you will desire to help disseminate this knowledge across the globe. To be of assistance, however, it is necessary that you select several people you consider qualified thinkers, with or without a title, so that they can also become part of the chain reaction. Once a sufficient number of people understand the principles, then this knowledge will become part of every school curriculum, and it won't be but a relatively short period of time before our New Earth can be officially launched.

This book was not meant to satisfy the connoisseur of style, grammar, punctuation, vocabulary and form in general (I'm quite sure this book is shot through with errors when measured by the standards of whether a certain word should have been capitalized, or a comma should have gone here instead of there) but was written primarily to reveal knowledge never before understood. I don't deny that others could have done a better job in explaining it, and their services are still welcome if they can clarify it even more. My job was to make known this discovery, which I have done to the best of my ability.

And so, my friends, I bid you adieu. If God is willing, perhaps we shall, one day, meet again, to herald in A New Earth.

Did you love *A New Earth*? Then you should read *View From The Mountaintop*[1] by Seymour Lessans!

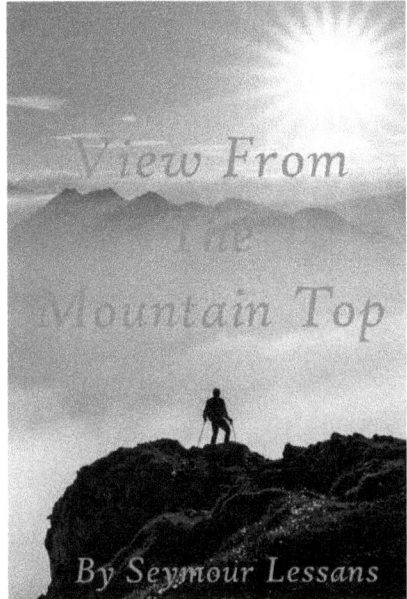

In view of the fact that the first chapter must be studiedthoroughly before any other reading is done, not only because it is akey that will unlock a door to the greatest treasure in the history ofmankind (the long awaited GOLDEN AGE that has been hoped andprayed for since time immemorial), but also because chapters two tosix, though much easier, will not make any sense otherwise, I amurging the reader to refrain from reading in a desultory manner. Youwill know why this is necessary soon enough. However, should youfind this chapter a little difficult don't be discouraged fromcontinuing, simply because what follows will help you understand itmuch better the second time around.

When you have finally grasped the full significance andmagnitude of this apparently brief work (ten years in the making) byreading it at least twice, and further realize there has never been, andwill never be, another

1. https://books2read.com/u/31R0ED

2. https://books2read.com/u/31R0ED

like it because of what is undeniably achieved,you will treasure it throughout your entire life.

Read more at www.declineandfallofallevil.com.

# Also by Seymour Lessans

Decline and Fall of All Evil
This Is An Urgent Message From A Visitor To Your Planet
Beyond the Framework of Modern Thought
The Secret
View From The Mountaintop
A New Earth
Inception of the Golden Age: A Scientific Discovery
A New Earth: From Conflict to Unity - The Road to Lasting Peace

Watch for more at www.declineandfallofallevil.com.